Contents

List of Figures

List of Tables

List of Contributors

J. Bamford

Management Process Improvement Officer
Phase II Theatres
Manchester Royal Infirmary

R.J. Boaden

Senior Lecturer in Operations Management
Manchester School of Management
UMIST

Nesrin Çilingiroğlu

Associate Professor
Faculty of Medicine
Hacettepe University
Department of Public Health
Ankara
Turkey

Natasa V. Daniilidou

Research Fellow
Department of Health Economics
National School of Public Health
Department of Health Economics
Greece

Jean-Louis Denis

Professor and FCRSS/IRSC chair
Department of Health Administration and Groupe
de recherche interdisciplinaire en santé
University of Montreal
Canada

Pamela H. Donaghy

Research Assistant
Healthcare Management Initiative
INSEAD
France

Carl-Ardy Dubois   Department of Health Administration and Groupe
                        de recherche interdisciplinaire en santé
                        Faculty of Medicine
                        University of Montreal

Karleen Everitt   Project Manager
                        Te Tai Tokerau MAPO Trust
                        Whangarei
                        New Zealand

Colin Fisher   Department of Human Resource Management
                        Nottingham Business School
                        The Nottingham Trent University

Mattia J. Gilmartin   Senior Research Programme Manager
                        INSEAD
                        France

Richard Gleave   Development Team, Department of Health and
                        Social Care – South
                        Bristol

Lynette Harris   Department of Human Resource Management
                        Nottingham Business School
                        The Nottingham Trent University

Maria M. Hofmarcher   Institute for Advanced Studies – IHS
                        Vienna
                        Austria

Susan Kirk   Department of Human Resource Management
                        Nottingham Business School
                        The Nottingham Trent University

Louise Kuraia   Strategic Projects Manager/Senior Policy
                        Analyst
                        Te Tai Tokerau MAPO Trust
                        Whangarei
                        New Zealand

John Kyriopoulos
Professor
Director of the Department of Health Economics
National School of Public Health
Greece

Federico Lega
Researcher
CeRGAS, Research Center on Health Care
Management
Bocconi University
Milan
Lecturer on Health Services Management at
SDA
Bocconi Business School
Milan

John Leopold
Department of Human Resource Management
Nottingham Business School
The Nottingham Trent University

Yvonne Leverment
Department of Human Resource Management
Nottingham Business School
The Nottingham Trent University

Bryan A. Liang
Professor
University of Houston Law Center
Health Law and Policy Institute
University of Texas Medical Branch-Galveston
Institute for Medical Humanities
Houston

Christine Lietz
Institute for Advanced Studies – IHS
Vienna
Austria

Chris McCabe
Senior Lecturer, Medical Care Research Unit
School of Health and Related Research
University of Sheffield

David Melzer

Senior Clinical Research Associate
Department of Public Health and Primary Care
University of Cambridge

Elaine Moss

Deputy Director of Corporate Affairs
Nottingham City Hospital NHS Trust and
Visiting Fellow
The Work Institute
Nottingham Business School

Paula Nicolson

Reader
Medical Care Research Unit
School of Health and Related Research
University of Sheffield

Jason Nickels

University of Wales College of Medicine and
Centre for Health Leadership (Wales)

Hilal Özcebe

Associate Professor
Faculty of Medicine
Hacettepe University
Department of Public Health
Ankara
Turkey

Gareth J. Parry

Senior Research Fellow
Medical Care Research Unit
School of Health and Related Research
University of Sheffield

Thomas G. Rundall

Henry J. Kaiser Professor of Organized Health
Systems
University of California
Berkeley

Mehdi Russel

Centre for Health Planning and Management
Keele University

Kyriakos Souliotis   Research Fellow
Department of Health Economics
National School of Public Health
Department of Health Economics
Greece

Lynette Stewart   Chief Executive Officer,
Te Tai Tokerau MAPO Trust
Whangarei
New Zealand

William Tarnow-Mordi   Professor
Westmead and New Children's Hospital
University of Sydney

Peter Totterdill   Director of The Work Institute
Nottingham Business School
The Nottingham Trent University

Janet S. Tucker   Senior Research Fellow
Dugald Baird Centre
Department of Obstetrics and Gynaecology
University of Aberdeen

Acknowledgements

We wish to thank, first of all, the participants in the Fifth International Conference on *Strategic Issues in Health Care Management* held at the University of St Andrews, Scotland in spring 2002. Over 20 countries were represented from many disciplines, and this eclectic mix ensured rich and varied debates on the problems facing health care in the twenty-first century.

Central to the conference planning and management was our conference secretary, Claire Topping. Claire performed wonders before, during and after the meeting, for which we are eternally grateful. In addition, Barbara Lessels and Liz Brodie also contributed to the conference management, and we thank them for their assistance. Appreciation is also due to our colleagues in the Department of Management at the University of St Andrews.

Finally, Pat FitzGerald, contributed great skill and considerable patience in the preparation of the text, and our publishers Ashgate greatly smoothed the production process: we thank them both.

Of course, none of the above can be held responsible for the final product. The presence of any errors or omissions lies solely with the editors and the contributing authors.

Huw Davies
Manouche Tavakoli

Preface:
Strategic Issues in Health Care
Management

In the pleasant environs of St Andrews, Scotland, scholars of health systems from across the world gathered in April 2002 to explore health care policy, system performance and issues of financing. From over 100 presentations at the Strategic Issues in Health Care Management (SIHCM) conference we have drawn this collection of papers as contributions to some enduring debates. While health care systems change with seeming ever-increasing rapidity, and problems appear perennial, we hope that you will agree that the extent, depth, subtlety and insightfulness of current health research offers policy makers and managers a better evidence-base than ever before to inform both strategic decisions and detailed actions.

Health Policy and Technology Assessment

Managing scarce resources remains a central concern across all health systems, and many countries have put in place ambitious programmes of health technology assessment (HTA). Gilmartin et al. suggest that, despite extensive efforts, HTA programmes are only rarely able to deliver definitive policy guidance, citing the paucity of the primary research base as a major obstacle. Richard Gleave homes in on the guidance emanating from the UK's primary mechanism for synthesising HTA outputs: the National Institute for Clinical Excellence (NICE). In doing so he highlights that providing robust guidance still leaves unanswered many difficult questions of local implementation. Building on this, Parry and Tucker then show, using a Bayesian analysis, how little impact even strong evidence may have on local beliefs.

Thus, even in these days of 'evidence based everything' significant challenges exist across the whole spectrum – from creation of evidence, through synthesis, communication and implementation. Fortunately significant resources are now accumulating to help us understand better these challenges – see, for example, recent web-based resources on research utilisation.[1]

Policy and Performance

For many countries, the 1990s was a decade when issues of health care quality and performance came to the fore. Medical errors, medical scandals, and a growing availability of comparative data on health care performance all pointed to significant concerns with the ability of health care providers to deliver consistent high quality care. Performance is now firmly on the global health care agenda.[2]

Crucial to the delivery of high quality care is the ability of doctors and managers to work together. Thomas Rundall explores how managers and doctors view each other and finds some marked areas of divergence. Jason Nickels looks in turn at the invisible costs of repeated cycles of organisational reform, shedding light on how organisational upheaval can have important counter effects that impact on performance. As one aspect of performance, medical errors have proved a significant rallying point for those concerned to address health care quality deficiencies.[3] Bryan Liang takes a thorough systems view of errors in explaining how error disclosure may contribute to improved patient safety.

Hand-in-hand with an awareness of quality deficiencies and performance problems goes the need for accountability. In a careful series of case studies Dubois and Denis explore the different models of accountability that have emerged in Canadian health care. They conclude that there is no one best way to frame accountability and therefore suggest that some degree of overlap in accountability systems may be no bad thing. Moss and Totterdill then explore the organisational frameworks designed to support accountability in UK health care. Clinical governance, they assert, may be distorted in implementation leading to an undue emphasis on quality assurance and a comparative neglect of quality improvement.

International Policy Innovation

Health care is an international business, and the diversity of arrangements around the globe offers intriguing opportunities for cross-national learning.[4] Half a dozen papers provide us with useful perspectives from the international scene.

Daniilidou et al. explore Roemer's Law ('a bed built is a bed filled') in Greece, showing, 40 years on from Roemer's original postulate, that the assertion remains robust. Çilingiroğlu and Özcebe take a broader perspective, providing an analysis of the impact of globalisation on public health, illustrating their arguments with local changes in Turkey.

The theme of international reform links the next two papers. In an impassioned piece, Stewart et al. analyse the New Zealand health reforms and Maori health development. In contrast, Federico Lega asks important questions about the organisational design of hospitals. Answers may be in short supply, but better analyses, such as this, at least enable the posing of better questions and the surfacing of important (but perhaps inappropriate) assumptions.

Effective access to medicines troubles most health care systems. Even the richest countries with the largest spend on health care struggle to provide affordable access. Hofmarcher and Lietz explore these difficulties in 'transition countries', looking in particular at Slovakia, Georgia and The Ukraine. While implementation of medicines policies remain diverse, affordability problems do not seem to be being resolved. Still in the context of transition, Mehdi Russel explores the development of the national health insurance scheme in Iran, locating it within the socioeconomic climate surrounding its development. Financial innovations that enable affordable access thus remain another core concern for international health policy.

Organising Innovation

Whatever the method of finance, all health care delivery organisations are concerned to squeeze more output from the same level of inputs. Boaden and Bamford demonstrate how both qualitative and quantitative analyses are important for identifying and removing blockages to more efficient use of operating theatre resources. Such analyses, around scheduling and delay, contrast with the explorations of Fisher et al. who focus instead on job satisfaction and performance, issues at the heart of the UK government's 'Modernisation Agenda' for the NHS. Finally, Tucker et al. provide some important new contributions to the debates about relationships between volume, staffing, workload and performance. Examining the work of UK neonatal intensive care units, they conclude that larger units are different in important ways from smaller units, but are not necessarily any better at delivering good health outcomes. Their analysis, in its careful execution, points the way to more nuanced explorations of organisational performance.

Looking Forward

That problems in health care policy, performance and finance are perennial does not necessarily make them intractable. Analyses such as those included in this collection go some way to providing insight, areas for action and a focus for further enquiry. Spreading learning across international boundaries, and seeking to accumulate knowledge into robust understanding can both contribute to a more informed set of health care stakeholders. We hope that these contributions contribute to those goals, and we look forward to working with you on future insights at the next SIHCM meeting in St Andrews in September 2004.

Huw Davies
Manouche Tavakoli
St Andrews, May 2003

Notes

1   For example, see the *Getting Research into Practice and Policy* web site resource (www.gripp-resources.org/), or the *Research Unit for Research Utilisation* (www.st-andrews.ac.uk/~ruru/).
2   See *World Health Report 2000* (www.who.int/whr2001/2001/archives/2000/en/index.htm).
3   See *To Err Is Human: Building a Safer Health System* (2000) (www.nap.edu/books/0309068371/html/).
4   For example, see *The Commonwealth Fund International Programme* (www.cmwf.org).

SECTION I
HEALTH POLICY AND
TECHNOLOGY ASSESSMENT

Chapter 1

Health Technology Assessment: More Questions than Answers for Clinical Practice?*

Mattia J. Gilmartin, David Melzer and Pamela H. Donaghy

In the current era of scarce economic resources, health care systems face the challenge of improving the effectiveness, efficiency and quality of their services. From a health policy perspective, there is a growing interest in assessing technologies so as to improve the management of technological change (Jacob and McGregor, 1997). Health Technology Assessment (HTA) is an emerging approach to develop information on the impact of new and existing health care interventions, promote clinical decision making based on evidence, and inform investment choices (Jonsson and Banta, 1999). A comprehensive health technology assessment examines four aspects of a technology: safety, efficacy/effectiveness, cost /benefits, and social impact (Jacox et al., 1990). HTA is not defined by a set of methods, but by its intention to provide evidence-based information ensuring value for money in health care. HTA is a structured analysis activity that relies on primary studies, such as prospective randomised trials, small area variation studies and technology diffusion studies, as well as economic evaluation studies and decision analysis (Perleth et al., 2001). HTA is a key component in the growing quality movement that focuses on improving efficiency in health care by influencing the use and diffusion of health technologies used in clinical practice (ibid.).

Several European countries have developed HTA programmes to inform policy decision-making on the coverage, reimbursement and implementation of health technologies (Banta and Oortwijn, 2000; Cranovsky et al., 1997; Goodman, 1997). Working in a collaborative manner, a comprehensive international strategy to HTA has been developed to ensure: 1) the systematic identification and prioritisation of health care technologies requiring assessment; 2) synthesis of existing research findings and production overviews or meta-analysis; 3) coordination of empirical studies where research evidence is lacking, and; 4) dissemination and implementation of the HTA findings (Jonsson and Banta, 1999).

Technology assessment is designed to determine a technology's value, making it possible selectively to adopt or abandon medical interventions (Garber, 1994). Limitations of HTA to manage technological change include: the number of clinical interventions and technologies needing evaluation; the focus of assessment on the technology rather than health outcome gains; the focus on 'big ticket' durable and pharmaceutical technologies that excludes comparative cost or efficacy information; and, the lack of consumer, health care professional and purchaser/end-user involvement in the priority setting and research process (Banta and Oortwijn, 2000). Additionally, the usefulness of HTA to control the adoption, diffusion, distribution and utilisation of clinical technologies is limited by the integration of findings into purchasing, reimbursement and clinical practice decisions.

Although a number of ambitious HTA programmes exist, there remains a fundamental question regarding the influence of these programmes in producing recommendations that can inform clinical practice and quality improvement initiatives. More specifically, we address the robustness of the findings and recommendations of HTA to change clinical practice and improve the quality of care. The purpose of this study is to determine the extent to which HTAs are producing recommendations that can, and should, affect clinical practice.

We address the following research questions:

• what conclusions and clear recommendations for practice have HTAs produced?
• are HTA recommendations useful for practice?

We organise the chapter as follows. First we describe the context and sampling frame for the study. Next, we describe the study's design and method. We then present our findings and conclusions regarding the robustness of HTA findings to affect changes in clinical practice. And finally, we discuss the implications of our findings for clinical practice development and research.

Context for the Study

The British HTA Programme is one of the most ambitious national strategies for the systematic and comprehensive evaluation of existing and emerging health technologies. In 1991 the National Health Service (NHS) launched the Research and Development (R&D) Strategy to improve the NHS' capacity for innovation. The NHS R&D strategy seeks to shift the NHS from being a passive recipient of new technologies to a research-based Health Service in which reliable and relevant information will be used for decisions on policy, clinical practice and management of services (NHS, 1991; Peckham, 2000). The R&D programme established the Cochrane Collaborative, a data repository of systematic reviews; the Technology Scanning Centre, to identify emerging technologies; and the National Coordination Centre, to support the systematic review of existing clinical research. The Health Technology Assessment Programme (HTAP) is a part of the National Coordination Centre.

The overall aim of the NHS R&D Health Technology Assessment Programme is to ensure that those who use, manage and work in the NHS have high-quality research information on the costs, effectiveness and broader impact of health technologies. Research is undertaken to provide evidence leading to the greatest benefits to patients, either through improved patient outcomes or resource efficiency (www.HTA.nhsweb.nhs.uk). Health technologies considered in the NHS programme are broadly defined to include all interventions used to promote health, prevent and treat disease, and improve rehabilitation and long-term care, independent of the setting for care. The NHS HTAP reviews a range of health technologies in use on a daily basis such as: outpatient services for chronic pain; interventions to promote the initiation of breast feeding; geriatric rehabilitation following fracture; the debridement of chronic wounds; and the management of post operative analgesia and vomiting in day-case surgery.

Since the launch of the NHS R&D Health Technology Assessment Programme in 1993, a total of 131 reviews have been conducted in the technology areas of pharmaceuticals (n = 19); diagnostic technologies and screening (n = 33); therapeutic procedures (n = 25); as well as a series of projects commissioned on behalf of the National Institute for Clinical Excellence (n = 19). As part of its larger mission of education and training to promote the uptake of health technology assessment, 35 methodological reports have been produced.

Method

Of the existing 16 European health technology assessment programmes, we decided to focus on the British National Health Service HTAP. We selected the

NHS HTAP because it evaluates a range of durable and service-based clinical technologies used in daily practice and because the results of these HTAs are readily available in the public domain in published monographs.

Of the four technology areas addressed in the NHS HTAP, we focus on those used in clinical practice once a disease process is identified or diagnosed. Although our a priori criteria limit the breath of available health technologies, our evaluation focuses on the dominant technology categories in use in the contemporary medical care system. For example, technologies evaluated under the therapeutic procedures area include: educational and psychosocial interventions for adolescents with diabetes; domiciliary health visiting; intravascular ultrasound-guided interventions in coronary artery disease; and methods of dialysis therapy for end-stage renal disease. Concomitantly, examples of technologies assessed in the pharmaceutical area include: laxatives in the elderly; antimicrobial prophylaxis in total hip replacement; management of dyspepsia; and inhaler devices for asthma and chronic obstructive pulmonary disease. Our sample included 64 HTAs in the technology areas of pharmaceuticals, therapeutic procedures, and those commissioned by the National Institute of Clinical Excellence available on the NHS website in January 2002.

The National Health Service maintains a website to disseminate HTAs (www.HTA.nhsweb.nhs.uk). The website includes Adobe Acrobat PDF files of executive summaries and monographs for each completed HTA. Monographs are also available in printed form by mail order. Executive summaries are two to three page documents that describe the background; objectives; data sources, extraction, quality and synthesis; results; and conclusions, including recommendations for research and practice for each technology. Full monographs are documents of approximately 100 pages that include detailed information on the design and method used for data collection and synthesis as well as analysis of the quality and limitations of the primary studies used as source data for the individual HTA.

The Executive Summary of each HTA was accessed, downloaded and assigned an identifying number. Each summary was read once for content, and additional information was retrieved from the body of the full HTA report. Two reviewers coded each HTA.

We developed a 12-item scoring sheet to gather data about the known effectiveness of each clinical technology. We scored five items to assess the dimensions of research design that each HTA includes, research measures, technology efficacy, economic evaluation, and technology development. These items were scored on a 1 to 4 categorical scale. The lower the score, the more developed the evidence base for the technology. We define these variables in the following manner:

- *research design*: the method used by the commissioned research team to achieve the stated objective of the HTA (1 = meta analysis; 2 = systematic review; 3 = rapid systematic review; 4 = primary research);
- *research measures*: the standardisation of concepts and instruments used to study the focal phenomena in the body of primary studies (1 = consistent valid and reliable measures; 2 = non-uniform measures, validity and reliability known; 3 = non-uniform measures, validity and reliability unknown; 4 = unknown);
- *technology efficacy*: the extent to which an intervention or group of related interventions demonstrates a change in clinical status ultimately improving people's health. (1 = known with certainty; 2 = known for specific components; 3 = uncertain with available evidence; 4 = unknown);
- *economic evaluation*: the demonstration of the monetary costs and benefits of a technology as compared to similar alternatives. (1 = cost-benefit known; 2 = cost-benefit known for specific components; 3 = cost-benefit uncertain with available evidence; 4 = cost-benefit unknown);
- *technology development*: the extent to which the specific application, efficacy and effectiveness of a technology is known. (1 = robust; 2 = promising; 3 = more development evidence needed; 4 = unknown).

We coded recommendations for practice with one item using a four-point scale. This item assessed conclusions to support the adoption or discontinuation of a particular technology (1 = technology should be the standard of care; 2 = implement this technology with continued evidence; 3 = implement in controlled situations; 4 = discontinue practice).

Recommendations for research were coded using binomial yes/no (yes = 1; no = 0) scores to capture the mutual exclusivity of recommendations. Recommendations included four types of further study: economic evaluation; information on specific components of the technology; randomised control trials to understand or compare technologies, and; primary/basic research to understand the underlying mechanisms of the disease process or clinical phenomena.

Data on the development of the literature base for each technology were gathered by recording the number of research papers found for review, the number of research papers used in the technology assessment and the total number of subjects participating in the primary studies/trials.

We categorised the purpose of each HTA to gain information on the focus and intent of the assessment. Assessments were categorised as evaluation of an individual intervention; package of care; relative effectiveness of a group of related interventions; or service. The objectives were classified as effectiveness; cost-effectiveness; modelling, and; cannot be categorised. It was possible for the assessment to include multiple objectives.

Finally, we coded each technology using Knight's (1967) taxonomy of organisational innovation. This taxonomy has four categories, each of which refers to a different type of innovation in products, processes, organisational structure or people. We used this taxonomy to develop information on the depth and breath of the health technologies evaluated in the NHS HTAP.

We conducted a pilot study to assess the reliability and validity of our coding method. The two reviewers coded a random sample of ten HTAs (five therapeutic and five pharmaceutical). Working independently of one another we met at regular intervals to discuss interpretations of the text and coding decisions. After the pilot work we achieved an inter-rater reliability (Pearson's r) of 0.72 to 1.0 on the seven variables requiring interpretation (Burns and Grove, 1993).

Data were entered into an excel database that included the citation and identifying number for each HTA. Primary studies commissioned for the NHS HTA programme were excluded from the analysis, yielding a final sample of 53 technologies. We analysed the data using descriptive statistics. Throughout the course of the study we kept a journal to record decisions, observations, interpretations and questions.

Findings

In this section we present the results of our analysis addressing the extent to which health technology assessments produce recommendations that can and should affect clinical practice. We describe the general characteristics of the sixty-four health technologies examined in our sample. Next we focus on the robustness of evidence demonstrating the effectiveness, maturity and cost benefit of these interventions, products, services and packages of care used in daily practice. And finally, we examine the recommendations for clinical practice and research generated by this particular national HTA programme to inform quality improvement initiatives.

The following attributes characterise this group of health care technologies (Table 1.1): of the 64 complex health care technologies in our sample 29 (54 per

Table 1.1   Results

	Individual interventions	Groups of related interventions	Package of care	Service
Types of technologies evaluated in the NHS HTA Programme (n = 64)	n = 13 (24%)	n = 29 (54%)	n = 8 (15%)	n = 4 (7%)
Research design used in the HTA (n = 64)	Meta analysis n = 1 (2%)	Systematic review n = 33 (51%)	Rapid systematic review n = 19 (30%)	Primary research n = 11 (17%)
Technology efficacy (n = 53)	Known with certainty n = 2 (4%)	Known for specific components n = 26 (49%)	Uncertain with available evidence n = 24 (45%)	Unknown n = 1 (2%)
Economic evaluation (n = 53)	Cost benefit known n = 0 (0%)	Cost benefit for specific components n = 7 (13%)	Cost benefit uncertain with available evidence n = 25 (47%)	Cost benefit unknown n = 21 (40%)
Technology development (n = 53)	Robust n = 1 (2%)	Promising n = 28 (53%)	More development/evidence needed n = 23 (43%)	Unknown n = 1 (2%)
Practice recommendations (n = 53)	Standard of care n = 1 (4%)	Implement with continued evidence n = 24 (45%)	Implement in controlled situations n = 27 (51%)	Discontinue practice n = 0 (0%)
Research recommendations (n = 53)	Economic evaluation n = 38 (71%)*s	Specific component n = 42 (79%)	RCTs to understand technology n = 30 (56%)	Primary research to understand tech/disease n = 14 (26%)

* Research recommendations for individual technologies are not mutually exclusive and fall into more than one category.

cent) were evaluations of groups of related interventions, such as combination therapy of interferon alfa and ribavirin in the treatment of chronic hepatitis. Thirteen (24 per cent) of the technology assessments evaluated individual interventions such as the use of coronary artery stents in the treatment of ischemic heart disease. Packages of care such as community based postnatal support services were the focus of eight (15 per cent) of the assessments, while; four (7 per cent) examined service configurations, such as centralised vascular services and primary care cooperatives for after hour emergency care.

HTA Methods

The ultimate intent of HTA is to provide information about the clinical and economic value of both emerging and existing health technologies. Based on this intent, HTAs rely on a number of qualitative and quantitative methods and draws on a range of primary data sources to accomplish a stated objective. The majority of the technologies in this sample were evaluated using either systematic review (n = 34) or rapid systematic review (n = 18). The systematic review is a qualitative method in which empirical studies on a given pharmacological agent, clinical intervention, durable medical device, etc. are compared and contrasted to evaluate the strengths, weakness and gaps in that body of knowledge. The rapid systematic review uses the same techniques but is limited by the exhaustiveness of the data searched and collated for analysis, or the time frame in which the analysis occurs.

HTAs also use quantitative techniques such as meta analysis and economic modelling. Meta analysis is a synthetic technique used to determine the efficacy of a clinical technology. The method involves quantitative and statistical combination of results of several random clinical trials to estimate the results of therapy, when no one of the single trials may be sufficient in number of patients to yield a statistically significant result (Goldschmidt, 1986). In this sample of HTAs only one technology had a sufficient evidence base to conduct a meta-analysis. Repeatedly, the most frequently stated limitation of the body of primary studies was their heterogeneity, which made it impossible to pool results.

Where sufficient primary data did exist, modelling exercises were conducted to extrapolate the economic impact of the diffusion of the health technology. Eleven of the 53 HTAs included modelling exercises. The remaining 11 HTAs in the sample were primary studies commissioned to gain information on the effectiveness and economic efficiency of services that are a priority to the NHS for which this type of information is lacking. The primary studies used randomised controlled designs to compare the effectiveness of specific interventions or technologies in a package of care.

Technological Efficacy

One of the main goals of HTA is to determine the extent to which a drug, device, procedure or intervention demonstrates a change in clinical status with the ultimate aim of improving health status. Efficacy is one dimension of technological evaluation used to either limit the diffusion of new technologies or discontinue the use of existing technologies. In this group of health technologies only two have a sufficient evidence base to demonstrate clinical effectiveness with certainty; antimicrobial prophylaxis in colorectal surgery, and antimicrobial prophylaxis in total hip replacement surgery.

Twenty-six (49 per cent) technologies in this sample demonstrate effectiveness for specific components within a group of interventions used to treat a disease process. For example, the HTA on interventions to promote the initiation of breastfeeding sought to evaluate which promotion programmes are effective, and reviewed the impact of such programmes in increasing the rate and duration of women breastfeeding. Clinical efficacy of small group antenatal health education is known to increase the initiation of breastfeeding, however the efficacy of this intervention in comparison to alternatives such as media campaigns, peer support groups and baby-friendly hospitals remains uncertain given the currently available evidence.

Clinical effectiveness for 24 (45 per cent) of the health technologies in this sample is uncertain. Insufficient sample sizes to detect statistically significant changes; lack of head to head comparative studies; and heterogeneity of outcome measures were the most often cited limitations of the primary research. Of the 53 HTAs, only one review explicitly stated that the efficacy of the health technology was unknown. Based on the current body of reliable research, there is no evidence to support the prophylactic removal of disease-free impacted wisdom teeth.

Cost and Benefits

Another goal of HTA is to provide information on the cost and value of technological investments to support the rational use of scarce health care resources. The economic benefit of health technology investments compares the monetary costs, such as purchase price or long-term cost savings of a particular technology, to the standard of care or similar alternative. The cost benefit of these 53 health technologies is largely unknown. Cost benefit was unknown for 21 (40 per cent) and uncertain for 25 (47 per cent) of the technologies we evaluated. Seven (13 per cent) of the technologies demonstrate cost benefit for components of the service or intervention. Examples of these technologies include certain types of hip prosthesis in primary hip replacement in the elderly, effectiveness of inhaler devices for the treatment of asthma and chronic obstructive pulmonary disease, and community-based services for the provision of hearing aids.

The efficacy of these interventions, devices and procedures is inconclusive, reflecting the limitations of the existing clinical evaluation model. Given the limitations of the primary research to produce definite information on clinical efficacy, we examined the extent to which the specific application, efficacy and effectiveness of a given health technology is known. Based on the existing information contained in the primary studies, 28 (53 per cent) of the health technologies were categorised as promising, while 23 (43 per cent) require further study to demonstrate statistically significant changes in clinical status leading to health improvement. Only one of the health technologies, antimicrobial prophylaxis in colorectal surgery, has a sufficient body of evidence to demonstrate clinical benefit with certainty.

HTA Recommendations

The purpose of this study was to determine the extent to which HTAs are producing information that yields useful recommendations to influence clinical practice. Specific recommendations for clinical practice derived by this group of technology assessments are limited. Of the 53 health technologies in our sample it was recommended that 27 (51 per cent) technologies should be implemented in controlled situations, while 24 (45 per cent) should be implemented with continued evidence. Only one technology was recommended as a standard of care. The use of pressurised metered-dose inhalers (pMDI) for persons with asthma and chronic obstructive pulmonary disease was recommended as the first-line standard of care. If a person was unable to use a pMDI device or was non-responsive to pMDI treatment, only then should measured dose inhalers be deemed appropriate as an alternative therapy (for details, see Brocklebank et al., 2001).

Finally, national HTA programmes seek to synthesise existing research findings and coordinate empirical studies where research evidence is lacking to inform clinical practice and health policy decision-making. Research recommendations generated by the NHS Health Technology Assessment

Programme include the commissioning of primary research studies to understand the technology or disease process (n = 13); randomised clinical trials to understand conditions under which the clinical technology should be used (n = 32); the evaluation of specific technology components (n = 42) to gain information of relative effectiveness, and; economic evaluations (n = 38) to determine pecuniary and non-pecuniary aspects of these technologies. Research recommendations for the health technologies were not mutually exclusive, and could be classified in more than one category.

Discussion

The purpose of this study is to determine the extent to which HTAs produce recommendations that can, and should, affect clinical practice. In this section we present our conclusions regarding the robustness of HTA findings as a tool to manage technological change in the health care sector. We also discuss the implications of our findings for clinical practice development and research.

A number of limitations come to light regarding the usefulness of HTA recommendations to inform health policy and clinical quality improvement decisions. The robustness of evidence demonstrating the effectiveness, maturity and cost benefit of these interventions, products, services and packages of care used in daily practice are startling. The demonstrated effectiveness of a large proportion of these health technologies to improve clinical status or health outcomes was unknown or uncertain. More importantly, information of the costs and benefits of these technologies revealed a similar lack of information on the comparative advantage of one treatment approach or set of interventions over another. Although definitive information on the clinical or cost effectiveness of these technologies is lacking, a scant amount of information on the potential of these technologies does exist.

HTA recommendations for practice remain vague due to the limitations of the primary research base namely; the key problem is that the studies are themselves flawed. The primary studies suffer from methodological problems such as small sample sizes, invalid or diverse outcome measures or inappropriate data analysis techniques. Secondly, the studies tend to focus on component technologies such as specific drug treatments, dressings, or prosthesis, while the evaluation of comparative costs and clinical effectiveness remains unconsidered. Third, the heterogeneity of the primary studies used in the HTA limits meta-analysis and integrated review.

There is an increasing need to define the effectiveness of health technologies in order to set policies and maximise system performance at the organisational, national and international levels (Jonsson and Banta, 1999; Fleurette, 1996; Uphoff, 1998). As an analysis activity HTA is a systematic and independent method to examine the technical performance, safety, clinical efficacy and effectiveness, costs, cost effectiveness, organisational impact, social consequences, legal and ethical aspects of a health technology (Perleth et al., 2001). However, our findings highlight the limitations of HTA to provide answers to these policy and practice questions. Given the level of investment in primary research and organised analysis programmes such as HTA in Europe and North America, why are the evaluations of health technologies so weak?

Firstly, comparative evaluations of complex health care interventions are technically difficult to conduct. The gold standard of clinical research is the randomised clinical trial (RCT) to evaluate the efficacy of health care interventions. However, RCTs are conducted in artificial and ideal situations that make generalisations to regular clinical practice difficult. Additionally, randomisation of patients to 'normal' and 'experimental' conditions require large sample groups to gain adequate statistical power to compare the effects of the intervention to determine changes in clinical or health status. Recruitment and retention of patients, practitioner skill and competence and institutional environment are factors in successful RCTs.

Secondly, the existing model of academic-led clinical research lacks incentives and structures to develop interventions or packages of care to a point where the effectiveness of the technology is known with certainty. Research and development to refine and evaluate complex interventions to improve health is a long-term and iterative process (MRC, 2000). Issues of research funding, productivity and performance in academia are factors contributing to the fragmented nature of the existing knowledge base (Perleth et al., 2001). A related problem of incentives underpinning the robustness of health technology assessment is the lack of fit between researchers' and policy makers' work. The positivist approach to science means that every assertion must be verifiable, while policy making is an interpretive process using diverse sources of information to develop a broad picture. Concomitantly, the political process of promoting or limiting the use of health technologies runs counter to the ethic of clinical practice autonomy for the clinician researcher or unbiased observer and reporter for the social scientist.

If health systems require a good primary evidence base on innovations, and undertaking clinical evaluation is complex and expensive, then resource availability and economic incentives to innovators is clearly the crucial factor, rather than post hoc HTA programmes. In general, society depends on two main approaches to encouraging innovation: public funding and intellectual property rights. Patents and copyright have been extraordinarily successful in producing large scale capital to fund the development of complex technologies. In health care, we depend on this model for pharmaceuticals, but especially in Europe, most other forms of health technology are excluded from this support by law. Radical policy thinking on improving the flow of innovations with good quality primary evaluative studies should reconsider the current heavy dependence of health care on academic funding, as this has clearly not delivered an adequate evidence base, as illustrated by our results. Melzer has previously argued (Melzer, 1998) that a widening of intellectual property rights in health care is perfectly feasible, and would require new policy on three main components: 1) an appropriate expansion of intellectual property rights in health care; 2) regulatory requirements that placed a burden on the intellectual property holders to provide evaluative information on their innovations; and 3) avoidance of monopoly power to block access to new health technology at patient level.

Increasingly, system based health care reform and performance improvement initiatives focus on using technologies that are both clinically and cost effective. HTA is one component of the quality and performance improvement movement addressing the rational use of scarce health care resources. Despite the weakness of this study, our findings highlight the limitations of HTA to produce recommendations to change clinical practice. Although the existing model of health care innovation has produced technologies that exceeded all expectations we highlight a number of limitations in the current research, development, and evaluation system. Our analysis shows that HTA recommendations for practice remain vague due to the limitations of the primary research base in providing evidence on comparative cost and clinical effectiveness. This analysis highlights the current state of technological development on a range of health technologies used in daily practice. Based on these findings, is health care in need of a new model of evaluating technologies in the clinical arena?

Conclusions

Health technology assessment programmes are designed to clarify the evidence on technologies, and support evidence based decision-making. In this study we have examined the output of one of the most ambitious HTA programmes based in Britain. Our analysis shows that HTA alone seldom produces definitive conclusions, because of the paucity of the primary research base. Policy makers need to consider ways of improving the flow of innovation with appropriate primary evaluation in health care. Policy initiatives will have to provide a more effective alignment of resources and incentives to those who innovate and evaluate in health care, rather than depend on the systematic review of weak primary evidence.

Note

*   This project was made possible by the support of the Johnson & Johnson research fund, Healthcare Management Initiative, INSEAD.

References

Banta, D. and Oortwijn, W. (2000), 'Health Technology Assessment and Health Care in the European Union', *International Journal of Technology Assessment in Health Care*, 16 (2), pp. 626–35.

Brocklebank, D., Ram, F., Wright, J., Barry, P., Cates, C., Davies, L., Douglas, G., Muers, M., Smith, D. and White, J. (2001), 'Comparison of the Effectiveness of Inhaler Devices in Asthma and Chronic Obstructive Airways Disease: A Systematic Review of the Literature', 5 (26), HTA, http://www.ncchta.org/execsumm/summ526.htm.

Burns, N. and Grove, S. (1993), *The Practice of Nursing Research: Conduct, Critic, and Utilisation*, 2nd edn, Philadelphia: W.B. Saunders.

Cranovsky, R., Matillon, Y. and Banta, D. (1997), 'EUR-ASSESS Project Subgroup Report on Coverage', *International Journal of Technology Assessment in Health Care*, 13 (2), pp. 287–332.

Fleurette, F. (1996), 'Confusion over whether New Technologies should be Regulated at European or State Level', *British Medical Journal*, 313 (7070), pp. 1486–7.

Garber, A.M. (1994), 'Can Technology Assessment Control Health Spending?', *Health Affairs*, 13 (3), pp. 115–26.

Goldschmidt, P.G. (1986), 'Information Synthesis: A Practical Guide', *Health Services Research* 21 (2 Pt 1), pp. 215–37.

Goodman, C.S. (1997), 'Closer Inspection: The Recent Evolution of Technology', *Health Systems Review*, 30 (2), p. 38.

Jacob, R. and McGregor, M. (1997), 'Assessing the Impact of Health Technology Assessment', *International Journal of Technology Assessment in Health Care*, 13 (1), pp. 68–80.

Jacox, A., Pillar, B. and Redman, B.K. (1990), 'A Classification of Nursing Technology', *Nursing Outlook*, 38 (2), pp. 81–5.

Jonsson, E. and Banta, D. (1999), 'Management of Health Technologies: An International View', *British Medical Journal*, 319 (7220), pp. 1293+.

Knight, K.E. (1967), 'A Descriptive Model of the Intra-Firm Innovation Process', *Journal of Business*, 40 (4), pp. 478–96.

Melzer, D. (1998), 'Patent Protection for Medical Technologies: Why Some and Not Others?' *Lancet*, 315 (14 February), pp. 518–19.

NHS (1991), *Research For Health: A Research and Development Strategy for the NHS*, London: UK Department of Health.

Peckham M. (2000), *A Model for Health: Innovation and the Future of Health Services*, London: The Nuffield Trust.

Perleth, M., Jakubowski, E. and Busse, R. (2001), 'What is "Best Practice" in Health Care? State of the Art and Perspectives in Improving the Effectiveness and Efficiency of the European Health Care Systems', *Health Policy*, 56 (3), pp. 235–50.

Uphoff, M.E. and Krane, D. (1998), 'Hospital Based Technology Assessment', *Public Productivity and Management Review*, 22 (1), pp. 60–70.

Chapter 2

NICE Works? A Case Study of the Local Implementation of NICE Guidance

Richard Gleave

Introduction

In 1997 the newly-elected Labour government proposed that a new special health authority be created to provide guidance to the NHS on health care interventions. The National Institute of Clinical Excellence (NICE) was established to produce reviews of assessments of health technologies, produce clinical guidelines and deliver a national clinical audit programme. By the end of March 2001 NICE had produced 21 sets of technology appraisals.

The roots of the work of NICE were the Development and Evaluation Committees (DECs) which were established in three regions to assist health authorities in the implementation of EL(95)55. This circular required these authorities to identify effective and ineffective interventions and use this knowledge in making investment decisions. The creation of NICE was widely welcomed (Smith, 1999) as an attempt to prevent unacceptable geographical variations in the implementation of new technologies, which was colloquially called 'postcode prescribing'. However, subsequent papers have been critical both of the method and results of NICE's early work (Smith, 2000; Hutton and Maynard, 2000; Cookson et al., 2001). These commentaries have focused on the work of NICE and there has been little work on the implementation of the results of NICE publications. NICE issued a draft booklet for comment in September 2000 ('Effective Implementation of NICE Guidelines'), which was finally published 12 months later (NICE, 2001).

This chapter summarises the conclusions of a study into the early implementation and impact of NICE appraisals in one health community in England. The research question was 'How are the conclusions of the appraisals of health technologies undertaken by NICE being implemented in a local health community and what is their impact on local service provision?' Although the two terms are often used interchangeably, there is a distinction between the implementation and impact of policy. Implementation is the process by which policy is put into practice and impact is the effect that the policy has upon local practice and can usually be measured using quantitative data.

Methods

Literature Search

The literature review was undertaken through a systematic search using Medline (1990 to 2000), Cochrane, HMIC and NHS Economic Evaluation databases. The key search terms were 'impact' and 'health technology assessment' and the alternative search terms were 'implementation' and 'economic evaluations'. Searches on impact/implementation were cross-referenced with health technology assessment and economic evaluation to identify relevant articles.

Study Design

This study examined the local implementation of NICE appraisal conclusions through a case study design. A controlled study, say using a case-control or a before-and-after design, was not possible as it would be impossible to create the control because all trusts and health authorities have to implement the final recommendations of an appraisal published by NICE. Although there are problems in generalising the conclusions of a case study, Keen and Packwood (2000) argued that the case study is ideally suited to studying the complex issues that arise in evaluating the implementation of health policy.

The research design brought together qualitative and quantitative research methods within the case study. Although there are epistemological and methodological problems with this approach, Bryman (1988) argued that one of the three ways in which the two approaches can be combined is when quantitative and qualitative research produce a general picture of a topic.

This study used this approach with qualitative data collected from semi-structured interviews and participant observation combined with quantitative data collected to assess the measurable impact of the NICE publications. The method is a small-scale version of the approach adopted by Smith and Robbins (1982) in their study of the implementation of education policy in US schools which they called 'structured ethnography'.

Qualitative Data – Collection and Analysis

Eight semi-structured interviews were conducted using a schedule that had been piloted and the interviews were taped. Interviews were held with a senior manager at director level or equivalent and with a senior clinician who also fulfilled a managerial role from each of the key health organisations (the health authority, the primary care groups and each of the two largest acute trusts). This data was supplemented by data collected from an analysis of key documents and participant observation by the author, who was a Director in one of the Trusts.

The interview data was analysed using an adaptation of the approach described by Ritchie and Spencer (1994) called 'framework analysis'. Framework analysis is specifically designed for the qualitative investigation of policy questions and has been used in the health service context.

Quantitative Data – Collection and Analysis

Quantitative data was collected on planned and actual impact of six NICE recommendations across the health community. The selection of appraisal reports sought a balanced range of technologies and settings. Implantable cardioverter defibrillators (ICDs) are a single item of high cost cardiac equipment, with relatively low costs for insertion. Taxanes are high cost cancer drugs which had been subject to explicit rationing decisions in the past. Proton pump inhibitors (PPIs) are a range of antacid drugs used mainly in primary care. Glycoprotein inhibitors (GPIs) are high cost cardiac drugs where practice in trusts has often differed. Wisdom teeth extraction is a dental procedure. Stents are items of equipment inserted during a cardiac procedure which have been adopted over several years.

Data on the position before the publication of the NICE report was collected, and compared with data on anticipated usage and costs submitted as part of the annual planning process (called the Service and Financial Framework or SaFF) for 2001–02. Thus there may be a danger of bids being inflated and not representing an accurate assessment of anticipated costs. Data on actual usage and costs subsequent to the NICE report was also collected for some technologies. Additional data, such as results of local audits and a study undertaken by an independent research company on behalf of a commercial drug company was also collected. Local data was compared with the information on 'implications for the NHS' published in the NICE report, which was reduced to the size of the local population. This approach could be subject to inaccuracies from the 'scaling down' of general data without allowing for local epidemiology and treatment rates.

Data

Chronology of the Decision-making Process

The health community is one of the largest in England and had five Primary Care Groups (PCGs) which were moving to Primary Care Trust status. Among the NHS Trusts are two large acute Trusts providing both local and regional specialist services.

The SaFF for 2000–01 had identified a reserve of £2m for NICE reports due to be published, though the precise arrangements for the management of this reserve were not finalised. This led to an exchange of correspondence between one of the Trusts and the Health Authority over several months expressing mutual frustration using the so-called 'NICE reserve'.

A paper was submitted to the August Health Authority meeting, setting out the proposed approach to the application of the reserve. It proposed that the reserve was used to address NICE recommendations in chronological order until it was exhausted with subsequent guidance which required additional funding, delayed for the next SaFF round. There was considerable debate about this proposal and a Working Group was convened to produce an amended proposal. The HA members were concerned that a system to implement NICE needed to be fair and consistent in covering guidance issued towards the end of the financial year and balancing secondary and primary care interventions.

A further paper was approved at the November HA meeting. It set out a process consistent with the draft NICE guidance on implementation with advice to the HA from the Prescribing and Therapeutics Committee. It also proposed that the £2m reserve represented £1m available in 2000–01 and an additional £1m in 2001–02 for the consequences of three interventions (GPIs, taxanes and interferon beta, even though this last report was not yet published). Other technologies were not funded and decisions were delayed until the SaFF round for 2001–02.

In January the planning process for 2001–02 commenced. Both Trusts identified some indicative costs for NICE but at the end of January clear advice from the NHS Executive Regional Office was that NICE recommendations had to be met immediately and in full. Davies (2001) had recently reported that an article in the *Daily Telegraph* on the approach being adopted in Wiltshire

HA had led to a firmer line about full implementation. The NHSE advice was later refined so that the 'must do' requirement was meeting 2000–01 recommendations in full and plans needed to be agreed for the implementation of recommendations due in 2001–02.

The HA produced a schedule of costs amounting to £5.7m covering both 2000–01 and 2001–02 recommendations but the projections identified by the Trusts were greater. This was partly because the Trusts took a different view of what NICE might recommend (for example based on combined treatment programmes for chemotherapy drugs rather than monotherapy) and partly because the Trust included additional costs for delivering the technologies, such as nursing, pharmacy and non-pay costs. The final SaFF for 2001–02 included £2.7m for NICE recommendations but there was no methodology in reaching this sum.

Qualitative Data about the Implementation and Impact of NICE Recommendations

a) Implementation of NICE guidance The interviews revealed a variety of approaches to implementing NICE recommendations between the different organisations, though there was universal agreement that the process was difficult. All organisations saw the prime responsibility as resting with a clinician-manager (Director of Public Health, Trust Medical Director or PCG Clinical Governance Lead) but stressed the need for corporate ownership through links between clinical, financial and planning teams.

The Health Authority approach was set out in the paper that went to the November HA meeting, but this was not referred to explicitly in the interviews. A less clear process involving exchanges of correspondence between organisations was described and this was seen as 'administratively heavy' and leading to delays. The Health Authority staff saw the difference between the timetable of the NICE workplan and the annual planning and budgetary cycle as a key problem which the reserve had attempted to address.

PCGs did not yet have a process but some ideas were emerging. The likely process put the main emphasis on education and dissemination supported by an analysis of the financial and workload consequences.

NHS Trusts were looking to adapt existing approaches. One Trust had a formal and systematic approach to planning and clinical practice and saw NICE recommendations as fitting into its business planning process. The other Trust believed its current approach was ad hoc, usually based on whether the recommendation had significant financial implications. However, it was proposing a formal system of 'knowledge management' which saw NICE as one sort of information on best practice which needed to be disseminated, adopted and audited.

From the interviews there appeared to be two key themes about the national context within which NICE operates. Firstly, although there was universal support for the principle of a body which made national recommendations on the adoption of health technologies, there was a gap between the ideal and the current practice. NICE was seen as causing as many problems for those involved in local implementation particularly because of the financial consequences of its work.

Secondly there was a conflict between the desire of local managers and clinician-managers to receive national advice, which allowed local flexibility, and wanting to receive an instruction or requirement, which would give consistency in implementation.

The scope for local flexibility in the implementation of NICE recommendations was a key feature of all interviews. One interviewee felt that health communities were 'hostages to the NICE workplan' and several interviewees sought some discretion not over whether to implement or not, but how, when and, in one case, to whom. The NHS Trusts were clear about how they would handle the situation when clinical staff argued against the implementation of NICE recommendations – one described an internal panel based on the 'three wise men' as traditionally used in consultant clinical performance issues while the other set out three criteria that needed to be met (no excess cost, no detriment to patients and no unethical decisions).

Within the local context there was a lack of clarity about the roles and responsibilities of different organisations in the implementation process. The role of dissemination was most clearly recognised by PCGs and the Health Authority, while NHS Trusts saw analysis of the implications as a key role for themselves. Monitoring was mentioned by the Health Authority as part of their Performance Agreement with the Regional Office and the role of CHI was unclear.

The 'culture' of the health community was alluded to by all interviewees and the degree of trust between organisations and their respective views about risk, especially financial risk, were seen as crucial to the approach to implementation. All interviewees believed that some form of financial risk-sharing was required though this meant different things between organisations. For Trusts this meant commissioners appropriately funding the costs of any NICE recommendation whereas for commissioners it meant identifying the risk and being clear with which organisation it sat.

There was a wide range of views over the role of the public in the implementation of NICE recommendations. Interviewees frequently described a process of information sharing, through the Community Health Council, the media or in the future through the Patients' Forums, and believed this was public involvement. The more detailed engagement and involvement work was seen by interviewees from all three sorts of organisations as best being undertaken at a health community level and there was a general recognition of the different needs of individual patients, patients' support and pressure groups and the wider public. One interviewee believed all that was possible was to 'manage the politics', especially the media and pressure groups.

b) Impact of NICE guidance All interviewees felt that NICE had reached essentially positive recommendations on health technologies. Most of the interviewees believed there were direct links between the political dimension in the workings of NICE and the positive nature of the decisions. However the way in which NICE used research data was also a factor as it was argued that NICE placed a strong emphasis on the clinical efficacy data which led to what were perceived as small changes in clinical measures leading to a positive recommendation. These two views were not mutually exclusive. However, there was no mention of a need for better economic or financial data but there was a wish to see individual technologies put in the context of both other treatments for that disease and the wider context of other health care interventions.

All interviewees saw the significant impact of financial framework on decisions about NICE recommendations. The interviews were conducted during the SaFF process which may have affected this emphasis. The key local financial dimension was related to which organisation would bear the main proportion of the risk. Some people believed that the Health Authority's approach was that in-year risk rested with the provider organisations while the providers, especially the NHS Trusts, clearly saw the responsibility for funding NICE recommendations which required additional resources sitting with the commissioners. There was a recognition that the responsibility for releasing savings (or what was described by one interviewee as the opportunity costs), where appropriate, was the provider's.

The impact of NICE recommendations upon clinical practice and upon clinical and managerial relationships was an area of divergent opinions. Some interviewees believed that the nature of the decision was seen as crucial in determining the nature of the response from clinicians. Some recommendations were uncontroversial and described widely accepted best practice, and thus the impact was likely to be minimal. In the new technologies in secondary care, the positive recommendations were seen to tap into a desire among clinical staff to use the new technology but in primary care, the recommendations to both adopt, and potentially to stop, were seen as a stimulus to change. One interviewee believed that the clarity of the information for GPs and the relevance of the clinical context were crucial in determining the speed of adoption.

Some interviewees had an essentially optimistic perspective as NICE recommendations were an opportunity to improve discussions between managers and clinicians, and between primary and secondary clinicians. An alternative pessimistic perspective was also proposed in which NICE recommendations were obstacles for managers (who in the words of one interviewee 'would have nowhere to hide') or as challenges to existing clinical practice. However the phrases 'clinical freedom' or 'clinical autonomy' were not used by any of the interviewees. Both 'optimists' and 'pessimists' commented that the historical scope of managers to influence clinical practice had been as small and believed that NICE was not likely to change the degree of 'control'. The impact on clinical practice was seen as not simply whether the NICE recommendations were seen as controversial but largely related to the national expectations on local managers.

Some of the interviewees saw NICE decisions as 'non-decisions' limited to processing the implementation of the central guidance. This view was expressed most strongly by lay managers who, despite their support the principle of NICE, felt that NICE added yet another set of 'must dos' from the centre.

Quantitative Analysis of Specific NICE Reports

Six Technology Appraisal Guidance Reports were examined and the national data on usage and cost of the technology compared with data collected within the local health community. This is summarised in Table 2.1.

a) Removal of wisdom teeth The actual number of removals in secondary care in the HA was very close to level of removals indicated in the NICE guidance (1029 procedures p/a compared to 1014). NICE estimated between 22 per cent and 44 per cent of removals were 'inappropriate'. Local data from a clinical audit (of 50 consecutive records immediately before the publication) showed that about 30 per cent of removals did not meet the NICE recommendations. A follow-up audit six months later showed no change in local practice compared to the guidance but local clinicians felt that some removals (such as those following trauma) were clinically appropriate even if they were outside the NICE guidance. This category accounts for all but one case of the 'inappropriate' removals in the second audit.

NICE estimates of savings are significantly above those that could be identified locally because NICE guidance used a unit cost which was 27 per cent above the unit costs produced by the Trusts.

b) Taxanes for cancer treatment The use of docetaxol (for breast cancer) was the subject of considerable debate and after the publication of the NICE report, the relevant Trust decided to start routinely using docetaxol without additional funding secured.

Table 2.1 shows that the estimated cost for the health community of docetaxol was over twice the NICE estimate. The NICE analysis did not cost the additional workload resulting from docetaxol, which is used as an additional not a replacement therapy. Thus about half the increase was funding for the extra day case activity needed to administer the drug and the remainder was because the local data on episodes per course was substantially above the data used by NICE.

Table 2.1 shows that the additional costs for pacliataxol (for ovarian cancer) were also above the NICE estimate, primarily because the current expenditure in Avon was below the level that NICE would have expected.

The local position was not unusual as a study by Cancer BACUP (2000) reported that implementation was patchy with only 77 per cent and 86 per cent of HAs implementing the guidance on docetaxol and paciltaxol respectively.

c) Stents in percutaneous coronary interventions (PCIs) Before the publication of the guidance, the local position was that the stenting rate was 69 per cent, which was in line with the rest of the country, though the PCI rate was less than half the national average. However clinical practice was substantially above the level of funding in the contracts, which reflected an explicit policy by the Health Authority not to invest substantially in PCIs nor in stenting as CABGs were seen as offering a more clinically and cost effective revascularisation procedure. With the publication of the 'National Service Framework for Coronary Heart Disease' (DoH, 2000), the HA policy to PCIs changed and the Trust used additional investment in 2000–01 to increase the funding to meet the actual stenting rate. Further investment in the 2001–02 SaFF doubled the PCI rate and marginally increase the stenting percentage.

Table 2.1 shows that the local costs of implementing the guidance was about 50 per cent less than the NICE estimated cost at an 85 per cent stenting rate.

Table 2.1   Summary of net estimated local financial impact

	NICE estimate	Local estimate
Wisdom teeth	−£95,000	−£19,000
Taxanes – breast	£324,000	£769,000
Taxanes – ovarian	£142,000	£100,000
Stents	£263,000	£391,000
PPIs	−£765,231	−£1,389,387
ICDs	£860,000	£629,000
GPIs – electives	£330,000	£336,000
GPIs – emergencies	£290,000	£310,000

Note: wisdom teeth and PPIs are estimated savings while others are estimated additional expenditure.

d) Proton pump inhibitors Expenditure on PPIs locally in 1998 was 20.1 per cent below the level estimated by NICE yet the conclusions of the modelling exercise undertaken locally was that the potential savings were 81.6 per cent greater than that estimated by NICE. The main reason for these savings was the reduction in low dosage prescriptions of PPIs. Unfortunately recent data on the trend in prescriptions and expenditure was not available so it is not possible to establish whether the 15 per cent reduction in usage estimated by NICE has occurred.

e) Implantable cardioverter defibrillators The 1999/2000 local rate of implantation was 13 per million, just below the national average quoted by NICE of 17 per million, but the existing expenditure was £878,000 below the level indicated by NICE.

NICE used a cost of £25,000 to cover the costs of the ICD and implantation. The local unit cost in 1999/2000 of the procedure and the defibrillator was £28,568 but, due to an improved purchasing agreement, this fell to £20,167 in 2000–01. The saving was redirected to increasing the number of PCIs undertaken.

The Eastern Region Specialist Commissioning Group concluded that it will take several years to reach the rate of 50 ICDs per million and the Trust proposed an increase in revascularisations of 35 for the 2001–02 SaFF but this was not fully funded in the SaFF.

The local experience suggests that the NICE estimate of £25,000 per ICD procedure is conservative and concerns have been raised that a lower national price for ICDs would be above the current price paid by some trusts.

f) Glycoprotein IIb/IIIa inhibitors The four Trusts had different approaches to the adoption of GPIs for treating emergency admissions of patients with unstable angina resulting in the costs ranging from £17,000 to £60,000 per 100,000 population. One Trust had started to use GPIs in 2000–01 without any agreement on funding, though this decision had been taken by the clinical staff without advice from the Trust's management. The detailed costing for this use of GPIs has costs only slightly below the level NICE estimated. This was purely fortuitous as the costing was based on an incorrect cost per case and a substantially lower number of cases than the actual number of episodes and than the NICE estimate of the expected number.

The costing for the use of GPIs as a treatment for patients undergoing PCIs was also only slightly below the NICE prediction which is entirely explained by the increase in the PCI rate, being below the historical national average used by NICE.

Discussion

'The Effective Implementation of NICE Guidance' (NICE, 2001) provides a clear idea of the approach to implementation that NICE believe should be adopted. It follows a 14-step model which is drawn from the same philosophy of scientific management as Easton's (1953) systems model and Whittington's (1993) 'classical' model. This is a rational approach that looks at the Institute's forward plan, dissemination, prioritisation, setting an action plan, managing change and monitoring and feedback. The document is a practical guide and uses examples of 'good practice' which fit into this rational process, though the majority of the examples have a primary care perspective. It is consistent with Charlton's (2000) concept of 'infostat' and Harrison and Dowdeswell's (2000) views on NICE as a 'bureaucracy'.

The case study has shown that there is a desire for a rational, planned process to implement NICE guidance locally. One trust has plans for a systematic process covering the range of evidence based guidelines and while the other seeks to put NICE within its business planning process. PCGs recognised their current limitations and the need to develop a process and the HA sought to steer the process through the Prescribing and Therapeutics Committee.

However, the experience has been that an unplanned, ad hoc process involving tensions, negotiations, disagreements in public and compromises has taken place. Examples include the need to reconsider the paper that was submitted to the August HA meeting and the decision by key staff in the HA which three recommendations to treat as priorities without data on the local cost implications. Thus Lindblom's (1959) ideas about 'incrementalism' and Whittington's (1993) 'processual' model are more consistent with the data in this case study. The findings in this limited study could be ascribed to 'teething problems' but the literature on the dynamics of local implementation in health communities over the past 20 years shows that this 'ad hoc' approach dominates.

Not only has the implementation process been unsystematic but the approach to costing the impact has varied. The idea of a standard approach to assessing workload and financial implications was agreed in principle by the Working Group but has not occurred. As a result funding allocated for GPIs varied hugely.

A discussion of the roles of stakeholders and of the nature of decisions about NICE demonstrates that the rational planned approach has not occurred in practice.

a) The role of stakeholders   Managers, clinicians and the public all have a vital stake in decisions on NICE guidance. The clinical community has been remarkably inactive on NICE decisions at a local level and thus far there have been no notable interventions by clinical staff in the case study. This is probably because the decisions have been uncontroversial and supportive of new technologies. This limited role for clinical staff is substantially different from the position described by Stocking (1985) where the 'local product champion' for a new technology was key in the dissemination and in attracting resources. The role described by Stocking usually took place in the absence of any policy whereas Lipsky's (1980) work on 'street level bureaucrats' highlighted the role of local staff in providing detail and discretion on the implementation of a policy. It is too early to see whether this sort of role for clinical staff will develop and the interviews highlighted a potential difference between primary and secondary care. In secondary care the NICE recommendations are fairly prescriptive, but do allow some scope for local discretion – for example on precise threshold levels for interventions. There are likely to be differences in interpretation and there are some clinicians who feel that the NICE guidance is too comprehensive. In primary care there appears to be greater scope for discretion and a recognition of longer delays in implementation. The independent contractor status of GPs give the PCG/Ts a less certain role in determining local policy on prescribing and the interviews showed the importance of persuasion and education to effect compliance with NICE recommendations.

The role of the public and pressure groups in local implementation has been small and the interviews showed there was no clear approach to their input. The input of the Community Health Council in the Prescribing and Therapeutics Committee was an attempt to provide a public perspective but there is the danger of 'tokenism'. There is no clear concept locally about public accountability for NICE decisions, which is consistent with Le Grand et al.'s (1998) conclusions on earlier reforms. However there is potentially an interesting contrast with the national role of NICE, which has a controversial public profile and taken great efforts to involve the public and patient groups.

Thus the implementation of NICE guidance has been an issue primarily for managers, though there are some important distinctions between the 'lay' managers and the 'hybrid clinician-managers' (Ferlie et al., 1996). The 'lay' managers have had to start to deal with clinical decisions which they rarely have the knowledge to understand and put NICE guidance alongside the delivery of other key national priorities. There is no evidence of the different 'hybrids' (GP, public health consultant or hospital medical director) forming alliances as the groupings observed were within organisations and there were probably greater tensions between different 'hybrid' managers than between the 'lay' managers in the different organisations.

b) The nature of NICE decisions Four key conclusions from the research can be drawn on the nature of NICE decisions:

1) Primary – secondary care differences
    Interviewees in the HA and in PCGs identified a clear difference between the implementation and impact issues in primary and in secondary care. In secondary care most of the recommendations had been about high cost technologies where there had been pressure from a small number of specialists to implement prior to the NICE guidance. Thus the recommendation could be easily costed and pressure put on the commissioner for additional funding. It was like taking the lid off a pressurised bottle with only limitations on physical capacity (as with ICDs) seen as a legitimate reason for delaying implementation.

In primary care the potential impact could not be clearly assessed in advance and thus additional resources would be difficult to obtain. The guidance would take a considerable time to be disseminated to a large number of GPs, who would vary in their speed of adoption. The financial impact would be hidden among other pressures on the prescribing budget and there would be a need to target a number of individuals who were slow to adopt the recommendation. This follows the classic 'S-shaped' adoption curve described by Stocking (1985). Unfortunately there was no data available to test whether these contrasting patterns of impact occurred in practice.

2) *National or local estimates*

The quantitative analysis identifies that the cost consequences estimated by NICE are not bourn out by local analysis. The two estimates of savings (wisdom teeth and PPIs) appear optimistic while local estimates of additional costs usually exceed the NICE projection. This is partly because NICE usually only calculated the cost of the new technology and not the 'delivery' costs but also because of their use of old data. Unfortunately data was not available to assess whether the actual trends were consistent with either the NICE or the local estimates. However informal discussions with staff at NICE indicate that they do not undertake a detailed or separate analysis of the estimated impact of the technology on the NHS.

3) *NICE and other HTAs*

One side effect of NICE was that it was seen having a detrimental impact on the influence of other HTA and EBM publications. It is almost as though there was only a limited amount of space on the organisation's agenda for EBM/HTA activity and NICE would prevent other guidance being implemented. The profile of NICE was seen as having a greater impact on managers than on clinical staff.

The feeling that NICE had approved most technologies to avoid controversy has been voiced by Smith (2000) as well as many of the interviewees in this study. Although Rawlins (2001) refuted this, he offered little evidence and it is difficult to conclude whether this is the case. One assessment could be on the use of economic data and Stevens et al. (1995) suggested that a cost per QALY of £3,000 to £20,000 should be supported by purchasers. However NICE has tended to use cost-effectiveness measures rather than cost-utility measures. This approach enables the new technology to be compared with existing interventions, though the NICE reports rarely provide data on the current comparison, but it does not allow comparison with other technologies.

The general conclusion of other studies is that HTAs have often been enthusiastically received but have had a very limited impact on decision-making. NICE is radically different from any other form of HTA seen in this country as the national political drive behind NICE reduces and even removes the significant barriers to adoption described by Drummond and Weatherly (2000). The tight central control of the NHS may lead to NICE having a greater impact than the long-running state-sponsored HTA systems in Canada and Australia. The comparative impact may be to bring UK expenditure on new technologies up to the levels of other countries quicker as they will be approved by NICE.

4) 'Simple' and 'complex' decisions

The experience in this case study leads to decisions on NICE being seen in two distinct ways. Firstly, the decisions are seen as a straightforward implementation decisions. Guidance is received and it needs to be implemented. The scope for local interpretation is limited and the decision is 'clean and simple'.

Secondly, NICE decisions are seen as 'rationing' decisions which require resources to be put into designated health technologies rather than other service pressures and needs. These decisions are 'complex' and require considerable negotiation and debate. McDonald (unpublished) argues that these sort of decisions for HAs display the features of 'puzzlement' as described by Harrison et al. (1992).

One hypothesis is that 'simple' decisions are those for local health communities and the pressure on the NHS after the publicity surrounding Wiltshire HA's proposed approach supports this. The 'complex' decisions can then be seen as those for NICE at a national level. However as Smith (2000) and Freemantle and Mason (1999) pointed out, by focusing on individual technologies in isolation, NICE's work does not address the 'rationing question'. This means that the 'rationing question' gets pushed down to health communities and links into the 'simple' implementation decision. 'Complex' decisions require the decision-makers to recognise that funding one technology has an opportunity cost, through not supporting other health care interventions, and represents a trade-off between achieving different health goals.

These two sorts of decisions cannot be easily separated. Within the case study there was a clear desire for a rational planning process to make the 'simple' decision. This process should assess the potential impact, disseminate and implement NICE recommendations but the reality both across the health community and within individual organisations was very different. The tension was neatly summed up by one interviewee as 'an attempt to make the unplannable, plannable'.

The evolution of a decision about only three of the appraisal reports seems to be well described by Lindblom's (1959) model of incrementalism at a micro local level (nicknamed 'muddling through'). A process of partisan mutual adjustment between the organisations and the stakeholders and incremental analysis of the data was crucial in reaching a compromise, which will soon need to be revisited.

This gap between ambition and reality and the evidence for elements of incrementalism show that the two sorts of decisions became entwined. What seems like a 'simple' decision is not simple because it cannot be separated from the complex 'rationing question'. The reason for this is because there are local resource constraints. This entanglement between the two decisions at a local level is inevitable and leads to the delays, confusion and frustrations that were seen in the case study.

Conclusion

The creation of NICE was a policy initiative to provide consistent national guidance on the clinical and cost effectiveness of health technologies and prevent 'postcode prescribing'. There is limited guidance about how local health communities should implement NICE guidance but it suggests that this should be a planned and rational process.

This study has shown that, in one health community, the profile of implementing NICE guidance is high among managers. However the practicalities of implementing the guidance was variable between trusts and costs differed significantly from those estimated nationally. The implementation process was difficult involving a range of stakeholders in complex decisions.

References

Bryman, A. (1988), *Quantity and Quality in Social Research*, London: Routledge.
Cancer BACUP (2000), 'Is NICE Removing Postcode Prescribing? Results from an Independent Survey of Health Authorities in England and Wales', http://www.cancerbacup.org.uk.

Charlton, B. (2000), 'The New Scientific Knowledge in Medicine: A Change of Direction with Profound Implications', in A. Miles, J.R. Hampton and B. Hurwitz (eds), *NICE, CHI and the NHS Reforms: Enabling Excellence or Imposing Control*, London: British Medical Association.

Cookson, R., McDaid, D. and Maynard, A. (2001), 'Wrong Sign, NICE Mess. Is National Guidance distorting Allocation of Resources', *British Medical Journal*, 323, pp. 743–5.

Davies, J. (2001), 'On Short Rations', *Health Service Journal*, 1 February, p. 16.

Department of Health (1997), 'The New NHS: Modern and Dependable', London: Department of Health.

Department of Health (2000), 'National Service Framework for Coronary Heart Disease', London: Department of Health.

Drummond, M. and Weatherly, H. (2000), 'Implementing the Findings of Heath Technology Assessments', *International Journal of Health Technology Assessment*, 16 (1), pp. 1–12.

Easton, D. (1953), *The Political System*, New York: Knoft.

Ferlie, E., Ashburner, L., Fitzgerald, L. and Pettigrew, A. (1996), *The New Public Management in Action*, Oxford: Oxford University Press.

Freemantle, N. and Mason, J. (1999), 'Not Playing with a Full DEC: Why Development and Evaluation Committee Methods for Appraising New Drugs may be Inadequate', *British Medical Journal*, 318, pp. 1480–82.

Harrison, S. and Dowdeswell, G. (2000), 'The Selective Use by NHS Management of NICE-promulgated Guidelines: A New and Effective Tool for Systematic Rationing of New Therapies', in A. Miles, J.R. Hampton and B. Hurwitz (eds), *NICE, CHI and the NHS Reforms: Enabling Excellence or Imposing Control*, London: British Medical Association.

Harrison, S., Hunter, D.J., Marnoch, G. and Pollitt, C. (1992), *Just Managing: Power and Culture in the National Health Service*, Basingstoke: Macmillan.

Hutton, J. and Maynard, A. (2000), 'A NICE Challenge for Health Economics', *Health Economics*, 9, pp. 89–93.

Keen, J. and Packwood, T. (2000), 'Using Case Studies in Health Services and Policy Research'. in C. Pope and N. Mays (eds), *Qualitative Research in Health Care*, London: BMJ Books.

Le Grand, J., Mays, N. and Mulligan, J.A. (1998), *Learning from the NHS Internal Market; A Review of the Evidence*, London: King's Fund.

Lindblom, C.E. (1959), 'The Science of Muddling Through', *Public Administration Review*, 19, pp. 79–88.

Lipsky, M. (1980), Street Level Bureaucracy, New York: Russell Sage.

McDonald, R. (unpublished), 'Rationing Rationally? Health Economics and the Politics of Decision-making in an English Health Authority', paper to the Autumn 2000 meeting of the Applied Health Economics Group, York University.

National Institute of Clinical Excellence (2001), 'Effective Implementation of NICE Guidance', NICE, London.

Rawlins, M. (2001), full response to *BMJ* Editorial on 2 December 2000 by Dr R. Smith, http://www.nice.org.uk.

Ritchie, J. and Spencer L. (1994), 'Qualitative Data Analysis for Applied Policy Research', in A. Bryman and R.G. Burgess (eds), *Analysing Qualitative Data*, London: Routledge.

Smith, R. (1999), 'NICE: A Panacea for the NHS?', *British Medical Journal*, 318, pp. 823–4.

Smith, R. (2000), 'The Failings of NICE', *British Medical Journal*, 321, pp. 1363–4.

Smith, A.G. and Robbins, A.E. (1982), 'Structured Ethnography: The Study of Parental Involvement', *American Behavioral Scientist*, 26 (1), pp. 45–61.

Stevens, A., Colin-Jones, D. and Gabbay, J. (1995), 'Quick and Clean: Authoritative Health Technology Assessment for Local Care Contracting', *Health Trends*, 27, pp. 37–42.

Stocking, B. (1985), *Initiative and Inertia: Case Studies in the NHS*, Nuffield Provincial Hospitals Trust, London.

Whittington, R. (1993), *What is Strategy – and Does it Matter?*, London: Routledge.

Chapter 3

The Effect of the United Kingdom Neonatal Staffing Study Results on the Prior Views of Neonatal Doctors: A Bayesian Analysis

Gareth J. Parry and Janet S. Tucker

Introduction

There has been much debate in recent years concerning the optimal configuration of service for providing neonatal intensive care. (International Neonatal Network, 1993; Field et al., 1990; De Courcey Wheeler, 1995; Field and Draper, 1999; International Neonatal Network, 2000) Much of this debate has centred on whether or not to further centralise the existing service. This is a very contentious issue with some smaller units viewing it as a threat to their existence. The United Kingdom Neonatal Staffing Study (UKNSS), with the endorsement of key professional organisations representing the neonatal intensive care staff, was conducted with the aim of obtaining a contemporary evidence-base to inform this debate (British Association of Perinatal Medicine, 1996; Parry, 1998; UK Neonatal Staffing Study Group, 2002). It became evident at an early stage of the UKNSS that one major factor in the acceptance of the results by doctors who work in the specialty would be their prior beliefs about performance differences between bigger and smaller units. For example, if a neonatal clinician has strong beliefs that there are performance differences between larger, medium and smaller units, then they would require considerably more persuasion (or stronger evidence) to change those views than somebody with less strong views. Before analysing the UKNSS data we obtained the beliefs and measures of the strength of conviction of doctors working in neonatal intensive care units as to what they felt was the difference in terms of risk-adjusted mortality between high, medium and low volume units. This information may be useful in identifying possible barriers to the acceptance of the results of the UKNSS, or over-ruling of service configurations suggested by its results.

Bayesian techniques have been proposed to illustrate how a person's quantifiable prior beliefs are modified in the light of new data. Consequently claims have been made that Bayesian techniques are superior to frequentist techniques at informing policy (Lilford and Braunholtz, 1996). The current paper examines the use of Bayesian techniques to illustrate how the prior beliefs of neonatal doctors may be amended in the light of the UKNSS results relating to the size of unit (Spiegelhalter et al., 2001).

Methods

The methodology and results of the UKNSS have been published elsewhere (UK Neonatal Staffing Study Group, 2002; Tarnow-Mordi et al., 1997). For the current study, the sample consisted of the consultant in charge at each of 54 NICUs participating in the prospective phase of the UKNSS, and a sampling ratio of 1 in 5 applied to the remaining medical staff listing of 685 for those units. Anonymous questionnaires were mailed in August 1999 to a subsample of 191 doctors, after the clinical data collection but before any planned frequentist analysis was started. The questionnaires asked staff to give their job title or position and had one item inviting any further comments. It was not possible to send reminders.

The items in the questionnaire focused on the primary hypotheses of the UKNSS. The questionnaire was piloted using face to face interviews with a group of 6 doctors to ensure that the questions were understood, and that they were filling in the questionnaire appropriately. The questionnaires asked staff to mark on a visual analogue scale the difference in risk-adjusted mortality they believed existed between units by the size and staffing levels used in the UKNSS (UK Neonatal Staffing Study Group, 2002). They were asked to provide their best estimate of the difference in terms of percentage mortality (W score) (Yates, 1990). Respondents were also asked to indicate how accurate or precise they felt their estimate was by marking an upper and lower limit on the scale (see Figure 3.1) An example of how to complete the questionnaire was also enclosed.

Any doctors whose estimated W score was 0 were defined as believing there was no difference in risk adjusted mortality between the unit types compared. Doctors whose estimated W score was not 0 were defined as believing there was some difference in the risk adjusted mortality between the unit types compared. Any doctors whose estimated W score was above 0, and whose upper and lower bounds were also above 0 were defined as having a very

For ALL infants admitted to NICUs

Please mark with a (X) on the line at the position of your estimate. Mark the lower and upper bounds of your estimate by making 2 marks (/) to either side, as in the examples.

Remember that you are always assuming that types of units are treating infants with similar levels of initial sickness.

What is your estimate of mortality outcomes in NICUs with *medium volume* compared with NICUs with *high volume?*

```
 -15%     -10%      -5%       0%        5%       10%       15%

                     ↓                           ↑
              Less mortality in NICUs    More mortality in NICUs
                with medium volume          with medium volume
                                    No difference
```

What is your estimate of mortality outcomes in NICUs with *low volume* compared with NICUs with *high volume?*

```
 -15%     -10%      -5%       0%        5%       10%       15%

                     ↓                           ↑
              Less mortality in NICUs    More mortality in NICUs
                 with low volume            with low volume
                                    No difference
```

Figure 3.1   The linear scale question to quantify doctors' beliefs about relative performance of NICU types in terms of risk-adjusted mortality outcomes

strong opinion in the direction indicated. Similarly if the W score, upper and lower bound estimates were all less than 0 then that doctor was defined as having a very strong opinion in the opposite direction.

The prior beliefs were then combined with the UKNSS data (which has been published elsewhere). (UK Neonatal Staffing Study Group, 2002) For each doctor's reply the estimate of the difference between unit types was used to indicate their central prior beliefs and the upper and lower bounds of their estimate used to indicate the strength of these beliefs. These prior belief values were combined with the UKNSS data using Bayes formula (Berry, 1996). The resulting values should provide the posterior beliefs of the doctors in the light of the new UKNSS data.

Doctors whose posterior W scores and associated upper and lower bounds did not include 0 were considered to have very strong posterior beliefs in the directions implied.

Results

Replies were received from 114 doctors (60 per cent). Table 3.1 summarises the results. For the comparison of low versus high volume units the mean W score was 3.7. This implied that on average, doctors believed that for all infants admitted, 3.7 more infants per 100 admitted died in small volume units compared to high volume units. The associated average lower estimate was –0.6 and upper estimate was 7.9. Seventy-four per cent of doctors believed that low volume units had higher risk adjusted mortality than high volume units, with 28 per cent indicating that they believed this very strongly. For the medium versus high volume comparison the mean W score was –0.2, with an average lower estimate of –4.3 and an average upper estimate of 4.0. Thirty per cent of doctors believed that medium volume units had higher risk adjusted mortality than high volume units, with 7 per cent indicating that they believed this very strongly.

The results of the UK Neonatal Staffing Study showed no difference in performance between low, medium or high volume units after adjusting for risk, but that mortality increased with workload in all types of units. (UK Neonatal Staffing Study Group, 2002) For low compared to high volume the W score (95 per cent confidence interval) was –0.4 (–0.9, 0.2) and for medium compared to high volume it was –0.2 (–0.7, 0.4).

When each of the doctors' beliefs were combined with the data using Bayes theorem, the posterior W score (95 per cent confidence interval) for low versus high volume units was –0.1 (–0.7, 0.6). In the light of the data 21 per cent of

Table 3.1 Prior beliefs of the doctors, the data from the UKNSS, and the posterior beliefs according to Bayes theorem of the doctors in the light of the UKNSS data

Valid response	(number)	W score Central	W score Lower	W score Upper	Central W scores > 0 Number	Central W scores > 0 Percentage	Lower W scores > 0 Number	Lower W scores > 0 Percentage
		(average of all responses)			(believe high volume better)		(believe high volume better very strongly)	
High vs medium volume								
Prior beliefs	98	−0.23	−4.30	4.03	29	30%	7	7%
Data		−0.18	−0.71	0.35	8	8%	0	0%
Posterior beliefs		−0.16	−0.81	0.50				
High vs low volume								
Prior beliefs	100	3.73	−0.64	7.88	74	74%	28	28%
Data		−0.35	−0.85	0.15				
Posterior beliefs		−0.05	−0.69	0.60	21	21%	8	8%

doctors should now still believe that low volume units have higher risk adjusted mortality than high volume units, but only 8 per cent should believe this very strongly. For medium versus high volume units, the posterior W score (95 per cent confidence interval) was −0.2 (−0.8, 0.5), with 8 per cent of doctors now still believing medium volume units had higher risk adjusted mortality than high volume units but 0 per cent believing this very strongly.

Discussion

This study indicates that although one of the largest studies of neonatal intensive care provision performed in the United Kingdom to date, found no difference in risk adjusted mortality between low, medium, and high volume units, almost a quarter of neonatal intensive care doctors will still believe that low volume units perform worse than high volume units. Furthermore just under 10 per cent will believe this very strongly.

The 10 per cent who still very strongly believe that risk adjusted mortality is lower in high than low volume units will have these beliefs for what they will believe are fully justifiable reasons. They may have individual experiential evidence that has led them to their very strong beliefs. Such evidence may not easily be quantified and integrated into large scale studies.

The questionnaire used in this study has not been tested elsewhere, and there may still be problems in the interpretation of the questions that we were not aware of (Chaloner, 1996). For example, it is not easy to ensure that the concept of risk adjustment was made clear enough. The UKNSS found there was no evidence of mortality being any worse than expected in medium or smaller units, nor any better than expected in larger units. The UKNSS also found that neonatal intensive care appeared to operate already on a networked basis, such that the sickest infants in smaller units were often, but not always, transferred to larger units soon after birth. This may suggest that smaller units either felt that care of very sick infants is best delivered in larger units, or that they were complying with local network protocols based on that belief. In the questionnaire, we asked people to assume that the illness severity of infants was accounted for in comparisons. The results from the prior belief questionnaire may be consistent with existing policy and doctors believing that the sickest infants are best cared for in larger units.

Bayes theorem provides an indication of how new data may affect prior opinions or beliefs. However it does not tell us how long it might take a person to change their beliefs, nor describe the processes by which people may or may not change their beliefs. It assumes people behave in a rational manner and employ purely scientific reasoning, which may not be the case in practice. Individuals with strong beliefs and who have publicly stated that belief or have a stakeholder interest, may find it more difficult to revise their beliefs in the light of new evidence, compared to those who have been less public or have invested less heavily in those beliefs. It would be useful to qualify prior beliefs by providing some information on why those beliefs are held.

The problems outlined above may be eased by adopting methodology used in qualitative research. For example, qualitative researchers regularly attempt to recognise and understand how their own position, perspective, prior beliefs or prejudices may affect the research process (Britten, 1996). Furthermore, there may be a role for utilising qualitative research methods in more reliably and informatively obtaining prior beliefs (Lilford and Braunholtz, 2000). Such methodology may provide invaluable insights as to why certain beliefs are held and the nature of the barriers to changing those beliefs (Chard et al., 1999).

Adopting Bayesian techniques in general can also be problematic. Just as Bayesian methods can be used to temper over-inflated claims for new interventions, groups with a vested interest in a new intervention or a certain policy may attempt to use the prior beliefs of a selected sample to artificially increase the appeal of their case. With care however, appropriately chosen prior beliefs may be invaluable in indicating the likely acceptance or not of a new treatment, intervention or policy.(Lilford, 1994) That said, the use of Bayesian analysis presented here, should not be confused with that of more sophisticated empirical methods, which are less susceptible to accusations of gaming.

Ultimately it is a combination of the clinical care staff, health service managers, and patients to decide on how to act in the light of new results or evidence. It must also be recognised that the views and beliefs of those individuals who represent each of these groups may be equally or more important in deciding future policy decisions than any large research study that they may wish to be involved in.

If the 60 per cent respondent neonatal intensive care doctors in this study are representative and have behaved consistently with Bayes theorem, we would predict that the results of the UKNSS will be broadly accepted. We would also predict and accept that a small number of doctors will still express considerable disagreement with the UKNSS results. If, on the other hand, a large number of doctors still express strong disagreement with the UKNSS results, then we must conclude that there is still some methodological work to be done before Bayesian techniques can be used in this way as a practical tool for informing health policy decisions.

References

Berry, D.A. (1996), *Statistics, a Bayesian Perspective*, Belmont, CA: Duxbury Press.

British Association of Perinatal Medicine (1996), *Standards for Hospitals providing Neonatal Intensive Care*, London: British Association of Perinatal Medicine.

Britten, N. (1996), 'Qualitative Interviews in Medical Research', in N. Mays and C. Pope (eds), *Qualitative Research in Health Care*, London: BMJ Publishing Group, pp. 28–35.

Chaloner, K. (1996), 'Elicitation of Prior Distributions', in D.A. Berry and D.K. Stangl (eds), *Bayesian Biostatistics*, New York: Marcel Dekkler, pp. 141–56.

Chard, J., Lilford, R. and Gardiner, D. (1999), 'Looking beyond the Next Patient: Sociology and Modern Health Care', *Lancet*, 353, pp. 486–9.

De Courcy Wheeler, R.H.B., Wolfe, C, Fitzgerald, A.,Spencer, M., Goodman, J.D. and Gamsu, H.R. (1995), 'Use of the CRIB (Clinical Risk Index for Babies) Score in Prediction of Neonatal Mortality and Morbidity', *Archives of Disease in Childhood and Fetal Neonatal Edition*, 73, F32–6.

Field, D. and Draper, E.S. (1999), 'Survival and Place of Delivery following Preterm Birth: 1994–96', *Archives of Disease in Childhood and Fetal Neonatal Edition*, 80, F111–14.

Field, D., Hodges, S., Mason, E. and Burton, P. (1990), 'Survival and Place of Treatment after Premature Delivery', *Archives of Disease in Childhood and Fetal Neonatal Edition*, 66, F408–11.

International Neonatal Network (1993), 'The CRIB (Clinical Risk Index for Babies) Score: A Tool for Assessing Initial Neonatal Risk and Comparing Performance of Neonatal Units', *Lancet*, 342, pp. 193–8.

International Neonatal Network and Scottish Consultants and Nurses Collaborative Study Group (2000), 'Risk Adjusted and Population-based Studies of Outcome for High Risk Infants in Scotland and Australia', *Archives of Disease in Childhood and Fetal Neonatal Edition*, 82, F118–23.

Lilford, R. for the Fetal Compromise Group (1994), 'Formal Measurement of Clinical Uncertainty: Prelude to a Trial in Perinatal Medicine', *British Medical Journal*, 308, pp. 111–12.

Lilford, R.J. and Braunholtz, D. (1996), 'The Statistical Basis of Public Policy: A Paradigm Shift is Overdue', *British Medical Journal*, 313, pp. 603–7.

Lilford, R.J. and Braunholtz, D. (2000), 'Who's Afraid of Thomas Bayes?', *Journal of Epidemioligal Community Health*, 54, pp. 731–9.

Parry, G., Gould, C.R., McCabe, C. and Tarnow-Mordi, W.O. (1998), 'Annual league Tables of Mortality in Neonatal Intensive Care Units: Longitudinal Study', *British Medical Journal*, 316, pp. 1931–5.

Spiegelhalter, D.J., Myles, J.P., Jones, D.R. and Abrams, K. (2001), 'An Introduction to Bayesian Methods in Health Services Research', in N. Black, J. Brazier, R. Fitzpatrick and B. Reeves (eds), *Health Services Research Methods. A Guide to Best Practice*, London: BMJ Books, pp. 150–62.

Tarnow-Mordi, W.O., Tucker, J.S., McCabe, C.J., Nicolson, P. and Parry, G.J. (on behalf of the UK Neonatal Staffing Study Collaborative Group) (1997), 'The UK Neonatal Staffing Study: A Prospective Evaluation of Neonatal Intensive Care', *Seminars in Neonatolology*, 2, pp. 171–9.

UK Neonatal Staffing Study Group (2002), 'A Prospective Evaluation of Patient Volume, Staffing and Workload in Relation to Risk-adjusted Outcomes in a Random, Stratified Sample of all UK Neonatal Intensive Care Units', *Lancet*, 359, pp. 99–107.

Yates, D.W. (1990), 'Scoring Systems for Trauma', *British Medical Journal*, 301, pp. 1090–94.

SECTION II
POLICY AND PERFORMANCE

Chapter 4

Hospital–Physician Relationships: Comparing Administrators' and Physicians' Perceptions

Thomas G. Rundall

Introduction

The growth of managed care in the United States has had, and continues to have, a profound impact on hospitals and physicians. Managed care organisations attempt to reduce both the unnecessary use and cost of hospital and physician services. Additionally, managed care plans collect performance data from medical care providers and monitor their quality of care. Negotiating with managed care plans and competing with other hospitals and physicians on the basis of documented performance and cost-effectiveness has been a new and formidable challenge to most hospitals and physicians. Hospitals responded to these pressures in a variety of ways, depending on the penetration of managed care plans in their market and the constraints and opportunities available to them. Some common responses were to merge with other hospitals in order to gain power in negotiations with health plans; to reduce expenditures on in-patient services, including downsizing the number of hospital-employed personnel; and to implement patient care protocols and other techniques to control utilisation of hospital resources. Physician responses also varied. But common physician responses were to merge into group practices or independent practice associations in order to gain power in contractual negotiations with health plans, and to seek ways of capturing more revenue by setting up clinics and even specialty hospitals to compete for patients with community hospitals (Rundall et al., 1998; Robinson, 1999; Shortell et al., 2000; Scott et al., 2000; Ginsburg and Lesser, 2001).

Although many of the responses of hospitals and physicians were primarily aimed at strengthening their negotiating positions with managed care plans, in some cases hospitals and physicians acted in ways that the other party perceived not to be in their interest. Indeed, a 1991 study of hospital–physician relationships suggested that the organisational and system changes described above may have undermined long-established cooperative relationships between hospitals and physicians (Shortell, 1991). A decade later, it is timely to ask: 'what is the current state of hospital–physician relationships in the United States?' This study addresses that question. We assess the current state of hospital–physician relationships in a sample of hospitals located in the western United States, and identify ways to improve those relationships. The study compares physicians' and administrators' opinions of the hospital–physician relationship overall, and of specific aspects of hospital and physician performance. Two other key features of the study are the identification of important barriers to building effective hospital–physician relationships, and the identification of key facilitators for building more effective relationships between hospitals and physicians.

Background

In the United States' health system, the hospital and the physician are loosely coupled yet interdependent entities. The success of one depends upon the effectiveness of the other. Hospitals rely on general practitioners and specialists to refer patients to ambulatory care departments, admit patients for inpatient care, provide diagnostic services and medical and surgical care, and oversee the nursing and rehabilitative services provided to patients in the hospital. Hospitals are paid for the non-physician services they provide to patients by private and public insurance plans, and to a lesser extent by individuals from their personal funds. If hospital revenues exceed expenses the surplus revenue is used to upgrade facilities, invest in new technologies, expand capacity, and in the case of for-profit hospitals pay dividends to investors. Historically, hospitals have sought to attract the loyalty of physicians by establishing a reputation as a high quality institution and by having the technology and specialised technical staff that would allow physicians to provide advanced, state-of-the-science care to their patients. The reputation of the hospital depended to a significant extent upon the effectiveness of the physicians in treating patients and upon the ability of the hospital to offer highly technical care for complex illnesses and injuries (Burns et al., 1993).

Physicians rely upon hospitals to provide care for their patients that cannot be provided in the physician's office-based practice. Hence, physicians refer their patients to the hospital for diagnostic exams requiring expensive technology, medical or surgical procedures requiring the use of technology and specialised personnel not available in the physician's practice, and intensive medical and nursing care for patients. A physician may admit patients to a hospital after their qualifications have been reviewed and approved by the hospital's credentialing committee. In communities served by several hospitals, physicians are likely to have admitting privileges at more than one hospital, thereby creating a competitive climate among hospitals for the physician's 'business'.

In spite of this interdependence, many non-governmental hospitals, which make up about 75 per cent of all US hospitals, do not employ physicians. Indeed, in many states there are laws prohibiting community hospitals from directly employing physicians (with limited exceptions for some specialties, such as pathology). The constraint against hospital employment is deeply rooted in the institutionalised beliefs that physicians should be solely accountable to their patients and should have unfettered autonomy and authority to make decisions in the best interests of their patients. Hence, physicians and hospitals in the United States evolved a special set of relationships, including business ties based upon hospital admitting privileges, dual hospital administrative and medical staff authority structures, and a shared goal of building the hospital's capacity and technical capabilities (Burns et al., 1993; Eisele et al., 1985; Fifer, 1987). These relationships were in harmony with the environment for medical care services from the 1940s through the 1982. In particular, during this time period fee-for-service reimbursement for both hospitals and physicians provided incentives for physicians to admit patients to hospitals, to order the use of expensive technologies to diagnose and treat patients, and for hospitals to provide intensive in-hospital nursing care and support services. Since 1982, the environment for medical care services has changed dramatically. In 1982 the federal government approved a major change in the way it pays for hospital care for Medicare beneficiaries. The new payment scheme, the prospective payment system (PPS), pays hospitals a fixed amount of money for each patient in a diagnostically related group (DRG). PPS opened the door for the private sector health plans to also develop managed care schemes that placed hospitals (and physicians) at financial risk and demanded greater accountability from both parties. By 2000, 30 per cent of the US population was enrolled in HMOs. In some states the market penetration of HMOs was much higher. For example, 54 per cent of the California population was enrolled in HMOs (Interstudy, 2000).

Five key elements of managed care health plans as they unfolded in the United States from 1982–2000 were:

1   payment from health plans to hospitals and physicians in a manner other than fee-for-service, such as capitation, per diem, or discounted fee-for-service;

2   limitations on the health plan member's choice of hospital and physician (selective contracting);

3   adoption of drug formularies by health plans to constrain expenditures on pharmaceuticals;

4   increased demands for provider accountability for medical service utilisation, resulting in implementation of required prior approval from the patient's health plan for certain expensive referrals, tests, and procedures (gatekeeping).

5   competition among hospitals and among physician groups for covered lives: persons enrolled in managed care plans.

The rise of managed care, and the related increasing demands for greater efficiency in providing hospital care, posed two major challenges for hospital administrators: 1) placing limits on the use of hospital resources in order to achieve financial profitability while 2) not alienating the physicians who refer patients to the hospital. The actions hospital administrators might take to limit the use of hospital resources, such as declining to purchase an expensive piece of new diagnostic technology or refusing to expand the number of operating theatres, could easily threaten the perceived autonomy and authority of attending physicians (Georgopoulos et al., 1987; Burns et al., 1999; Morrisey et al., 1999; Shortell et al., 2001).

Differing Perspectives of Hospital Administrators and Physicians

This study examines the state of hospital–physician relationships during 2000, a year marking the end of a decade of growth in managed care plans throughout the United States. We assume that the state of hospital–physician relationships is at least partly manifested in the opinions of hospital administrators and physicians in leadership positions in the hospital's medical staff. We expect administrators and physician leaders to react differently to managed care pressures and incentives. Their respective cultural beliefs and values, forged by their education, training, and socialisation, are inherently different. Table 4.1 presents the key cultural differences between hospital administrators and physicians.

Given their differing values, beliefs and foci, in managed care environments we expect physicians to express more negative views about the hospital–

Table 4.1   Cultural differences between hospital administrators and physicians

Attribute	Hospital administrators	Physicians
Basis of knowledge	Primarily social and management sciences	Primarily biomedical sciences
Exposure to relevant others while in training	Relatively little exposure to physicians, nurses, other health care professionals, or patients	Great deal of exposure to nurses, other health professionals, and patients; little exposure to broader business/economic world of health care
Patient focus	Broad: all patients in the organisation and the larger community	Narrow: one's individual patients
Time frame of action	Middle to long run; emphasis on positioning the organisation for the future	Generally short run; meet immediate needs of patients
Decision-making	Fewer, larger decisions taken, usually by or in groups, often requiring negotiation or compromise, with many organisational constraints	Many clinical decisions taken every day, mostly by individual clinicians with few constraints on their decision
Rules of evidence	Understand the need to act on 'soft' qualitative information; loose-linked cause-effect relationships that may not be well understood	'Soft' qualitative information viewed with scepticism; prefer 'hard' facts; tightly linked cause-effect relationships that are well understood
View of resources	Always limited; challenge lies in allocating scarce resources efficiently and effectively	Resources essentially unlimited or at least should be unlimited; resources should be available to maximise the quality of care
Professional identity	Much less professionalised, with much less formal body of knowledge	Highly professionalised, with a strong formal body of knowledge

Source: Adapted from Shortell, 1991 and Walshe and Rundall, 2001.

physician relationship generally and about constraints on the availability of hospital resources in particular.

Key Questions Addressed in the Study

The data collection and analyses for this study were organised around seven questions that were suggested by previous research (Shortell, 1991) and from preliminary discussions with hospital managers and physicians. These questions and the responses derived from the survey and interview data described above are used as the format for presenting the study's key findings.

1   What is the current state of hospital–physician relationships as perceived by hospital administrators and physicians?
2   Are there specific aspects of hospital–physician relationships for which less than a majority of both administrators and physicians agree that performance is supportive of a strong hospital–physician relationship?
3   Are there specific aspects of hospital–physician relationships for which less than a majority of physicians (only) agree that performance is supportive of a strong hospital–physician relationship?
4   Are there specific aspects of hospital–physician relationships for which less than a majority of administrators (only) agree that performance is positive?
5   Are there specific aspects of hospital–physician relationships where there is a substantial difference of opinion regarding performance?
6   What do administrators and physicians feel are the most significant barriers to improving hospital–physician relationships?
7   What do administrators and physicians feel are the most significant facilitators for improving hospital–physician relationships?

Study Design

This study consisted of two related data collection efforts: 1) a mail survey sent to a sample of managers and physician leaders in 96 hospitals and seven health systems within the VHA, West Coast network; and 2) interviews with 18 senior managers and physician leaders in five different hospitals. The hospitals participating in this study were all affiliated with VHA, West Coast, Inc., a network of not-for-profit hospitals. Although the majority of the hospitals are community general hospitals, several major medical centres and teaching hospitals were included in the sample. The hospitals ranged in size from 15 to 564 available beds, and included rural, suburban, and urban facilities. The following lists the states in which the hospitals are located and lists the per cent of each state's total population enrolled in HMOs:

State	HMO market penetration
Arizona	31%
California	54%
Hawaii	30%
Oregon	41%
Washington	15%

A 67-item self-administered questionnaire was developed, building on previous research on hospital–physician relationships (Shortell, 1991). The questionnaire addressed a number of specific aspects of the hospital–physician relationship, such as perceptions of the hospital's support of physician practices; physician autonomy; cost-efficiency of patient care; physician equipment and technology needs; quality of care; physician participation in hospital management and governance; hospital facilities; physician leadership; incentives and risks in managed care contracts; and joint ventures between the hospital and physicians. The questionnaire also asked respondents to rate hospital–physician relationship at their institution and asked about the barriers and facilitators to strengthening hospital–physician relationships. The questionnaire is attached to this chapter as Appendix A.

During March and April 2000, the questionnaire was mailed to 323 senior administrators and physician leaders in 96 hospitals. The individuals to whom the questionnaire was sent varied somewhat depending upon the number of managerial and physician leader roles in the hospital. Typically, the questionnaire was sent to the hospital's chief executive officer, chief financial officer, chief operating officer, chief of staff, and medical director. Follow-up reminder cards were sent, and later reminder telephone calls to each person in the sample were placed to request that each recipient complete the questionnaire and return it to the investigators. A total of 117 out of 323 questionnaires were returned for a 36 per cent response rate. Completed surveys were returned from 65 administrators and 52 physicians. At least one questionnaire was returned from 61 of 96 hospitals in the sample (64 per cent).

To gain more in-depth and detailed information about hospital–physician relationships, interviews were conducted with 18 senior administrators and physician leaders at five hospitals. In each case, the hospital chief executive officer, chief of staff, and/or medical director were interviewed. In some hospitals an additional manager, physician, or nurse executive was interviewed. Seventeen individuals were interviewed in person at their hospital. In one case the interview was conducted via telephone. The interviewees were sent the interview guide in advance of their interview so they could reflect on the key interview questions prior to the meeting. The interviews averaged 45 minutes to one hour in length and covered topics related to the history of the hospital; the status of hospital management and board relations with the medical staff; the roles played by physicians; the trust between the hospital and its physicians; specific accomplishments, barriers, and facilitators of hospital–physician relationships; specific approaches used to improve relationships; and the extent of physician influence over the hospital's strategic and operational decision-making. The interviewee's responses to questions were recorded in notes taken by one of the investigators.

All survey respondents and interviewees were assured that information they provided would remain anonymous.

The cross-sectional survey design provides a 'snapshot' of the hospital–physician relationship and of the key factors affecting this relationship during the spring of 2000.

Study Sample Characteristics

Characteristics of the survey respondents are shown in Table 4.2. Overall, 117 surveys were completed by 65 hospital administrators (56 per cent) and 52 physicians (44 per cent). The majority of respondents were male (77 per cent) and Caucasian (91 per cent); the mean age of the sample was 51.7 years. Survey respondents filled a variety of roles within the hospital setting, including physician executives (38 per cent), chief executive officers (28 per cent), chief financial officers (9 per cent), attending medical staff (5 per cent), quality managers (1 per cent), and other hospital employees (18 per cent). Respondents indicated an average of 6.3 years in their position and 13.1 years affiliation with the hospital.

As seen in Table 4.2, physician respondents had been affiliated with the hospital nearly twice as long as the administrators surveyed (17.9 years vs. 9.3 years, respectively). The respondent's primary role in the hospital also differed by type of respondent, with physicians primarily serving as physician executives (85 per cent) and attending medical staff (11 per cent); hospital

Table 4.2   Characteristics of survey respondents

	Administrators (n = 65)	Physicians (n = 52)	Total (n = 117)
Percent of total respondents	56%	44%	100%
Sex			
Male	73%	82%	77%
Female	27%	18%	23%
Ethnicity			
Caucasian-white-non-Hispanic	92%	90%	91%
Asian/Pacific Islander	5%	8%	6%
Latino	3%	2%	3%
Mean age (years)	50.0	53.6	51.7
Respondent's primary role in hospital			
Physician Executive	0%	85%	38%
Chief Executive Officer	52%	0%	28%
Chief Financial Officer	17%	0%	9%
Attending medical staff	0%	11%	5%
Quality Manager	2%	0%	1%
Other hospital employee	30%	4%	18%
Mean years in position	6.3	6.3	6.3
Mean years affiliated with hospital	9.3	17.9	13.1

administrators were more likely to fill the role of chief executive officer (52 per cent), chief financial officer (17 per cent), and other hospital positions (30 per cent).

Table 4.3 provides additional characteristics of the physician subsample only. Physicians in the sample were well distributed across specialty areas, with the largest proportions in internal medicine (37 per cent), general/family practice/general internal medicine (17 per cent), and surgery (12 per cent). These respondents indicated a relatively high level of participation in hospital governance, with 27 per cent being a member of the hospital board and 70 per cent serving on an executive committee of the hospital. The majority of physicians surveyed were compensated by salary (55 per cent). A variety of practice types were represented, including group practice (47 per cent), solo practice (23 per cent), hospital-based physician (15 per cent), and other (15 per cent).

Interviews

Interviews were conducted with a total of 18 senior administrators and physician leaders in five different hospitals within the VHA, West Coast network. Interviewees included chief executive officers (7), physician executives (6), hospital administrators (4), and one director of nursing.

Findings

1   What is the Current State of Hospital–physician Relationships as perceived by Hospital Administrators and Physicians?

A person's overall assessment of the hospital–physician relationship will influence their demeanour, decision-making, and commitment to the institution. In any given hospital, opinions regarding this relationship will differ among its administrators and medical staff members. Across hospitals, opinions will also differ due to local circumstances and the historical development of the hospital. We will not try to examine all the complexities introduced by these role and community differences. Rather, our intent is to provide an assessment of the current state of opinion regarding overall hospital–physician relationships that cuts across all the hospitals in our sample. We do compare, however, the opinions expressed by two groups of respondents: lay administrators and

Table 4.3   Characteristics of physician survey subsample (n = 52)

	Percent
Specialty area	
Internal medicine	37
General/family practice/general internal medicine	17
Surgery	12
Obstetrics/gynecology	7
Pediatrics	5
Emergency medicine	5
Anesthesiology	2
Other	15
Member of hospital board (% yes)	27
Serves on executive committee of hospital (% yes)	70
Compensation arrangement with hospital	
Salary	55
Fee for service	10
Departmental revenue/capitated	3
Other	32
Type of practice	
Medical group practice	47
Solo practice	23
Hospital-based physician	15
Other	15
Medical group's relation to hospital (among those respondents who indicate being part of a medical group)	
Owned by hospital	5
Other	95

physician leaders, most of whom are the chiefs of staff or medical directors in their hospitals.

While the majority of respondents rated the current hospital–physician relationship positively, a substantial minority did not. However, the relationship is complex and not easily summarised in a single measure. Interview data from administrators and physicians indicated that the hospital–physician relationship varies depending on the issues being addressed at any point in time and on the particular subgroup of physicians of concern. Moreover, it is apparent that the relationship is dynamic, evolving over time as all parties learn to adjust to the new environment for medical care.

Table 4.4 reveals that only 56 per cent of respondents rated hospital–physician relationships at the positive end of the response scale (4 or 5). Higher proportions of physicians than administrators rated the hospital–physician relationship at the extremes of the response scale. Physicians were more likely to say that the hospital–physician relationship was poor, but they were also more likely to say that the relationship was excellent. However, these differences were not large enough to be statistically significant.

Table 4.4   Overall rating of hospital–physician relationship

Q55 Overall, how would you rate hospital–physician relationships at this institution?	Percent of respondents reporting	
	Administrators	Physicians
1 (Poor)	3%	13%
2	9%	10%
3	28%	25%
4	54%	37%
5 (Excellent)	6%	15%

This bifurcation of physicians' views of the hospital physician relationship was reflected in comments from physician leaders in our interviews. One physician emphasised how positive the relationship had become in the recent past:

> On a scale from one to ten, the hospital–physician relationship here is about 8.5. The administration is very supportive of the medical staff, and the medical staff works well with the administration. This is due to a lot of recent work to develop a collaborative culture and to the individuals currently involved. The medical staff actually brings initiative proposals to the hospital. This is a big improvement in comparison to four or five years ago. We have made improvements in clinical care in the ER, treatment of cardiovascular patients, and in our working relationships with nurses. In each case the medical staff proposed the improvement initiative and the hospital supported it.

Physicians also expressed negative views of the hospital–physician relationship. For example, one doctor stated:

> Those on the medical staff who voice an opinion say that the relationship is adversarial and that they do not trust the hospital management. The hospital administrators consider the medical staff as a fact they have to live with. As a group, management's opinion is not positive or respectful.

The qualitative interviews indicate that the hospital–physician relationship is unusually complex, dependent on factors external to the hospital and on individuals and circumstances within the hospital. For example, a number of persons interviewed commented that the state of the hospital–physician relationship varied depending on the issue under discussion and the subgroup of physicians with whom discussions are being held. As one administrator noted:

> The relationship is very complex, depending on the issue and whether the physician is a member of the hospital's IPA. Historically, community physicians have been suspicious of the IPA. Also, in the past specialists were closer to hospital management. With managed care, the hospital is closer to the primary care physicians.

Other interviewees commented on the importance of the values and management style of the individuals in leadership positions, especially the hospital chief executive officer and the chief of the medical staff, in building a strong hospital–physician relationship.

> At the present time relationships are good. Much improved over the past four years. This is mostly due to a change in the CEO four years ago. The key to improving relationships was open communication. It was important to share sensitive financial information with the medical staff. When this information was kept from the physicians, suspicion was generated. The doctors thought there was a lot more profit than there was. They now know the hospital's financial picture is positive but fragile.

Finally, one administrator emphasised the transition that hospital and physicians are in as managed care arrangements redefine longstanding relationships and roles:

> Relationships here are as good as they could be given the pressures of the environment. CEOs have tried hard to build relationships. Money always becomes a barrier. Each side wants things (e.g. new technology, taking consultations in the ER, etc.) that the other does not want or cannot deliver. The hospital and the medical staff are still in transition from the old way of doing things when there was more generous revenue to today's environment.

2   *Are there Specific Aspects of Hospital–physician Relationships for*
    which less than a Majority of both Administrators and Physicians
    agree that Performance is Supportive of a Strong Hospital–physician
    Relationship?

It is important to understand not only the overall status of the hospital–
physician relationship, but also the perceptions of specific aspects of hospital
and physician performance that affect the relationship. The self-administered
questionnaire asked administrators and physicians their opinions about a
large number of such aspects of their relationship, such as to what extent
did they agree or disagree with the statement: 'Hospital administrators and
physicians are in agreement on the overall goals of the institution.' (A few
statements were reverse-worded, in which case we identified those statements
where less than a majority of administrators and physicians *disagreed* with
the statement.) Table 4.5 identifies statements on which less than a majority
of *both* administrators and physicians agreed. In these cases there is a clear
mandate to examine the reasons for such negative opinions and pursue
strategies to improve performance and communicate about this issue with
administrators and physicians. Early intervention to discuss those areas of
performance of mutual concern, and to improve performance, will strengthen
the hospital–physician relationship.

3   *Are there Specific Aspects of Hospital–physician Relationships for which*
    less than a Majority of Physicians (Only) Agree that Performance is
    Supportive of a Strong Hospital–physician Relationship?

With respect to some aspects of the hospital–physician relationship, it may be
the case that while the majority of administrators may agree performance is
supportive of a strong hospital–physician relationship, a majority of physicians
may not agree. Table 4.6 presents the statements on which a majority of the
physicians (only) disagreed. In their responses to three of these four statements
the physicians are expressing concern that the hospital will undermine the
physicians in their dealing with managed care plan. In the fourth case, the
physicians expressed disagreement with the assertion that there is an adequate
number of nurses to provide quality of care, a major issue in managed care
environments.

Table 4.5   Statements for which less than a majority of administrators and physicians express agreement

Statement	Percent of respondents who agree or strongly agree	
	Administrators	Physicians
Q6 The hospital administration gets things done quickly	49%	41%
Q30 Physicians perceive the hospital's decision-making process to be fair	42%	46%
Q33. The hospital responds quickly to purchase requests	48% *	29%
Q36 The hospital and physicians work collaboratively to try to obtain 'fair' contracts with payers	38%	37%
Q41 The financial incentives in managed care contracts for the hospital and the physicians are in alignment	20%	12%
Q42 The hospital and physicians collaborate effectively in negotiating managed care contracts	30%	19%

*   Difference of proportions test for administrators vs physicians significant at p < .05.

Table 4.6   Statements for which less than a majority of physicians express agreement

Statement	Percent of respondents who agree or strongly agree	
	Administrators	Physicians
Q29 There is an adequate number of nurses to provide quality patient care.	52% *	25%
Q44 The hospital's involvement with prepaid plans (HMOs) takes into account physician interest.	65% *	42%
Q45 The hospital facilitates partnerships with physicians that are 'win-win.'	74% *	43%
Q46 The hospital's involvement with PPOs takes into account physician interest.	55% *	44%

* Difference of proportions test for administrators vs physicians significant at p < .05.

4 *Are there Specific Aspects of Hospital–physician Relationships for which less than a Majority of Administrators (Only) Agree that Performance is Supportive of a Strong Hospital–physician Relationship?*

Table 4.7 identifies the only statement on which less than a majority of administrators (only) agreed. Only 49 per cent of hospital administrators agreed that 'The hospital enjoys strong physician leadership.'

5 *Are there Specific Aspects of Hospital–physician Relationships where there is a Substantial Difference of Opinion Regarding Performance?*

Table 4.8 identifies those statements on which there was at least a twenty percentage point difference between administrator and physician responses. These finding reveal fairly deep divisions in the perceptions of administrators and physicians regarding the availability of hospital resources, the 'fairness of the hospital–physician relationship,' and the strength of the hospitals physician leadership. Five statements have to do with the availability of various hospital resources: operating rooms, beds, nurses, and other personnel. In each case a significantly higher percentage of administrators agreed that the supply was adequate. Two items state that the hospital supports 'win-win' partnerships with physicians, and that the hospital's involvement with HMOs takes into account physician interests. Again, a significantly higher percentage of administrators agreed with these statements. Interestingly, a higher percentage of physicians agreed with the statements indicating that the hospital enjoys strong physician leadership, and that physicians bear more risk that the hospital in current managed care contracts.

6 *What do Administrators and Physicians feel are the most Significant Barriers to Improving Hospital–physician Relationships?*

Questions on both the survey and the interview guide asked about the barriers to effective hospital–physician relationships. The majority of survey respondents identified the rather broad category 'external economic and regulatory forces' as the barrier to effective hospital–physician relationships. Interestingly, the next most frequently identified barrier was the 'other' category. The survey provided respondents with an opportunity to specify what these 'other' barriers were. The most frequently mentioned barriers are noted below.

Table 4.7   Statements for which less than a majority of administrators express agreement

Statement	Percent of respondents who agree or strongly agree	
	Administrators	Physicians
Q35 The hospital enjoys strong physician leadership	49% *	73%

* Difference of proportions test for administrators vs physicians significant at p < .05.

Table 4.8   Statements for which there is at least a 20 percentage point difference between administrator and physician agreement

Statement	Percent of respondents who agree or strongly agree	
	Administrators	Physicians
Q4 The hospital provides the needed personnel to support quality care	88% *	67%
Q9 There is adequate availability of operating rooms	76% *	46%
Q12 There is adequate availability of beds	69% *	49%
Q29 There is an adequate number of nurses to provide quality patient care	52% *	25%
Q34 The relative degree of power and influence among the hospital board, management and medical staff is appropriate	74% *	53%
Q35 The hospital enjoys strong physician leadership	49% *	73%
Q39 In general, physicians bear more risk than the hospital in current managed care contracts	16% *	39%
Q44 The hospital's involvement with prepaid plans (HMOs) takes into account physician interest	65% *	42%
Q45 The hospital facilitates partnerships with physicians that are 'win-win'	74% *	43%
Q48 The hospital provides the needed personnel to support cost-efficient care	78% *	54%

* Difference of proportions test for administrators vs physicians significant at p < .05.

Barrier	**Number of mentions**
Lack of alignment of incentives between the hospital and physician	5
Conflict among hospital board, management and physicians	4
Lack of trust between physicians and the hospital's management	1
The hospital's need to control the care process	1

The damage done to hospital–physician relationships by external market forces was frequently noted in interviews with physicians and administrators. One physician described the nature of these market forces:

> It is due to the partnership of insurance carriers and business groups. Insurance carriers have the ability to drive a wedge between the hospital and the physician groups. A solid hospital–physician relationship can be broken down by the carrier/business group market pressure. [Another barrier is] Wall Street. They have the money to make things happen. Wall Street Investors can fund satellite hospitals and strain former hospital–physician alliances.

The financial pressure created by market forces may put physicians and hospitals at odds over quality of care issues. One physician described the most important barrier to improving hospital physician relationships as:

> The philosophy of management. Management is focused on sustaining economic viability/reducing costs; physicians think about caring for patients and about costs later.

A hospital administrator agreed with this observation.

> The biggest problem is reduction in reimbursement from managed care – 'the big squeeze'. This can interfere with achieving agreement on clinical guidelines, for example.

Declining revenue for physicians and hospitals was a frequently mentioned barrier to hospital–physician relationships. But, it is interesting to note that many of the respondents linked reduced revenue to another barrier, less time to work on building relationships. For example, one administrator said:

An important barrier is reduced revenue. As MDs incomes have shrunk, MDs must spend more time in patient care. They don't have time to work on developing relationships.

A physician respondent agreed with this view. At his hospital:

Time demands are a problem. MDs do not have time to attend meetings and participate in planning.

One administrator identified a package of four barriers:

Managed care and the Balanced Budget Act have reduced revenue to the hospital. The hospital is not making a profit. The financial incentives between hospitals and physicians have become less aligned in recent years. … Physician's believe that the whole managed care process treads on their autonomy. Before, central issues were about equipment and technology, issues only indirectly related to physicians' incomes. Now, with managed care, it is about personal income of the physicians and their autonomy. This has become a personal struggle for the physicians. … Also, Compliance laws thrust on the hospital serve to 'sanitise' the relationship between the hospital and physicians. How do you pay doctors to be the head of a unit without putting the hospital in a position of liability with respect to utilisation, referrals, etc.? … Finally, the lack of good information systems is a barrier. There is a greater need to communicate with physicians than ever before, but the cost of developing the information systems is a barrier. The appetite for information is 'insatiable' and there is a high cost to achieving connectivity – everybody wants everything now.

Other themes frequently mentioned in interviews were communication and trust. One administrator emphasised the difficulties that arise from poor interpersonal skills:

The most important barriers are inability to communicate well with one another in contract negotiations, inability to trust one another, and lack of skill in negotiation.

A physician echoed these sentiments:

Open communication and trust are still developing; lack of these is still a barrier.

7   What do Administrators and Physicians feel are the most Significant
Facilitators for Improving Hospital–physician Relationships?

Perhaps the single most important question addressed by this study is what are the factors that facilitate building a strong hospital–physician relationship? We will address this question with data from both the survey and interviews of hospital administrators and physicians.

The survey asked respondents to identify factors that would strengthen hospital physician relationships. Many facilitators were suggested. The ten most frequently mentioned facilitators are listed below.

Facilitator	Number of mentions
Communication between the hospital and physicians	15
Alignment of hospital and physician financial incentives	11
Physician educational programmes and leadership development	8
Physician involvement in committees and decision-making	6
Focus on improving the quality of patient care	4
Trust between administrators and physicians	3
Sharing hospital financial information with physicians	3
Reduce administrative work physicians are required to perform	3
Efficient delivery of patient care services	3
Formal, paid role for Chief-of-Staff and VP Medical Affairs	å

The most frequently mentioned facilitator in our survey data and in our interviews was communication. Some typical comments from administrators were:

> Communication and dialogue are the answers; get the physician engaged and make them part of the solution.

> More communication between physician leaders and the hospital management [is the key].

The facilitators for better hospital physician relations are open communication, honest sharing of views, a forthright approach to dealing with people, and building trust.

Open communication. Partnership in decision-making. These things help even if feelings get hurt.

One-on-one communication (is the key). Administrators need to develop personal relationships with physicians and develop multiple channels of communication, including phone calls, e-mails, meetings, and open-door availability.

Our CEO makes rounds up on the floor, talking to staff and physicians. This communicates interest and understanding.

One CEO summed up many of these findings in his three key facilitators for a strong hospital–physician relationship:

Physicians must have active meaningful involvement in governance. They must participate in the management process by serving on committees and sharing in decision-making. The hospital must share information with physicians about its finances and other indicators of performance with physicians.

The other facilitators that were frequently listed by survey respondents were also identified by interviewees. Numerous comments were made regarding the value of alignment of hospital and physician financial incentives; programs to educate physicians on policy and management issues; getting physicians involved in committees and decision-making; formalising the paid role of the Chief-of-Staff and/or Vice President for Medical Affairs, and more generally paying for physicians' time to be on-call in the emergency department and to work on hospital committees and projects.

Conclusion

Strong, effective hospital–physician relationships are essential for the future success of both hospitals and physicians. Although external factors such as third party payment arrangements and increasing regulations to prevent fraud and abuse were the most commonly cited barriers to improving hospital–physician relations, other factors more easily controlled within the hospital setting were also deemed important. Our findings suggest that by working

Table 4.9　Barriers to effective hospital physician relationships

Q49 What do you feel is the most significant barrier to effective hospital–physician relationships at this institution?

	Percent of respondents reporting	
	Administrators	Physicians
External economic and regulatory forces	70% *	56%
Internal disagreements among board management and medical staff	11%	15%
Time demands hospitals place on physicians and the loss of income that may result	5%	10%
Other	14%	19%

* Difference of proportions test for administrators vs physicians significant at p < .05.

together to: 1) align the incentives facing hospitals and physicians; 2) improve the quality of patient care; 3) enhance the cost-efficiency of patient care; 4) support physician participation in hospital governance and management; and 5) cultivate physician leadership, hospital administrators and physicians would do a great deal to strengthen hospital–physician relationships.

Finally, the quality of interpersonal relationships were found to be important facilitators of strong hospital–physician relationships. Frequent communication, mutual respect, trust, and the cultivation of a collaborative and participative organisational culture are important facilitators for effective hospital–physician relationships. We conclude then, with a call for comprehensive efforts to improve hospital–physician relations through work on health policy, individual and organisational performance, and interpersonal dynamics and organisational culture. The difficulty of achieving success should not be underestimated. However, many administrators and physicians in our study suggested that fundamental improvements in quality, cost control, and provider and patient satisfaction could be expected from improved hospital–physician relations. These are benefits worthy of such a challenging task.

Acknowledgements

This study was conducted under the auspices of the Center for Health Management Studies at the University of California, Berkeley. The study was funded by the Center's Research Partners Program. VHA, West Coast, Inc. is a member of the Research Partners Program, and through its financial contribution to this Program, provided funding for this research. I am grateful to VHA, West Coast for this financial support. I am thankful for the collaboration of the leadership of VHA, West Coast, Inc. on important aspects of this study. I am especially indebted to Michelle van Zuiden, Senior VP/Executive Officer, Karen Oppliger, CHE, Director, Managed Care, and Alan H. Rosenstein, MD, MBA, Vice President/Medical Director for their contributions to the development of the research questions and study instruments, the selection of study hospitals, and the identification of hospital managers and physicians to be surveyed and interviewed. These contributions were crucial to the success of this study. I greatly appreciate the assistance of Sherrie Tye, who compiled the computer database and produced the statistical tables for the analysis. I am also thankful for the cooperation of over 130 hospital managers and physicians who willingly took time to complete our questionnaire or to be interviewed for this study. In every case these dedicated men and women cordially welcomed us into their busy world and generously shared their time to respond to our questions thoughtfully and with candour.

References

Burns, L.R., Andersen, R.M. and Shortell S.M. (1993), 'Trends in Hospital/Physician Relationships', *Health Affairs*, Fall, pp. 213–23.

Burns, L.R., Andersen, R.M. and Shortell, S.M. (1999), 'The Effect of Hospital Control Strategies on Physician Satisfaction and Physician-Hospital Conflict', *Health Services Research*, 25:9 (3), pp. 527–60.

Eisele, C.W., Fifer, W.R. and Wilson, T.C. (1985), *The Medical Staff and the Modern Hospital*, Englewood, CO: Estes Park Institute.

Fifer, W.R. (1987), 'The Hospital Medical Staff of 1997', *Quality Review Bulletin*, June, pp. 194–7.

Georgopoulos, B.S., D'Aunno, T.A. and Saavadra, R. (1987), 'Hospital–physician Relations under Hospital Prepayment', *Medical Care*, 25, pp. 781–95.

Ginsburg, P.B. and Lesser C.S. (2001), *Understanding Health System Change: Local Markets, National Trends*, Chicago: Health Administration Press.

Interstudy (2000), *The Interstudy Competitive Edge 10.2. Part II: HMO Industry Report*, St Paul, MN: Interstudy Publications.

Morrisey M.A., Alexander, J., Burns, L.R. and Johnson, V. (1999), 'The Effects of Managed Care on Physician and Clinical Integration in Hospitals', *Medical Care*, 37 (4), pp. 350–61.

Robinson, J.C. (1999), *The Corporate Practice of Medicine*, Berkeley, CA: University of California Press.

Rundall, T.G., Starkweather, D.B. and Norrish, B.R. (1998), *After Restructuring: Empowerment Strategies at Work in America's Hospitals*, San Francisco: Jossey Bass.

Scott, W.R. (1982), 'Managing Professional Work: Three Models of Control for Health Organizations', *Health Services Research*, 17, pp. 213–40.

Scott, W.R., Ruef, M., Mendel, P.J. and Caronna, C.A. (2000), *Institutional Change and Healthcare Organizations*, Chicago: The University of Chicago Press, 57–95.

Shortell, S.M. (1991), *Effective Hospital–physician Relationships*, Ann Arbor, MI: Health Administration Press.

Shortell, S.M., Alexander, J.A., Budetti, P.B., Burns, L.R., Gillies, R.R., Waters, T.M. and Zuckerman, H.S. (2001), 'Physician-system Alignment: Introductory Overview', *Medical Care*, 39 (7), I–1–I–8.

Shortell, S.M., Gillies, R.R., Anderson, D.A., Erickson, K.M. and Mitchell, J.B. (2000), *Remaking Health Care in America*, 2nd edn, San Francisco: Jossey Bass.

Walshe, K. and Rundall, T.G. (2001), 'Evidence-based Management: From Theory to Practice in Health Care', *The Milbank Quarterly*, 79 (3), pp. 429–57.

Appendix

Survey of Hospital–physician Relationships

This survey is part of a collaborative study conducted by VHA West Coast, Inc. and the University of California, Berkeley, Center for Health Management Studies. The purpose of the study is to gain a better understanding hospital–physician relationships and to identify strategies for building more effective and positive linkages between hospitals and physicians.

In today's rapidly changing health care environment, the hospital–physician relationship faces increasing pressures and strain. A number of technological, economic, market, and regulatory forces pose new challenges for hospitals, physicians, and their relationships. In order to realise success providing health care to our communities, it is critical for both administrators and physicians to break down communication barriers and to work to establish positive working alliances.

Your participation in this study will provide critical information on the current status of hospital–physician relations, as well as existing or planned strategies to improve these relationships. A central objective is to uncover the level of satisfaction, needs, and recommendations from the perspective of various groups within the health care sector (i.e., physicians, hospital administrators, nursing staff, etc.). Your feedback and insights are invaluable toward this goal.

Please be assured that your responses to this survey will be kept strictly confidential. All answers will be recorded anonymously and no names or other identifying information will be used in any reports that emerge from the study.

After completing the survey, please return it and the signed informed consent form in the enclosed pre-addressed, postage-paid envelope.

Finally, it is our hope to share study results with you and other study participants through a roundtable and learning network meeting to be held at a central location. Survey results will be aggregated and written summaries of findings will be made available to VHA West Coast member hospitals at this time.

**Thank you very much for sharing your perspectives and insights with us.
Your help is greatly appreciated.**

Hospital–physician Relationships Survey

Instructions: Please circle the number that corresponds to *your* degree of agreement or disagreement with each of the statements below. We are interested in your honest, candid opinion of each statement. All statements and questions you are asked to respond to refer to your hospital or medical center.

Statement	Strongly agree	Agree	Neither agree nor disagree	Disagree	Strongly disagree
SECTION A					
1　Physicians are adequately involved in care management activities	5	4	3	2	1
2　The hospital gives physicians sufficient autonomy to practise medicine	5	4	3	2	1
3　There is adequate maintenance of current equipment	5	4	3	2	1
4　The hospital provides the needed personnel to support quality care	5	4	3	2	1
5　The hospital administration ensures cost-efficient operations and use of resources	5	4	3	2	1
6　The hospital administration gets things done quickly	5	4	3	2	1
7　The hospital CEO has confidence in physician leadership capabilities	5	4	3	2	1
8　The hospital is more interested in financial survival than clinical quality	5	4	3	2	1
9　There is adequate availability of operating rooms	5	4	3	2	1
10　Medical staff are consistently of high quality	5	4	3	2	1

Statement	Strongly agree	Agree	Neither agree nor disagree	Disagree	Strongly disagree
11 The hospital is willing to form joint ventures/partnerships with physicians	5 å	4	3	2	1
12 There is adequate availability of beds	5	4	3	2	1
13 The hospital exerts pressure to *not* use certain ancillary tests/services	5	4	3	2	1
14 The hospital provides the needed information technology to support quality care	5	4	3	2	1
15 There is adequate availability of ancillary services (x-ray, lab, etc.)	5	4	3	2	1
16 The hospital purchases equipment/technology requested	5	4	3	2	1
Section B					
17 The hospital encourages physician leadership development	5	4	3	2	1
18 The hospital provides the needed structure and resources to support cost-efficient care	5	4	3	2	1
19 Hospital ambulatory care programmes compete with physicians	5	4	3	2	1
20 Sufficient numbers of physicians are involved in hospital management and governance	5	4	3	2	1
21 Hospital administration and physicians are in agreement on the overall goals of the institution	5	4	3	2	1

Statement	Strongly agree	Agree	Neither agree nor disagree	Disagree	Strongly disagree
22 Hospital ancillary services (x-ray, lab, etc.) are consistently of high quality	5	4	3	2	1
23 The hospital encourages new programme development opportunities with physicians	5	4	3	2	1
24 Payment and compensation provisions in managed care contracts have created conflicts of interest between the hospital and physicians	5	4	3	2	1
25 Hospital diagnostic services compete with physicians	5	4	3	2	1
26 Inflexible rules hamper physician discretion in treating crisis cases	5	4	3	2	1
27 The hospital purchases the needed equipment/technology to support cost-efficient care	5	4	3	2	1
28 A key component of future success will be joint hospital–physician collaborations	5	4	3	2	1
29 There is an adequate number of nurses to provide quality patient care	5	4	3	2	1
30 Physicians perceive the hospital's decision-making process to be fair	5	4	3	2	1
31 The hospital uses performance profiling in the credentialing process	5	4	3	2	1
32 The hospital provides the needed information technology to support cost-efficient care	5	4	3	2	1

Statement	Strongly agree	Agree	Neither agree nor disagree	Disagree	Strongly disagree
SECTION C					
33 The hospital responds quickly to purchase requests	5	4	3	2	1
34 The relative degree of power and influence among the hospital board, management and medical staff is appropriate	5	4	3	2	1
35 The hospital enjoys strong physician leadership	5	4	3	2	1
36 The hospital and physicians work collaboratively to try to obtain 'fair' contracts with payers	5	4	3	2	1
37 The hospital supports the physician's private practice (e.g., physician referral service, practice management assistance, etc.)	5	4	3	2	1
38 The range of clinical services offered is adequate	5	4	3	2	1
39 In general, physicians bear more risk than the hospital in current managed care contracts	5	4	3	2	1
40 The physicians and hospital work well together as a team	5	4	3	2	1
41 The financial incentives in managed care contracts for the hospital and the physicians are in alignment	5	4	3	2	1
42 The hospital and physicians collaborate effectively in negotiating managed care contracts	5	4	3	2	1
43 The hospital exerts pressure to discharge/transfer patients early	5	4	3	2	1
44 The hospital's involvement with prepaid plans (HMOs) takes into account physician interest	5	4	3	2	1

Statement	Strongly agree	Agree	Neither agree nor disagree	Disagree	Strongly disagree
45 The hospital facilitates partnerships with physicians that are 'win–win'	5	4	3	2	1
46 The hospital's involvement with PPOs takes into account physician interest	5	4	3	2	1
47 There is good communication between hospital management and physician leadership	5	4	3	2	1
48 The hospital provides the needed personnel to support cost-efficient care	5	4	3	2	1

49 What do you feel is the most significant barrier to effective hospital–physician relationships at this institution? (Circle one)
1. External economic and regulatory forces.
2   Internal disagreements among board management and medical staff.
3   Time demands hospitals place on physicians and the loss of income that may result.
4   Other (Please explain): _____

50 How do you think the hospital primarily views the physician at this hospital? (Circle one)
1   As a competitor
2   As a partner
3   As an independent contractor
4   As an employee
5   Other (Please explain):_____

51 How satisfied are you with the time, resources and energy devoted to nurturing effective hospital–physician relationships at this institution? (Circle one)
1   Very satisfied
2   Somewhat satisfied
3   Not very satisfied
4   Not at all satisfied

52 How do you see hospital–physician relationships evolving over the next year? (Circle one)
1   Hospital–physician relations are likely to *improve*.
2   Hospital–physician relations are likely to *deteriorate*.
3   Hospital–physician relations are likely to *stay the same*.

53 What, if anything, would you recommend to further strengthen hospital–physician relationships?
What do you feel would be the greatest benefits of strengthening hospital–physician relations?

54 Overall, how would you rate hospital–physician relationships at this institution? (Circle one)

1	2	3	4	5
Poor				Excellent

55 What is your primary role within the hospital? (Circle one)
1 Chief Executive Officer
2 Chief Financial Officer
3 Chief Nursing Officer
4 Quality Manager
5 Physician Executive (e.g., Medical Director, VPMA, Department Chair or Director)
6 Attending medical staff
7 Other hospital employee (Please briefly indicate):_____

56 How long in this position?   _____Years

57 How long have you been affiliated with this hospital? _____Years

58 Sex: M F

59 What ethnicity best describes you? (Circle one)
1 African-American – Black
2 Asian/Pacific Islander
3 Caucasian – White – Non-Hispanic
4 Latino – Hispanic – Chicano
5 Native American Indian
6 Other: _____

60 What is your age?   _____Years

Additional Questions for Physicians:

61 What is your specialty area? (Circle one)
1 Surgery
2 Internal Medicine
3 Obstetrics/Gynecology
4 Pediatrics
5 Psychiatry

6   General/family practice/general internal medicine
7   Radiology
8   Anaesthesiology
9   Pathology
10 Emergency medicine
11 Other (Please briefly indicate): _____

62 Are you a member of the hospital's board?
1   Yes
2   No

63 Do you serve on an executive committee of this hospital?
1   Yes
2   No

64 What is your compensation arrangement with this hospital? (Circle one)
1   Fee for service
2   Departmental revenue/capitated
3   Salary
4   Other (Please briefly indicate): _____

65 Which of the following best describes your practice? (Circle one)
1   Solo practice
2   Medical group practice
3   Independent practice association
4   Hospital-based
5   Other (Please briefly indicate): _____

If you are part of a medical group practice:

66 What is your medical group's relationship with the hospital? (Circle one)
1   Owned by the hospital
2   Under contract with the hospital
3   Other (Please briefly indicate): _____

Thank you for your time.

Chapter 5

The Invisible Costs of Repeated Cycles of Organisational Restructuring: A Theory of (Dis)engagement

Jason Nickels

Introduction

On the 1 February 2001 'Improving Health in Wales: A Plan for the NHS and its Partners' was published. 'The Plan' articulated the central ideal that the Welsh NHS would become more democratic and simpler to understand. However, few health care managers dared imagine that these strategic ideals would equate to the dissolution of the five 'archetypical' Welsh Health Authorities.

During the last decade the Welsh NHS has seen a total of seven organisational restructures. Some would argue that the rationale is based upon the strategic assumption, that this will inject new interest, life and enthusiasm into the NHS system. Others, perhaps, a little too cynically, suggest that restructuring 'creates the illusion that something is happening' (Kets de Vries and Balazs, 1997, p. 8). Despite this fact the National Assembly for Wales continues to argue that the NHS staff remain 'its greatest asset'. The political rhetoric seemed reified when it became clear that there would be few, if any, redundancies resulting from the new strategic 'vision'.

As one can imagine, the human resource implications within the context outlined above, are in stark contrast with those whereby organisations engage in large-scale redundancies. Notably, within these latter contexts those employees 'fortunate' enough to remain employed often suffer from what has been termed as 'survivor sickness' (Noer, 1997). Put simply, the redundancy survivors report increased levels of stress, anxiety, and depression with the associated problem of decreased performance in relation to job satisfaction, morale and organisational commitment (Brockner, 1988). Evidently, from this perspective the National Assembly for Wales was incorporating 'best practice' into its human resource policies and methods, which is commendable.

Interestingly, however, there is a noticeable dearth of evidence that has critically examined the effects of repeated cycles of organisational restructures (RCOR) with respect to performance with the associated *absence* of redundancies. This inquiry seeks to address this gap. This chapter will outline the research more generally and a little later pay particular attention to the ways in which RCOR may have some important implications for group performance, more specifically, innovation.

Given the exploratory nature of this inquiry, this research utilised a grounded theory approach (Strauss and Corbin, 1995).

Methods and Data

The data are derived from 33 interviews (as reflected in Table 5.1). The research inquiry spans approximately 13 months (between May 2001 and June 2002). Grounded theory methods (Strauss and Corbin, 1995) were used to analyse the data. More specifically the steps taken included: 1) examining the interviews and developing open codes; 2) building a causal matrix; 3) conducting further theoretical sampling; 4) refining these concepts; 5) using axial coding in order to; 6) develop a theory.

Table 5.1   Data derived from interviews

Phase	Research objectives
1 Survey questionnaire (n = 50) The 'dissolution of a health authority' (case study approach)	To gauge the extent to which staff morale was impacted upon by the policy underpinning the dissolution of the health authority
2 Interviews (n = 15) discussion groups (n = 3) The 'dissolution of a health authority'	Open-ended interviews, and discussion groups to examine the negative impact of RCOR
3 Interviews Chief executives within Wales (n = 5)	To elicit the strategic view and the 'trade-offs' of RCOR. To research the nature of the 'new' psychological contract within NHS (Wales)
4 Innovations in care Interviews (n = 10)	To understand the nature, drivers and barriers to innovation within NHS (Wales)

There were four (overlapping) phases to the inquiry. These phases reflect the iterative nature of the inquiry process, as well as the ways in which this inquiry was informed and 'fed into' other research projects undertaken by the author.

Emergent Issues

In this section there are two important issues arising from the interview data. Firstly, for the majority of NHS managers RCOR was described as a positive way in which to 'open-up' new promotional opportunities and improved ways of working. As such, few participants thought that the practice would cease. Most thought that it would increase in its frequency and impact. Thus, the notion of perpetual motion (Baruch and Hind, 1999) is very much an internalised mental model for NHS management. This perception is consistent with global patterns (Marks, 1994; Burke and Nelson, 1997).

Secondly, consistent with the literature on group development (Srivastva et al., 1977; Jarrett and Kellner, 1996) it appears that RCOR yields a number of problems. In some circumstances RCOR *inhibits* both individual and group performance. It is to this latter set of problems that this research inquiry has found its energy. This sits neatly with the author's personal values of improving the quality of working life for NHS employees, in the belief that this will enhance long-term NHS organisational performance.

This chapter will now address and discuss the grounded theory of engagement. It is important to note that the most negative RCOR effect is a 'zone of disengagement', which precedes the engagement stage of group development and performance. Theoretically, the zone of disengagement is the total time period preceding the alignment of the four factors discussed below. By definition it is the *absence* of engagement. Some of the most prominent factors associated with the creation of the disengagement zone will also be highlighted. Some helpful ways in which to manage a group from a disengaged to a fully engaged 'state' will also be discussed.

Engagement Theory: A Conceptual Analysis

Analysis of the data indicates that a fully developed 'engaged stage' of group performance is the critical alignment and, at the same time, dynamic interplay between four critical, socially (intersubjectively) shared cognitive and emotional factors. These factors are outlined below:

- the genesis of group experiential 'interconnectedness';
- the occurrence of individual/group double-loop learning;
- a shared sense of empowerment relating to group objectives/ goals;
- the perception or 'bodily experience' that time and space have qualitatively changed.

Consistent with a phenomological perspective, it is important to understand the ways in which the research participants constructed these concepts within their daily work and talk (Shotter, 1994) with one another and the author (as the researcher). As such, this chapter will discuss (and attempt to define) each factor respectively.

One of the primary ways in which participants described an engaging experience was in the way in which they experienced a shared sense (Weick, 1997) of 'interconnectedness' between, and through, one another. Conceptually, interconnectedness rotates on a two-sided pivotal axis: mutual influence and reciprocated power-through-others. This axis is highly sensitive and when correctly calibrated provides the energy by which synergy and creative tension for high performance (for example, innovation) can be traced.

In contexts whereby one or more group member(s) is perceived to be exerting relatively too much influence or power, this theory predicts that such contexts would not be perceived as a fully engaging experience for the group present. In this respect, power is not conceptualised as 'residing in' individuals due to their job role or authority status. Power, herein, is seen as 'the ability to work through others in a spirit of cooperation and trust'. Similarly, mutual influence is the group perception that each member can exert a 'legitimate' influence by which one can, and ought to, shape the groups direction, work and energy. Legitimacy, in this respect, is an inter-subjective perception.

The second dimension of a fully 'engaged' state is the notion of double-loop learning. Although each participant described this entity in slightly different ways, in effect the notion of double-loop learning authentically conceptualises this dimension. For Argyris and Schon (1978) learning can take two main forms: single and double loop. Single loop learning is whereby those involved in the learning process instrumentally understand the goals and strategies being shared. However, the learning has a taken for granted quality. In contrast, double-loop learning has the added advantage that the learning strategies, values and goals are reflectively and critically examined for the underpinning assumptions and ideology. Thus, double-loop, rather than single-loop, learning will often be accompanied by changes in the groups' norms, policies and objectives. Put simply, it is learning *about* the learning that has taken place.

The notion of 'empowerment' is, unfortunately, developing into a conceptual nightmare (Thomas and Velthouse, 1990) or part of the on-going development of management fads and fashions (Carson et al., 1999). However, having said that, these research participants used the signifier in a specific 'fashion'. This is neatly summarised in this statement by one senior manager: '... we had the skills, the ability to change the environment, you know, we had what we needed to change this all around ... to get the job done'. Another added to this idea by stating that he knew that he could 'rely on (his co-workers) to play their part in realising the agenda'. In this way empowerment is 'the shared sense that the group has the necessary skills, expertise and desire to realise their objectives by working cooperatively together'.

Lastly, a definitive quality of an engaging work experience was the post-event evaluation, or perception, that *during the experience,* time and space had qualitatively changed. For example, one manager stated that he thought that his watch had broken. When he checked this with one of his colleagues, his colleague stated that she had noticed how time had appeared to pass quickly for her. This insight led the author to develop a theoretical sample of participants in which to elucidate this notion more fully. The author has found it to be a robust insight. These ideas, the author has later discovered, have something in common with the research of Csikszentmihalyi (1990, 1996) with flow theory.

Csikszentmihalyi (1990, 1996) wanted to understand the notion of creative genius. Therefore, he interviewed notable creative individuals and found that they would enter a state of happiness and fluid thought, which he termed 'flow'. Later this research (for example, Csikszentmihalyi, 1996) developed into an idea that humans can enter a 'stage' or 'state' of optimal experience. In such a state, we are very naturally energised, creative and at peace. In this way, he argues, flow involves a certain mind-set, emotional focus and our bodies exhibit physiological signs of being 'locked into' (and yet at peace with) our selves and our environment. In this way, we feel in total control of our actions, thoughts and emotions. The 'flow' encounter deeply locks the participant into a process of total absorption with the given flow activity. There is an accompanied sense of real value and purpose with such activity for the persons so involved.

However, unlike flow theory, the theory of engagement that has been generated from these participant's accounts is a *sociological* and not a psychological theory. In this way, it might well be that flow is being captured at the group, and not the individual, level.

Discussion

A summary thus far might be helpful. In effect, this research has found that RCOR has predominantly positive personal outcomes for the majority of NHS managers. However, RCOR has a destructive and disruptive affect. It is destructive in that it destroys (potentially) existing organisations and teams that are currently working within the 'zone of engagement'. It is disruptive in that it typically takes between seven to 12 months before organisations organically develop into the engagement zone. The data, therefore, implies a paradox: RCOR destroys and disrupts the very thing that it is seeking to enhance and improve. At least in the short to medium term. Therefore, one can only assume that the Health Authorities in Wales were not performing within an 'engaged' zone, and as a result, the National Assembly decided that the dissolution of the five Health Authorities was based on performance criteria of some sort or another.

There are a number of problems with this interpretation of events. Firstly, where is the evidence-base on which these performance judgements were made? To what extent were the Health Authorities ineffective? And ineffective for whom: patient-care or political (centralised) control?

Secondly, McClelland (2002) rightly claims that the National Assembly for Wales has the potential for a distinctive health policy making 'era', rather than a simple derivative of our English neighbours. However, there is a perception that this very desire for *distinctiveness* underpinned an irrational and illogical approach to the policy underpinning the restructural reforms within Wales. It was this desire to legitimate the policy-making role of the Assembly that created the necessary conditions to take a more 'radical' approach for its own sake, and not necessarily for a more patient-centred NHS. This, yet again, illustrates the tensions between the short-term need for re-election and media grabbing attention for Assembly members, and long-term rational and logical progression through service development and accompanying investment.

There is no evidence to suggest that with each RCOR cycle the aggregate performance level improve. This is currently a belief: 'an assumptive reality' (McClelland, 2002) presumably of NHS policy analysts. However, evidence from a survey of public sector managers' perceptions following a restructure (Worrall and Cooper, 1998) implies that RCOR is problematic. It creates slower decision-making speed and decreased overall participation in the short term. This is consistent with the theory of engagement in respect to the preceding zone of disengagement. However, for longer-term success, Nolan and Cronson (1995) argue that RCOR restructures introduce a necessary evil of 'creative destruction' (p. 12) by which organisations must evolve in order to continue in the longer term.

When participants were asked to reflect on the outcomes of an engaging experience most often they referred to new or novel ways of thinking and behaving as an outcome. Interestingly, an engaging experience acts as a group 'rite of passage' in relation to new, emerging group norms. These include risk-taking, initiative, coping with ambiguity and enhanced resilience when faced with challenging circumstances. The signifier 'innovation' has been selected for this concept. Thus, innovation is defined as 'the creation of something new within the groups problem-solving space'.

Lessons for the Future

This section of this chapter will examine some of the reasons *why* RCOR has an inhibitory affect in relation to engaging work experiences. The data has identified three major preceding factors: anxiety and stress, job role conflict and NHS politics. However, this section is intended to be open to consideration. As such, a conclusion section will raise some important *questions* for future research. Each of the three preceding factors will be discussed in turn. Each section will address key findings that will aid organisational developers and health policy analysts in informing their knowledge base within this increasingly important area.

Anxiety and Stress

Consistent with the available evidence, changing jobs (Ivancevich, 1986) can be a stressful event, particularly in the early transitional period. This influence is found even when one is promoted and enthused by the new post. This affect is compounded when the recipient is required to move geographically, or uproot family, and so on. There were two effective workplace methods referred to:

- access to an independent work counsellor;
- having a line manager/coach who made (achievable) specific and explicit job role expectations early in the job move.

Job Role Conflict

The second major constraint on developing into an engagement zone concerned what one research participant called the 'negotiated nature of NHS management'. Although each new/revised job had role parameters; too often managers thought that there were 'an excessive imbalance' between new and existing employees, with not enough existing managers to provide the sense of stability that they thought was a prerequisite for team development.

However, other managers' argued that the very introduction of this instability was a catalyst for new growth and welcomed it. There are four strategies in this regard:

- effective leadership to guide and direct the new structure and personnel;
- goal setting at both the group and individual level;
- linking the goals above with periodic (for example, six-monthly) performance appraisals. this seemed to help with job role clarity and its relation with other group members;
- having an external facilitator to assist in the early development of the new group.

As a Political Response

The literature on organisational justice (for example, Brockner et al., 1986) illustrates how National Assembly for Wales policies have as much an affect on employee's justice perceptions as do the relative personal outcomes. Conceptually, these are known as procedural and distributive justice respectively.

Within each wave of RCOR it would be best practice, from the available evidence-base, to build in systems and procedures whereby NHS employees could 'voice', in the truly democratic sense, their concerns. Too often the value of democracy is negated in practice as the anger, cynicism, frustration and embitterment is ignored and silenced. The evidence suggests that by giving employees a 'voice' acts as a method of catharsis (O'Neill and Lenn, 1995). For example, focus groups, consultative surveys (Cameron et al., 1991), and 'venting sessions' are effective mechanisms in this regard.

Importantly, the evidence from Noer (1997) suggests that organisations ignore this important dimension 'at their peril'. Concurring with that research, this inquiry discovered that those individuals who had *not* resolved these issues 'carried them' with them as part their NHS career trajectory. This small, but significant, minority were one of the most salient inhibitory engagement factors or forces. In effectively managing RCOR this is one of the most important findings.

Rousseau (1996) suggests that the notion of the psychological contract is helpful in analysing situations and contexts as that described above. It is only during critical moments (for example, the next RCOR implementation), that individuals are motivated to examine and look for information (Turnley and Feldman, 1998) regarding their psychological contracts. Consistent with equity theory (see Brockner et al., 1986) to the extent to which individuals feel their psychological contract has been 'violated' individuals will asymmetrically withdraw their 'hearts and minds' from the new NHS agenda. This will act as a significant inhibitory factor on the ability of the new group to move into the engagement zone.

There were four main factors why RCOR programmes were perceived as 'unfair or unjust'. These were:

- lowered promotional opportunities (career glass ceiling);
- lowered levels of quality of working life (for example, ruptured work friendships);
- the lack of a coherent National Assembly for Wales rationale for the RCOR programme;
- unfair 'job slotting' principles.

Each of the four issues will be discussed briefly in turn. The first problem is the perception that with the new RCOR programme the individual feels that they have 'not received a just or fair promotion'. This signifies to the individual that their NHS career now has a 'glass ceiling'. This, of course, may be completely true! As RCOR has an absence of redundancies, which is 'best practice' and commendable, the downside is that 'lower' performing managers have to be 'slotted' or assigned somewhere within the new structure.

Given the political nature of the NHS, the individual(s) concerned may have been 'loyal' within her/his career network and now feel that this loyalty has been overlooked, ignored or violated. Unfortunately, few in this position receive any candid discussion concerning this decision. The decision-making process appears to be couched in political 'symbolic' behaviours. Unfortunately, the individuals concerned then appear to 'read an awful lot into that' with obvious detrimental affects. Obviously, some very disaffected individuals leave (Fried, 1996) with a loss to social capital (Hambrick and Canella, 1993) and organisational learning.

Secondly, although some managers receive pay increases as part of the RCOR programme these are cognitively evaluated in a crude form of cost: benefit analysis. For example, some managers would rather remain in their current post, with the existing remuneration and, therefore, keep intact their valued work friendships and familial and travel arrangements. As one might anticipate this finding was particularly important in the most recent RCOR programme which signalled the dissolution of the health authority organisation and the total collapse for many long-term work relationships.

Thirdly, it is politically imperative that the rationale for any RCOR programme is articulated in such a way that it appears coherent, practical and based upon health care users' needs. It is, therefore, important that it is not simply a desire to 'create the illusion that something is happening' (Kets de Vries and Balazs, 1997) or simply as a way in which to appear distinctive rather than derivative (McClelland, 2002) of the English policy-making process, for its own sake. In this regard, it is vitally important for the National Assembly for Wales to use multiple media forms to convey the same message as NHS senior executives consistently. It is also commendable when systems are in place for 'real' consultation and debate.

Lastly, some managers felt that the current principles whereby individuals could be 'slotted' into new posts was less effective and that a spirit of open competition (whereby managers could apply for any job) within the complete new RCOR structure was more appropriate. However, there were equally as many managers who felt that the current arrangements were appropriate and effective.

Conclusion

In conclusion, the theory of engagement has been articulated from a grounded theory tradition. Attention has been paid to the ways in which repeated cycles of organisational restructures act as a disruptive and destructive inhibitory dynamic. This it has been argued thus prevents NHS organisations and groups therein from developing from a disengaged to an engaged state, or zone, of performance. However, RCOR has also been described as a 'necessary evil' or the 'destructive creative influence' that is deemed to be essential for revitalising the NHS and positively shaping electorate perceptions that 'something is happening' within the discourse or social construction of 'modernisation' or 'renewal' as its is called within Wales. The theory of engagement has been outlined with specific attention, by way of an exemplar, to group innovation.

Some practical ways in which to manage RCOR programmes have been outlined. It is the author's hope that individual/group quality of working life may be enhanced. It is the author's belief that this will assist in the successful enhancement of NHS effectiveness in both the short and longer term.

References

Argyris, C. and Schon, D. (1978), *Organisational Learning*, Reading, MA: Addison Wesley.

Baruch, Y. and Hind, P. (1999), 'Perpetual Motion in Organisations: Effective Management and the Impact of the New Psychological Contracts on Survivor Syndrome', *European Journal of Work and Organisational Psychology*, 8 (2), pp. 295–306.

Brockner, J. (1988), 'The Effects of Work Layoffs on Survivors: Research, Theory and Practice', *Research in Organisational Behaviour*, 10, 213–55.

Brockner, J., Greenberg, J., Brockner, A., Bortz, J., Davy, J. and Carter, C. (1986), 'Layoffs, Equity Theory and Work Performance. Further Evidence on the Impact of Survivor Guilt', *Academy of Management Journal*, 29, pp. 373–84.

Burke, R.J. and Nelson, D.L. (1997), 'Downsizing and Restructuring Lessons from the Firing Line for Revitalising Organisations', *Leadership and Organisation Development Journal*, 18 (7), pp. 325–34.

Cameron, K.S., Freeman, S.J. and Mishra, A.K. (1991), 'Best Practices in White Collar Downsizing: Managing Contradictions', *Academy of Management Executive*, 5 (3), pp. 57–73.

Carson, P.P., Lanier, P.A., Carson, K.D. and Birkenmeier, B.J. (1999), 'A Historical Perspective on Fad Adoption and Abandonment', *Journal of Management History*, 5 (6), pp. 320–33.

Csikszentmihalyi, M. (1990), *Flow: The Psychology of Optimal Experience*, New York: Harper and Row.

Csikszentmihalyi, M. (1996), *Creativity: Flow and the Psychology of Discovery and Invention*, New York: Harper.

Fried, Y., Tiegs, R.B., Naughton, T.J. and Ashford, B.E. (1996), 'Manager's Reactions to a Corporate Acquisition: A Test of an Integrative Model', *Journal of Organisational Behaviour*, 17, pp. 401–27.

Hambrick, D.C. and Canella, A.A. (1993), 'Relative Standing: A Framework for Understanding Departures of Acquired Executives', *Academy of Management Journal*, 36, pp. 733–62.

Ivancevich, J.R. (1986), 'Life Events and Hassles as Predictors of Health Symptoms Job Performance and Absenteeism', *Journal of Organisational Behaviour*, 7, pp. 39–51.

Jarrett, M. and Kellner, K. (1996), 'Coping with Uncertainty: A Psychodynamic Perspective on the Work of Top Teams', *Journal of Management Development*, 15 (2), pp. 52–66.

Kets de Vries, M.F.R. and Balazs, K. (1997), 'The Downside of Downsizing', *Human Relations*, 50 (1), pp. 11–50.

McClelland, S. (2002), 'Health Policy in Wales – Distinctive or Derivative?', *Social Policy and Society*, 1 (4), pp. 325–33.

Marks, M.L. (1994), *From Turmoil to Triumph*, New York: Lexington Books.

Noer, D.M. (1997), *Healing the Wounds: Overcoming the Trauma of Layoffs and Revitalising Downsized Organisations*, San Francisco: Jossey-Bass Publishers.

Nolan, R.L. and Cronson, D.C. (1995), *Creative Destruction: A Six-Stage Process of Transforming the Organisation*, Boston: Harvard Business School Press.

O'Neill, H.M. and Lenn, D.J. (1995), 'Voices of Survivors: Words that Downsizing CEOs should Hear', *Academy of Management Executive*, 9 (4), pp. 23–33.

Rousseau, D.M. (1996), 'Changing the Deal while Keeping the People', *Academy of Management Executive*, 10 (1), pp. 50–61.

Shotter, J. (1994), *Conversational Realities*, London: Sage.

Srivastva, S., Obert, S.L. and Neilson, E.H. (1977), 'Organisational Analysis through group processes: a theoretical perspective for organisational development', in C.C. Cooper (ed.), *Organisational Development in the UK and USA: A Joint Evaluation*, UMIST: Macmillan.

Strauss, A. and Corbin, J. (1995), *Basics of Qualitative Research*, Newbury Park, CA, Sage Publications.

Thomas, K.W. and Velthouse, B.A. (1990), 'Cognitive Elements of Empowerment', *Academy of Management Review*, 15, pp. 666–81.

Turnley, W.H. and Feldman, D.C. (1998), 'Psychological Contract Violations during Corporate Restructuring', *Human Resource Management*, 37 (1), pp. 71–83.

Weick, K.E. (1997), *Sensemaking in Organisations*, London: Sage.

Worrall, L. and Cooper, C.L. (1998), *The Quality of Working Life: 1998 Survey of Managers' Changing Experiences*, London: Institute of Management.

Chapter 6

Themes for a System of Medical Error Disclosure: Promoting Patient Safety using a Partnership of Provider and Patient

Bryan A. Liang

Introduction

Few issues engage the attention of health policy and management stakeholders like the quality of care rendered to patients. And justifiably so; the ethical duties that attend the promotion of health in any society require attention to determine whether care provided to patients is successful and whether there are means to improve it given the social resources available (Liang, 2000b). As part of this effort, policy makers and providers have attempted to assess the process and outcomes of care to identify means by which care may be enhanced, and thus patient health advanced. Further, such efforts seek to utilise scarce societal resources more efficiently to increase the benefit associated with each allocation.

Although quality efforts have been performed in the past, recently attention around the world has determined that medical error – a mistake, inadvertent occurrence, or unintended event in health care delivery that may or may not result in patient injury (Liang, 2001a) – is the primary cause of avoidable patient injury (Institute of Medicine, 1999; Tito, 1994; UK Department of Health, 2000; Wilson, 1993). This work, insightful and important as it is, also points out the dismal news: the presence, indeed, the epidemic of patient injuries in health care is a strong proxy indicating suboptimal quality of care. Such work also provides some hope to address the problem: the use of systems analyses focusing not on individual blame directed toward the last person who happened to touch the patient, but instead utilising a systems focus and root cause analysis methodology to determine the contribution of all facets of the delivery system so that intelligent system redesign can prevent errors from occurring and/or progressing to a point of patient injury (Berwick and Leape, 1999; Carroll and Edmondson, 2002; Institute of Medicine, 1999;

Kelly, 1999; Leape, 1994). These systems approaches, gleaned from other similarly complex industries such as aviation, nuclear power, and the military, have been exceedingly successful in reducing errors and injuries (Liang, 1999); their limited application in medicine has indicated that it, too, can similarly benefit (Cooper et al., 1984; Cullen et al., 1992; Gaba, 1989; Gaba and DeAnda, 1988).

However, due to the significant attention to medical errors and their associated adverse events, there have been widespread calls for error disclosure by patients and policy bodies (American College of Surgeons, 1998; American Medical Association, 1997; Hebert, 1999; Joint Commission on Accreditation of Healthcare Organizations, 2002; National Patient Safety Foundation, 2000; Rosner et al., 2000). Unfortunately, many of these calls reflect the individually-oriented shame and blame conception – to find someone to blame – which have been demonstrated to be so antithetical to effective reductions of error (Berwick and Leape, 1999; Leape, 1994; Reason, 1990). Indeed, disclosure calls at the present time appear geared towards disclosure for disclosure's sake; often these calls are based upon the ethical duties of (individual) physicians, the rights of patients, or the potential for reduced litigation costs (American College of Surgeons, 1998; American Medical Association, 1997; Hebert, 1999; Joint Commission on Accreditation of Healthcare Organizations, 2002; Kraman and Hamm, 1999; National Patient Safety Foundation, 2000; Rosner et al., 2000). However, in terms of information flow, they traverse only one way: only from provider to patient. Such calls and mandates do not engage the patient as part of the delivery system, do not integrate management and systems learning, nor do they attempt to militate against potential adverse legal consequences for such a disclosure.

Yet error disclosure as part of a *system* of medical error disclosure can promote quality of care. As part of this promotion, information flow can be instituted multi-directionally between administrators, patients, and providers in a marriage of organisational/system science and medical information (Merry, 2001). System concepts and ideals can be provided to all within the health delivery environment; a true partnership of patient and provider can result in an improved therapeutic relationship based upon rights and responsibilities shared; and conflict resolution costs may be decreased (Kraman and Hamm, 1999; Levinson, 1994). By instituting such an approach, patient, providers, and policy makers can become comfortable with system concepts and join together as a team to fight the battle and win the war against medical errors and the injuries that they cause.

Theme 1: Mutual Respect, Trust, Responsibility, and Partnership

No system will be effective without support from those it affects. In health care, an effective patient-provider partnership must be founded on mutual respect, trust, responsibility, and partnership. Fortunately, most health care entities already have statements to such effect in their statements of purpose or mission. To implement this approach in the context of medical error, when an error occurs due to system failures, the system must be accountable: all members of the system adversely affected should be informed about its occurrence as a fundamental matter of mutual respect, trust, responsibility, and partnership, and the members of the system must work together to address the error so as to understand it and implement corrective action.

Note that providers under such a system do not abdicate their ethical duty to take individual care. Indeed, because the system is the focus of quality, each member of the healthcare team assumes an even greater role as compared with an individually-oriented system; providers must be alert regarding all aspects of care and be aware of all actual or potential sources of error. Such an effort will hence go beyond traditional activities and observations. Further, patients who are involved in the process of error detection and system improvement should be an equal part of the team of healthcare system improvement, since they see the greatest breadth of system function. Although initially there may be some concern regarding error detection levels by patients, being a critical part of the system and being integrated and respected to bring systems issues to the forefront to a listening provider may result in patients responding favourably as they have in other similar efforts (Kraman and Hamm, 1999). However, both a systems focus and individual accountability must be integrated to promote safe health care systems.

Theme 2: Systems Education

Providers

Although recent research has identified systems as the appropriate focus to reduce errors and injury in the health delivery system, unfortunately medical care providers generally adhere to individually-oriented shame and blame methods in an effort to promote quality (Liang, 2000c). Senior and junior physician are practising or being trained in an environment where error is deemed moral failure and indicative of a lack of professionalism, poor individual preparation, and perhaps even an inability to accept the rigours of patient care (Liang, 2000c; Sharpe, 2000). Unfortunately, this very approach is the most ineffective to reducing error in complex systems (Moray, 1994; Reason, 1990).

Therefore the first step in any creation of a system of medical error disclosure as part of the quality process is provider education. Key to this approach is to emphasise the systems nature of error and outcomes in health care delivery quality. Although there are many ways to communicate this concept depending upon the delivery locale and environment, one important lesson to emphasise in this educational process is that physicians cannot claim full credit for a positive clinical outcome of a particular patient. The outcome is part of a team effort involving the physician, nurses, administration, support staff, and the patient; that is, the health care delivery team. In fact, it would be tremendously arrogant of a physician, or any other single member of the team, to claim sole credit for a positive clinical outcome. Similarly, if a negative clinical outcome occurs, any single member of the health care team cannot claim sole responsibility. Another example illustrating this concept is the aviation system: it is not solely the pilot that is responsible for the results of a particular flight; it is the pilot, the copilot, navigator, stewards, air traffic controllers, maintenance crews, and ground staff – in other words, the aviation system, which drives outcomes (Liang, 2000c). Being the last person to touch the patient or the aircraft controls does not give that person the full and sole responsibility for the outcome, good or bad. Such a basic systems understanding is essential so that providers understand systems-based error reduction methods and systems-focused error disclosure means (Liang, 2001a).

Patients

In addition, patients (including their families) must also understand systems concepts. Although much of the error disclosure literature focuses upon patients simply receiving this information (American College of Surgeons, 1998; American Medical Association, 1997; Hebert, 1999; Kraman and Hamm, 1999; National Patient Safety Foundation, 2000; Rosner et al., 2000), and indeed, patients should receive this information as part of their rights, with rights do come responsibilities. As part of a systems process, patients are an exceedingly valuable team member: they see by necessity the broad array of providers, staff, and others involved in health care delivery – the entire spectrum of health care – much more so than any individual provider or staff member (Liang, 2000c). Furthermore, there are many more patients than providers, staff, and others within the health care facility. Therefore, patients experience and can provide a broader range of observation, and integration of those observations, than any other single member of the health care delivery team. Thus, patients have a right to information on medical error, and as part of the health care team, must also be engaged to participate in working with health care providers to avoid errors and potential adverse events associated with them, be provided with information on the complexity of care and the systems nature of error and outcomes, and be encouraged to report errors and be part of the error reduction process.

To emphasise and educate patients on their critical role in error reduction, some form of a 'health care partnership agreement' should be signed by both a provider representative and the patient at the outset of care. This agreement might state that:

> Medical care is complex and sometimes complicated. We believe that patients are an equal partner in the delivery of care and essential for improving the health care system. We will do everything we can to provide safe and effective care to you. As our partner, please ask any question you have about your care, and, in particular, please let us know if you observe *any* issues in your care so we may use this important information as an opportunity to improve how we treat you and all patients. We want to work with you and make the best health delivery system for everyone! Thank you for your help and participation!

By expressly acknowledging the important role of the patient, patients are empowered to impact their own outcomes of care and are explicitly given a voice in their care. This may lead to improved communications and, of course, an improved therapeutic relationship, which is essential in avoiding error and promoting safety.

Theme 3: Clear Standard Operating Procedures

Current mandates for error disclosure are haphazard at best and do not contribute to a system of medical error disclosure that can provide information to improve safety. A foundation for an effective system of medical error disclosure requires an effective systems approach to error detection, analysis, and discussion. Aviation provides an analogy for this portion of a system of medical error disclosure. In formal policies and procedures within the facility, an 'error investigation team' should investigate any errors that lead to an adverse event. This team should have the relevant skills to assess errors using systems tools and root cause analyses; therefore, the team should have interdisciplinary membership including providers from all relevant parts of the spectrum (for example, nursing, medicine, technicians, and so on) as well as others from administration and management (for example, medical affairs, risk management, senior management, legal counsel). As well, like aviation, there should be on call members of the error investigation team available for immediate investigation of an adverse event, including sealing off the relevant sites and pathways of care for detailed review and analysis while evidence is still available and relatively undisturbed.

In addition to an error investigation team, an 'error disclosure team' should also be created. This error disclosure team, reflecting the systems nature of error and outcomes, should have systems representatives as its members. Administrative, clinical, and patient care liaisons should all be members of this team. Further, the provider who last touched the patient should not be a member of this team, at least initially. This provider will be under severe emotional strain due to the error and thus will likely be ineffective in discussing it (Brazeau, 2000; Christensen et al., 1992; Leape et al., 1999; Wu, 2001; Wu et al., 1993); further, his or her presence may result in provider-patient conflict during the error disclosure that may escalate into a harsh blame and finger pointing exercise. The provider should be part of the error investigation team; the information from this provider will likely be highly valuable and, as well, may assist in helping the provider sublimate the emotional turmoil into appropriate corrective action efforts that benefits the delivery system at large.

The error disclosure team must be trained in the 'three Cs': concern, commitment, and compassion. Since communication is such a critical issue, only those with appropriate sensitivity training should engage in the error disclosure effort (Allen and Brock, 2000; Buckman and Kason, 1992; Coiera and Tombs, 1998; Edwards et al., 1999; Rogers et al., 2000; Lefevre et al., 2000; Little et al., 2001). Such sensitivity training should have as its goal effective communication of all aspects of the error as well as the analysis (including the message that the error investigation team is immediately and unceasingly investigating the error), taking into account cultural factors, language, and gender (Hodge and Kress, 1993; Lakoff and Johnson, 1980; Tannen, 1986); in particular, such training should emphasise avoidance of defensive reactions by the members of the disclosure team. In relation to this latter component, it should be noted that there may be times where patients and their families will react with anger and hostility to error disclosure. Empathetic listening is important in these situations, keeping the three Cs in the forefront of any communications during these difficult circumstances.

One other aspect is essential in creating an effective error disclosure procedure: keeping the patient in the information loop – one area which has been ignored and often reported as a rationale for patient lawsuits (Hickson et al., 1992). The patient care liaison should communicate regularly with the patient and/or family regarding the progress of the error investigation; such actions reflect the mutual regard between the patient and/or family and provider as important parties to be included in the investigation as well as establish a continuous relationship between the parties that may assist in learning about the error. Finally, the patient care liaison should be responsible for assisting the patient and/or family with other necessary remedial aspects of care (for example, transportation, housing, phone calls, and so on), whether they are a direct result of an error or not, consistent with the mission of the entity.

Errors should not be disclosed when disclosure might harm a patient (for example, patients who are being abused or there are suspicions of patient abuse by family members which may be exacerbated by disclosure; when psychological factors make disclosure to the patient harmful), or in relevant circumstances of public welfare and policy (for example, police investigations). These situations should, however, be generally infrequent.

Finally, a system of error disclosure should be documented through a 'disclosure record.' All aspects of any meetings and discussions regarding the disclosure of the error, including subsequent patient care liaison updates to the patient and/or family, should be placed within this record, including all objective information discussed. Of critical import is that this disclosure record focus on only objective information; no blame, conclusions, or accusations/assessments of fault should be made.

Theme 4: Objectivity in Disclosure

The 'how' theme of error disclosure is objectivity. Using descriptive methods is paramount to ensure that patients and/or their families are not misled by premature conclusions and statements; as well, statements assessing or implying blame may be viewed by the legal system as an admission of fault (Campaigne et al., 2000).

If an adverse event occurs, two processes should be put into motion: the error investigation team should immediately begin assessment and the error disclosure team should meet with the patient and/or family, preferably as soon as the adverse event is detected or as soon as possible after that. The error investigation team should begin its detailed investigation, calling in other experts and relevant members of the team. The error disclosure team should indicate to the patient and/or family that there may have been a systems error that may have adversely affected the patient. Using the principles indicated previously, the latter team should communicate that the error is being investigated, and the investigation will continue until fully understood, including all root causes. The team should also describe the relevant systems tools and methods by which the error and event will be investigated (generally an overview of root cause analyses and critical incident techniques, relevant to the specific clinical situation (Fitzgerald, 2001; Flanagan, 1954; Luttman, 1998; Nelson et al., 2000; Weinberg, 2001; Wenzel, 1993)). The patient care liaison should expressly note that he or she will contact the patient and/or family at specific intervals to inform them of the investigation's progress and, again expressly, tell the family that they may contact the patient care liaison at any time. The patient care liaison should also indicate to the patient and/or family that he or she is available to assist with any remedial needs.

The error disclosure team should also request the assistance of the patient and/or family in investigating the potential error, either at the initial meeting, or at subsequent meetings depending upon the specific patient and/or family. The error disclosure team should request that the patient and/or family discuss with the error investigation team or representative all factors, problems, and/or observed errors that may or may not have contributed to the particular error. Such an activity should be tailored to the specific patient, provider, and injury. Thus, the encounter may be quite brief or involve a full debriefing of the patient and family before, during, and, potentially, after the event's resolution. However, by consistent involvement of the patient and family, the concept of partnership between provider and patient is stressed while also providing the patient and/or family a vested interest in corrective and corrected action at the facility.

Theme 5: Communication Through Mediation

One other aspect should be a fundamental part of any error disclosure effort: mediation. Patients and their families have consistently reported that they turn to litigation due to poor communication by providers when an adverse event occurs (Hickson et al., 1992; Hickson et al., 1994; Shapiro et al., 1989). Unfortunately, the high emotional and financial costs associated with litigation, the tremendous incentives it creates to limit communications, and the lack of any systems understandings that result from the process make it a poor quality methodology (Liang, 2001b; Meadows, 1999; Metzloff, 1991; Metzloff, 1992).

Further, it emphasises the individually oriented shame and blame approach that does not promote system safety.

Mediation therefore is an important patient advocacy tool to offer patients once error disclosure has been made. It promotes communications between parties in an open positive, and honest environment, which may in itself reduce settlement costs (Levinson et al., 1997), and allows for a virtually infinite array for conflict resolution beyond the simple monetary transfer available in court (Liang, 2000a ; Liang, 2001b). Indeed, patients often do not sue just for money; they desire a resolution of uncertainty, the opportunity to vent, an opportunity to be heard, and an acknowledgement of suffering (Beckman et al., 1994; Lester and Smith, 1993; Vincent et al., 1994). Further, in the context of patient safety, mediation allows for a prominent role for the patient and family in corrective action, which allows alternatives such as naming a corrective action policy after the patient and family that was subject to the error, public thanks for the patient and family's assistance in improving the delivery system, as well as other desired actions unavailable in litigation such as provider apology and a request for provider corrective action training.

Indeed, it should be noted that provider apology is an important aspect of the error disclosure process since it is an important sign of empathy. It thus should be used to reflect the systems nature of error and outcomes (for example, 'we are so sorry that this event has occurred to you') and be sincere; note that individually-oriented apology (for example, 'I'm sorry I made a mistake that hurt you') is inappropriate since it does not reflect the systems nature of error. However, it must be noted that apology raises significant legal issues associated with potential legal admission of fault (Campaigne et al., 2000). There are some jurisdictions that allow for such statements without such a conclusion (California Evidence Code, 2001; *Deese v. Carroll City County Hospital*, 1992; Massachusetts General Laws, 2000; *Phinney v. Vinson*, 1992; *Senesac v. Associates in Obstetrics and Gynecology*, 1982; Texas Civil Practice and Remedies Code, 2000), but practically speaking, assessment of the legal climate where the entity provides care is important before any blanket means of apology are used.

Through the use of mediation and open communications processes, it has been reported that settlement costs are reduced (Kraman and Hamm, 1999; Levinson, 1994). Although this may be true, use of such a system most importantly allows for the patient to avoid the difficult vagaries of litigation, including the time commitment and significant reduction in settlement due to legal fees, while providing relatively quick closure and resources to address his or her health care and social needs and allowing for a future outlook (Liang,

2000a). Just as important, this approach will also provide a greater opportunity to unearth important systems issues for corrective action, thus avoiding potential future accidents and errors that would not have been forthcoming under the traditional litigation system. Finally, it is important to note that both providers and patients have expressed satisfaction with mediation and buy-in of this approach is therefore likely (Dauer and Becker, 2000).

Conclusion

Health care quality, and its less desirable expression, patient injury, rightfully is a focus of public and private policy makers, providers, and patients. Important systems understandings have shown the culprit of error in a vast majority of patient injury. Although such understandings have been used in an effort to mandate error disclosure in a retrograde shift back to individually oriented shame and blame methods, implementing a system of medical error disclosure can promote quality of care. By engaging in mutual respect between all members of the health care enterprise, systems education, clear standard operating procedures, disclosure objectivity, and mediation to promote communication, system learning can be accomplished. And this learning can benefit all of us: those who need care today, and those who follow. As partners in the health care enterprise, we deserve no less.

Acknowledgements

This work was presented at the Fifth International Conference, 'Strategic Issues in Health Care Management', University of St Andrews, 11–13 April 2002, St Andrews, Scotland; the World Organization of Family Practice/Primary Care Physicians, London, UK, 9–13 June 2002; and the World Conference of Medical Law, 11–15 August 2002, Maastricht, The Netherlands. I thank the members of these forums for their insightful comments and suggestions. Thanks also to Shannon M. Biggs, JD, MA, MEd for editing assistance and Mary Anne Bobinski, JD, LLM for helpful comments on this work.

References

Allen, J. and Brock, S. (2000), *Health Care Communication Using Personality Type: Patients are Different!*, London: Routledge.

American College of Surgeons (1998), *Ethics Manual*, 4th edn, *Annals of Internal Medicine*, 128, pp. 576–94.

American Medical Association, Council on Ethical and Judicial Affairs (1997), *Code of Medical Ethics: Current Opinions with Annotations*, Chicago: American Medical Association.

Beckman, H.B., Markakis K.M. Suchman A.L. and Frankel R.M. (1994), 'The Doctor-Patient Relationship and Malpractice: Lessons from Plaintiff Depositions', *Archives of Internal Medicine*, 154, pp. 1365–70.

Berwick, D.M. and Leape L.L. (1999), 'Reducing Errors in Medicine', *British Medical Journal*, 319, pp. 136–7.

Brazeau, C. (2000), 'Disclosing the Truth about a Medical Error', *American Family Physician*, 62, p. 315.

Buckman, R. and Kason, Y. (1992), *How to Break Bad News: A Guide for Health Care Professionals*, Baltimore: Johns Hopkins University Press.

California Evidence Code (2001), 'Admissibility of Expressions of Sympathy or Benevolence', California Evidence Code §1160, St Paul, MN: West Publishing Co.

Campaigne, C., Costantino, J., Guarino, G. et al. (2000), 'Evidence; Particular Types of Evidence; Admissions and Declarations; Person Making or Affected by Statement; Agents and Employees', *American Jurisprudence*, 2d edn, Rochester: Evidence, Lawyers Co-operative Publishing Co.

Carroll, J.S. and Edmondson, A.C. (2002), 'Leading Organisational Learning in Health Care', *Quality and Safety in Health Care*, 11 (1), pp. 51–6.

Christensen J.F., Levinson, W. and Dunn P.M. (1992), 'The Heart of Darkness: The Impact of Perceived Mistakes on Physicians', *Journal of General Internal Medicine*, 7, pp. 424–31.

Coiera, E. and Tombs V. (1998), 'Communication Behaviours in a Hospital Setting: An Observational Study', *British Medical Journal*, 316, pp. 673–6.

Cooper, J.B., Newbower R.S. and Kitz, R.J. (1984), 'An Analysis of Major Errors and Equipment Failures in Anesthesia Management: Considerations for Prevention and Detection', *Anesthesiology*, 60 (1), pp. 34–42.

Cullen, D.J., Nemeskal, A.R., Cooper, J.B., Zaslavsky, A. and Dwyer, M.J. (1992), 'Effect of Pulse Oximetry, Age, and ASA Physical Status on the Frequency of Patients Admitted Unexpectedly to a Postoperative Care Unit', *Anesthesia Analgesia*, 74 (2), pp. 181–8.

Dauer, E.A. and Becker D.W. (2000), 'Conflict Management in Managed Care', in E.A. Dauer, K.K. Kovach, B.A. Liang, R.B. Mathews, P.S. Walker (eds), *Health Care Dispute Resolution Manual: Techniques for Avoiding Litigation*, Gaithersburg: Aspen Press.

Deese v. Carroll City County Hospital (1992), 416 S.E.2d 127 (Ga. 1992).

Edwards, A., Elwyn, G. and Gwyn, R. (1999), 'General Practice Registrar Responses to Use of Different Risk Communication Tools in Simulated Consultations: A Focus Group Study', *British Medical Journal*, 319, pp. 749–52.

Fitzgerald, R. (2001), 'Error in Radiology', *Clinical Radiology*, 56 (12), pp. 938–46.

Flanagan, J.C. (1954), 'The Critical Incident Technique', *Psychological Bulletin*, 51 (4), pp. 327–54.

Gaba, D.M. and DeAnda, A. (1988), 'A Comprehensive Anesthesia Simulation Environment: Recreating the Operating Room for Research and Training', *Anesthesiology*, 69 (3), pp. 387–94.

Gaba, D.M. (1989), 'Human Errors in Anesthetic Mishaps', *International Anesthesiology Clinics*, 27 (3), pp. 137–47.

Hebert, P.C. (1999), 'Patients must be told of Unintended Injuries During Treatment', *British Medical Journal*, 318, p. 1762.

Hickson, G.B., Clayton E.W., Entman S.S., Miller C.S., Githens P.B., Whetten-Goldstein K. et al. (1994), 'Obstetricians' Prior Malpractice Experience and Patients' Satisfaction with Care', *Journal of the American Medical Association*, 272, pp. 1583–7.

Hickson, G.B., Clayton E.W., Githens P.B. and Sloan F.A. (1992), 'Factors that Promoted Families to File Medical Malpractice Claims following Perinatal Injuries', *Journal of the American Medical Association*, 267, pp. 1359–63.

Hodge, R. and Kress, G. (1993), *Language as Ideology*, New York: Routledge.

Institute of Medicine (1999), *To Err is Human: Building a Safer Health System*, Washington, DC: National Academy Press.

Joint Commission on Accreditation of Healthcare Organizations (2002), 'Standard RI 1.2.2', available at: http://www.jcaho.org/standards_frm.html.

Kelly, D.L. (1999), 'Systems Thinking: A Tool for Organizational Diagnosis in Healthcare', in *Making It Happen: Stories from Inside the New Workplace*, Waltham: Pegasus Communications, Inc.

Kraman, S.S. and Hamm, G. (1999), 'Risk Management: Extreme Honesty may be the Best Policy', *Annals of Internal Medicine*, 131, pp. 963–7.

Lakoff, G. and Johnson, M. (1980), *Metaphors We Live By*, Chicago: University of Chicago Press.

Leape, L.L. (1994), 'Error in Medicine', *Journal of the American Medical Association*, 272, pp. 1851–7.

Leape, L.L., Swankin D.S. and Yessian M.R. (1999), 'A Conversation on Medical Injury', *Public Health Reports*, 114(4), pp. 302–17.

Lefevre, F.V., Waters, T.M. and Budetti, P.P. (2000), 'A Survey of Physician Training Programs in Risk Management and Communication Skills for Malpractice Prevention', *Journal of Law, Medicine and Ethics*, 28, pp. 258–65.

Lester, G.W., Smith, S.G. (1993), 'Listening and Talking to Patients: A Remedy for Malpractice Suits?', *Western Journal of Medicine*, 158, pp. 268–72.

Levinson, W. (1994), 'Physician-Patient Communication: A Key to Malpractice Prevention', *Journal of the American Medical Association*, 272, pp. 1619–20.

Levinson, W., Roter, D.L., Mullooly, J.P., Dull, V.T. and Frankel, R.M. (1997), 'Physician-Patient Communication: The Relationship with Malpractice Claims Among Primary Care Physicians and Surgeons', *Journal of the American Medical Association*, 277, pp. 553–9.

Liang, B.A. (1999), 'Error in Medicine: Legal Impediments to US Reform', *Journal of Health Politics, Policy and Law*, 24 (1), pp. 27–58.

Liang, B.A. (2000a), 'Alternative Dispute Resolution', in B.A. Liang (ed.), *Health Law & Policy: A Survival Guide to Medicolegal Issues for Practitioners*, Woburn: Butterworth-Heinemann.

Liang, B.A. (2000b), 'Comment: Other People's Money: A Reply to the Joint Commission', *Journal of Health Law*, 33 (4), pp. 657–64.

Liang, B.A. (2000c), 'Promoting Patient Safety through Reducing Medical Error: A Paradigm of Cooperation between Patient, Physician, and Attorney', *Southern Illinois University Law Journal*, 24, pp. 541–68.

Liang, B.A. (2001a), 'The Adverse Event of Unaddressed Medical Error: Identifying and Filling the Holes in the Health Care and Legal Systems', *Journal of Law, Medicine and Ethics*, 29 (3/4), pp. 346–68.

Liang, B.A. (2001b), 'The Perils of Law and Medicine: Avoiding Litigation to Promote Patient Safety', *Preventive Law Reporter*, 19 (4), pp. 10–12.

Little, P., Everitt, H., Williamson, I. et al. (2001), 'Observational study of Effect of Patient Centredness and Positive Approach on Outcomes of General Practice Consultations', *British Medical Journal*, 323, pp. 908–11.

Luttman, R.J. (1998), 'Next Generation Quality, Part 2: Balanced Scorecards and Organizational Improvement', *Topics in Health Information Management*, 19 (2), pp. 22–9.

Massachusetts General Laws (2000), 'Admissibiity of benevolent statements, writings, or gestures relating to accident victims', *Massachusetts General Laws*, ch. 233, §23D, St Paul, MN: West Publishing Co.

Meadows, K.K. (1999), 'Resolving Medical Malpractice Disputes in Massachusetts: Statutory and Judicial Alternatives in Alternative Dispute Resolution', *Suffolk Journal of Trial and Appellate Advocacy*, 4, pp. 165–85.

Merry, M. (2001), 'The Past, Present, and Future of Health Care Quality', *Physician Executive*, 27, pp. 30–36.

Metzloff, T.B. (1991), 'Resolving Medical Malpractice Disputes; Imaging the Jury's Shadow', *Law and Contemporary Problems*, 54, pp. 43–115.

Metzloff, T.B. (1992), 'Alternative Dispute Resolution Strategies in Medical Malpractice', *Alaska Law Review*, 9, pp. 429–55.

Moray, N. (1994), 'Error Reduction as a Systems Problem', in M.S. Bogner (ed.), *Human Error in Medicine*, Hilldale, NJ: Lawrence Erlbaum Associates.

National Patient Safety Foundation (2000), 'Talking to Patients about Health Care Injury: Statement of Principle', 14 November, available at: http://www.npsf.org/statement.htm.

Nelson, E.C., Splaine, M.E., Godfrey, M.M. et al. (2000), 'Using Data to Improve Medical Practice by Measuring Processes and Outcomes of Care', *Joint Commission Journal of Quality Improvement*, 26 (12), pp. 667–85.

Phinney v Vinson (1992), 605 A.2d 849 (Vt. 1992).

Reason, J. (1990), *Human Error*, New York: Cambridge University Press.

Rogers, A.E., Addington-Hall, J.M., Abery A.J. et al. (2000), 'Knowledge and Communication Difficulties for Patients with Chronic Heart Failure: Qualitative Study', *British Medical Journal*, 321, pp. 605–7.

Rosner, F., Berger, J.T., Kark, P., Potash, J. and Bennett, A.J. (2000), 'Disclosure and Prevention of Medical Errors', *Archives of Internal Medicine*, 160, pp. 2089–92.

Senesac v. Associates in Obstetrics and Gynecology (1982), 449 A.2d 900 (Vt. 1982).

Shapiro, R.S., Simpson, D.E., Lawrence, S.L., Talsky, A.M., Sobocinski, K.A. and Schiedermayer, D.L. (1989), 'A Survey of Sued and Nonsued Physicians and Suing Patients', *Archives of Internal Medicine*, 149, pp. 2190–96.

Sharpe, V.A. (2000), 'Behind Closed Doors: Accountability and Responsibility in Patient Care', *Journal of Medicine and Philosophy*, 25, pp. 28–47.

Tannen, D. (1986), *Talking Voices: Repetition Dialogue and Imagery in Conversational Discourse*, New York: Cambridge University Press.

Texas Civil Practice and Remedies Code (2000), 'Communication of Sympathy', *Texas Civil Practice and Remedies Code*, §18.061, St Paul, MN: West Publishing Co.

Tito, F. (1994), *Compensation and Professional Indemnity in Health Care. Review of Professional Indemnity Arrangements for Health Care Professionals*, Canberra: Commonwealth Department of Human Services and Health.

UK Department of Health (2000), *An Organization with a Memory: Report of an Expert Group on Learning from Adverse Events in the NHS*, London: HMSO.

Vincent, C., Young, M. and Phillips, A. (1994), 'Why Do People Sue Doctors? A Study of Patients and Relatives Taking Legal Action', *Lancet*, 343, pp. 1609–13.

Weinberg, N. (2001), 'Using Performance Measures to Identify Plans of Action to Improve Care', *Joint Commission Journal of Quality Improvement*, 27 (12), pp. 683–8.

Wenzel, R.P. (1993), 'Beyond Total Quality Management', *Clinical Performance in Quality Health Care*, 1 (1), pp. 43–8.

Wilson, L.L. (1993), 'Quality Management: Prevention is Better than Cure', *Australian Clinical Review*, 13 (2), pp. 75–82.

Wu, A.W. (2001), 'A Major Medical Error', *American Family Physician*, 63, pp. 985–8.

Wu, A.W., Folkman, S., McPhee, S.F. and Lo, B. (1993), 'How House Officers Cope with Their Mistakes', *Western Journal of Medicine*, 159, pp. 565–9.

Chapter 7

Accountability in Canadian Health Care Systems: Fitting the Pieces of the Puzzle Together

Carl-Ardy Dubois and Jean-Louis Denis

Introduction

Over the last decades, the convergence of various factors has imposed accountability as a prominent element in the transformation of Canadian health care organisations. As the expansion of medical knowledge and technologies has never been so rapid, four recent commissions mandated by federal and provincial governments to survey the health services consistently reported difficulties in health care systems' provision of high quality, efficient and timely services to patients (Clair, 2000, Fyke, 2001; Mazankowski, 2001: Romanow 2002). Amongst others, waiting lists for services, nursing shortages and emergency room overcrowding have become perennial issues across the country. While citizens are facing difficulties in accessing health care and serious quality shortcomings, they are asked to contribute more in order to sustain the public health care systems. In most Canadian provinces, total health care spending accounts for almost 40 per cent of public expenditures. Although there is no doubt that pressures from technology, pharmaceuticals and the ageing population are all playing some part in the magnitude of health care expenditures, there is also substantial evidence of waste associated with various factors such as poor human resource management practices, variations in style of practices and inappropriate processes of care.

All these issues give rise to concerns about the sustainability of health care systems and raise questions regarding accountability. To address these issues, most Canadian provinces have, over the last decade, implemented major changes, including the regionalisation of health services, the strengthening of ambulatory care, and the reform of professional regulation. Enhanced accountability has concurrently been seen as a major objective and a way to improve performance. The aim of this chapter is to analyse the impact of the reforms on the practices of accountability. Several questions result: what forms of accountability are predominant in the Canadian health care systems within the current context of transformation; what are the relationships between them; and what are the mechanisms used to implement them?

To explore these questions, we start by outlining four competing models of accountability prevailing in the health sector. Then, we analyse the information gained from three case studies and elucidate what models of accountability are dominant in the Canadian health care systems, what their interrelationship is and what management practices they drive. Finally, we discuss key lessons learned from the case studies and we make recommendations to reframe accountability in health care organisations. Our analysis shows evidence of the coexistence of multiple forms of accountability in health care systems. The puzzle metaphor is used to portray the reality of accountability. We argue that fitting the pieces of this puzzle together requires that attention be paid to the size of each piece, intersection points, divergence points and complementarities.

Four Models of Accountability in the Health Sector

Though accountability, at its simplest, refers to processes by which one party justifies their activities and takes responsibility for them, research findings suggest it is not a cut-and-dried concept (Darby, 1998; Weber, 1999). Competing conceptualisations evolve from the answers to several specific questions: who is to be held accountable; to whom; for what; and through what mechanisms? Our review of the relevant literature highlights four main models of accountability in the context of the health sector: the political model, the professional model, the bureaucratic model and the managerial model.

The political model combines principles of participatory and representative democracy and fosters the input of the population in decision-making. Interaction between public servants, governing representatives, and citizens are therefore favoured. Governing representatives have to account to their constituents so they in turn have providers account for their services. The primary mechanism for accountability is 'voice' (Emanuel and Emanuel, 1997; Hirschmann, 1970). Citizens have the opportunity to express their dissatisfaction, to have regular accounts of health care provision and to influence health policies. Criteria to monitor performance mainly focus on inputs and outputs. The focus is not on health outcomes but on providing services required by population, on providing resources to offer these services, and on setting up procedures to enforce rules and regulations. Because goals are often conflicting and there is often no agreement on what results should be obtained, political accountability focuses more on processes and on responsiveness to public needs than on results (Deleon, 1998).

The professional model is built on the principle of self-regulation. The relationship between the different actors involved in health care is consequently based on the principle of deference to expertise (Romzek, 1996). Adherence to professional norms, training, and the use of scientific method contribute to reduce the uncertainty surrounding professional intervention. Thus, professional associations exert a strong influence by establishing standards, propagating them and disciplining those who deviate from them. Emphasis is on accountability of professionals to their clients and their peers. Health professionals are asked to account above all for their competencies. They are sanctioned not so much for failure to achieve a given result but for malpractice and for departing from professional standards.

The bureaucratic accountability in health care organisations is exercised through the hierarchy and is based on the principle of obedience to a superior. The main source of control and influence is at the top of the hierarchy. Supervisory control is applied intensively and represents the main procedure to account for responsibility. Employees are asked to comply with directions given by their superiors and can be called to account for any action taken. Central authorities in the ministries take the lion's share in the decision-making process and determine both programme objectives and the means for achieving these objectives. Performance monitoring focuses on the verification of processes and conformity to administrative rules.

In the managerial model, the relationship between the different actors is based on the principles of the market. As an economic model, managerial accountability considers health services a commodity subject to the principle of supply and demand based upon value for money (Emanuel and Emanuel, 1997). Providers have to account to both purchasers and consumers and the main procedures for accountability are based on the opportunity for 'exit' given to purchasers and consumers. Providers are induced into competition for client loyalty and attempt to offer the best services to consumers. Managerial accountability promotes contractual relationships between purchasers, providers and consumers and devotes huge efforts to clearly define the specific results that are expected from health interventions. Measures of output or outcomes are consequently used to manage performance.

Forms and Practices of Accountability in Canadian Health Care Organisations

Beyond outlining a theoretical framework, this chapter aims to empirically examine, from the perspective of senior managers and professionals, the forms and mechanisms of accountability associated with the transformation of health care organisations. Our premise is that a complete understanding of accountability must incorporate the perspectives of actors who experience it. Senior managers and health professionals play key strategic roles in health care systems and their perceptions are particularly relevant to convey the reality of accountability. We interviewed 49 key informants in three Canadian provinces: Quebec, Alberta and Ontario. These three provinces have in common the scope of changes in their health care systems in the last decade and the strong focus on accountability while implementing these changes. Since the mid-1990s, Quebec has been implementing a broad project of reform including regionalisation, restructuring of hospital services and strengthening of ambulatory care. Alberta had a similar agenda with a particular focus on performance monitoring. Ontario is the only province of Canada that did not devolve responsibilities for health services to regional authorities. Its reform programme emphasised hospital restructuring, improvement of cost-effectiveness and integration of health care services. The following sections will provide the main results drawn from the analysis of the data collected in these three province. Our informants included senior managers, senior officers in professional regulatory bodies, medical and nurse practitioners.

Quebec Case Study

Data collected from interviews in Quebec show evidence of a codominance of professional and bureaucratic forms of accountability with explicit attempts to introduce components of managerial and political accountability.

Many important features support widespread perceptions of the dominance of bureaucratic accountability. For respondents, power clearly lies with central health authorities and the ministry is viewed as the key institution that exercises the strongest influence both on the direction and the management of health services. Vested with ministerial responsibility, the Health Minister devotes huge efforts to control the administrative process and the implementation of health programmes. Our data suggests that all higher profile issues such as wage bargaining and strategic planning are confined to influential politicians and experts located at the central level.

Accountability of employees is to their hierarchic superiors or to their employers. Chief executive officers strongly emphasised their duty to account both to their Board as their employer and to the regional health authorities (RHA) as their hierarchic superior. The relationship between the different tiers of governance is described as hierarchically based and the regional health authorities are largely perceived as relaying directions coming from the central level. Neither central authorities nor RHA take advantage of their purchaser power to influence providers' behaviours. Resources are allocated mainly on an historical basis, regardless of the performance of providers and the specific needs of communities.

Another indication of the bureaucratic model dominance is provided by the domains senior managers are accountable for. Priorities defined by the central government are at the forefront. In recent years, the accounting process, strengthened by an anti deficit law, has been dominated by issues associated with balancing budgets. Financial statements, reports destined to the ministry, external and internal audits are described as mechanisms extensively used in order to ensure ministerial prescriptions are enforced at all levels. Prevailing performance management mechanisms are also consistent with this hierarchic approach. Respondents argued that, except for some very modest initiatives, little attention has been devoted to the technical functions of health care related to client satisfaction with services, effectiveness of health interventions, and health outcomes. Most attention has been paid to the institutional functions of the health care system that address compliance to institutional norms, that is, balancing the budget, respecting rules and laws, and following ministerial directions.

This strong dominance of bureaucratic processes does not reveal all accountability mechanisms in the health care system. Respondents argued that health professionals and their corporatist bodies exert an influence at least as powerful as the bureaucratic one. Taking advantage of their self regulation privileges, their organisational capacities, the legitimacy conferred to them by laws, traditions and culture, health professionals have shaped the current configuration of the health care system and their own patterns of accountability. The accountability of professionals, especially physicians, is to their individual patients and their peers. Whereas all other professional groups value not only accountability to their clients and their peers but also to their employer and their hierarchic superiors, doctors who generally have an independent status in their organisation, are frankly hostile to any mechanism departing from the principles of self-regulation. Domains for which health professionals have to account are mainly skills, behaviours, practice profiles, attitudes, all elements that refer to professional competencies. Procedures for reporting and promoting professional performance take the same orientation. All prevailing procedures cited aim to monitor and enforce compliance to professional standards and norms.

Our data suggests that reforms implemented have not radically altered the traditional forms of accountability in the health care system in Quebec. Nevertheless, reforms attempted to integrate democratic components that fit more with the political model. Reforms, supported by a new legislation, promoted public consultation, involvement of citizens in the governance of establishments and regional Boards, and utilisation of community competencies. Respondents assessed that accomplishments in these areas have not met expectations. Difficulties cited include: low participation in Board elections, embarrassment of citizens elected to Boards vis-à-vis technical debates dominated by experts, interference of the bureaucratic power with Board decision-making process, and colonisation of political forums by powerful interest groups that monopolise the political process to the benefit of their own interests. More recent initiatives aim to introduce other components valued by managerial model of accountability: primacy of results while managing performance, reliance on experienced managers recruited from the business industry, resource allocation based on productivity and population, and an approach to management based on performance contracts.

Alberta Case Study

In Alberta, major reforms of the health care system have fostered the codominance of managerial and professional forms of accountability whilst diverse initiatives have attempted to introduce components of the political form of accountability.

Several facts attest to the dominance of managerial accountability. Interaction between central authorities, RHA and providers is built on contractual relationships. Rather than relying upon its bureaucratic authority and legal prerogatives, the Alberta health ministry banks upon its resource allocation function to drive provider behaviour by asking for a demonstration of the value of services offered. All respondents agreed the RHA are not simply relaying orders coming from the ministry. Senior managers in RHA reported they have large room for manoeuvring while managing both human and financial resources allocated to their region. RHA that spend the bulk of the department budget take advantage of their purchasing power to ask providers, hospital executives, contracting groups to demonstrate what products will be delivered for the money they get.

In line with the managerial model, respondents put strong emphasis on accountability for financial management and efficiency, but they indicate that these economic concerns have been tightly associated with a strong attention to providing the services required by clients and ensuring the needs of the population are met in the best way possible.

Accountability of senior managers is mainly to purchasers. The ministry operates as purchaser vis-à-vis the RHA and they, in turn, vis-à-vis the providers of their region. The main procedure for accounting is regular reviews of performance rather than direct supervision. Once there is agreement on a business plan that specifies responsibilities of both parties, required resources, and performance expectations, purchasers count on periodic reports, meetings, and surveys to update providers' performance and ask, if necessary, for adjustments in the service delivery. All interviewees emphasised multiple opportunities that allow consumers to express their dissatisfaction. At the same time, they highlighted the complexity and size of health care organisations, the asymmetry between providers and consumers, and the lack of relevant information constitute serious obstacles to empowerment of consumers.

Prevailing practices of performance management depart from the traditional emphasis on processes. Respondents indicated that senior managers in RHA and health facilities have genuine latitude in the means used to achieve their results even if these means can sometimes upset the political authorities. Nonetheless, they regularly have to produce evidence of results they have achieved, based upon criteria that refer to health outcomes, productivity, quality, and economic performance.

Despite predominance of these managerial components promoted by the reforms, our data suggest that components of the professional model have been safeguarded via the self-regulation of professions and some adjustment of professionalism. Interaction of professionals with their patients and subsequently with their peers has been identified as the main locus of accountability for all health professionals and physicians in particular. The specificity of the doctor/patient relationship is brought up: no third party should interfere with this rapport, except for professional bodies whose mediation guarantees both the integrity of this rapport and an appropriate understanding of the intricacies of the professional services. Though respondents generally agree on the discretion that professionals should have while carrying out their tasks, they struggle with how to hold professionals accountable. While some emphasised accountability of professionals vis-à-vis their individual patients for their competencies and their behaviour, others suggested a broader responsibility that should take into consideration not only clients' expectations but also community needs and constraints in which health care organisations are operating. To deal with these tensions, Alberta health care leaders rely on the development of clinical leadership. The new organisational diagram associates administrative leaders and professional leaders (mainly physicians) at each tier of governance of the region, with the promise this new configuration will ensure better alignment between professionals' expectations for their individual patients and regional priorities. Professional prerogatives are thus safeguarded and are even viewed as providing a good check and balance in the health care system.

Reforms have also attempted to introduce components of the political model. Though the main procedure for accountability promoted in the reforms is based on giving purchasers the opportunity to exercise choice, several institutional mechanisms also promote citizen and community participation. Citizens may be involved through the governing bodies of RHA in which they are co-opted or through the regional planning process that ensure inputs from communities by means of focus groups, workshops, and surveys. Some respondents acknowledged that these mechanisms are closer to public consultation than to giving citizens a strong influence in the decision-making process. Election of two-thirds of RHA boards members is planned as an opportunity to shift to new arrangements where citizens could exercise a stronger influence.

Ontario Case Study

As in Alberta, data collected from interviews in Ontario indicate a codominance of the managerial and professional forms of accountability. Whereas professional accountability has traditionally been an integral part of the health sector in Ontario, respondents suggested that managerial components emerge from recent changes that have impacted on the health system.

Our data confirms the dominance of the managerial form of accountability from many angles. Senior managers exert a strong influence in health care establishments. All CEO interviewed reported having large room for manoeuvring independently of the ministry or any regional authority. The relationship between ministry and providers has been described as very much at arm's length. As the ministry funds providers according to an operating plan, it behaves as a purchaser of services and its regulatory role is reduced to a minimum. Data suggest that the boards in health care corporations have discretion for adjusting the composition of service supply, for hiring staff, for contracting services with external agencies, and for holding both staff and external agents accountable to them.

According to our respondents, another fact in the reforms in Ontario has been to shift the focus of accountability from ministry and politicians to consumers and corporate boards. Respondents challenged the policy option requiring health care corporations to account to a community. They argued that, firstly the health care system, as currently structured, is not organised to provide services to a geographic set of people, and secondly the leaders drawn from the industries, co-opted into the Boards or appointed to the posts of directors should be more competent and more familiar than elected boards with issues such as quality, cost-containment, and efficiency. Rather than collectively as the democratic process might suggest, influent persons mostly businessmen, academics, professionals, and community leaders are called to participate as individuals and to use their leadership to lobby for their organisation, secure resources via fundraising, and support interventions. Self-interest has been described as the nitty-gritty of accountability issues in health care. This point of view has been put forward to justify many opportunities currently offered to consumers in Ontario: publication of performance indicators, publication of client satisfaction survey results, reform of primary care aiming to link resource allocation with client services.

The process of accounting has also been focused on domains that are closer to managerial accountability. The quest for efficiency drives the relationship between health care corporations and the ministry. Health care corporations are challenged to restrict their spending within the resources allocated to them or, at least, to have plausible justification for any over expenditure as well as to provide their services at lower cost. Some respondents pointed out that the bureaucratic mechanisms of coercion are still present. Though health care corporations are in general independent, central authorities still have the legal prerogative to use administrative supervision in order to enforce compliance. Respondents reported frequent tensions between ministry expectations and priorities of the health care corporations that continually have to struggle with central authorities in order to obtain the required resources allowing them to respond to their clients' needs. Economic performance competes with technical performance. While health care corporations focus on client satisfaction indicators, quality indicators and patient outcomes, the ministry emphasises balancing the budget, meeting volumes, lowering costs of the services, all indicators related to productivity.

Even if these diverse components of managerial accountability have raised the pressure to reinforce managerial power and reduce professional autonomy, respondents clearly felt that the professional form of accountability is still strongly dominant in the Ontario health care system. Both labour organisation and division are still driven by a profession-based model and centred on professional preferences. Physicians, in particular, were kindly identified as wonderful guerrilla fighters that have the ability to deal with and circumvent any system aiming to control their behaviour. Though reforms have highlighted the corporate nature of the health care environment, boards and managers in health care organisations acknowledged difficulties in holding physicians directly accountable to them and are limited to relying on self-regulation processes to have physicians' account. Thus, self-regulation mechanisms are challenging the new managerial procedures of accountability emerging from reforms. Despite these perceptible tensions, respondents showed, in general, a strong commitment to maintain components of professional accountability in a renewed health care system, arguing that professionals as champions and advocates for their patients ensure a good balance in the system and compel governments to search good alignment between their economic expectations and the patients' needs.

Discussion

In summary, in the three provinces studied, reforms of health care systems have attempted to integrate managerial or political actions within a top-down, hierarchically controlled and professional-centred system of accountability. New arrangements promote empowerment of consumers and citizens, involvement of citizens in health care governance, managerial autonomy for managers and a sharing of power between professionals, bureaucratic experts, governing representatives and consumers. Efforts have been made to devolve influence to RHA or health care corporations. Reforms in the three provinces expanded the concept of expertise beyond scientific and bureaucratic expertise in order to include citizens' opinions, consumers' perceptions, community leaders input, and clients' claims. Many institutional arrangements aim to reduce the asymmetry between providers and consumers and give the latter the opportunity to influence health service delivery. Despite these developments, bureaucratic and professional accountability are still present in the three provinces and are valued because they ensure compliance with state regulations, government requirements, professionals standards. Reforms in the three provinces have broadened the frame of performance management in health care organisations. Instead of focusing only on verification of actors' conformity to rules and professional standards, new mechanisms overtly focus on policy results, on programme efficacy, on productivity, on efficiency and on health outcomes.

Whereas there has been some convergence of most of the initiatives, each of the cases display a distinct configuration of accountability. In the Quebec puzzle, the bureaucratic piece seems to have a larger size than the two other provinces and gives rise to a strong centralisation of the decision-making process. Since the mid-1990s have Alberta and Ontario explicitly initiated a managerial shift. These two provinces have devolved strong powers to senior managers in either RHA or health care corporations. Whereas in Quebec, administrative rules still drive the relationships between the different tiers of governance, Alberta and Ontario favour contractual relationships based on business plans or operating plans. Efforts to incorporate political components in the accountability puzzle have been variable in the three provinces. The decentralisation project in Alberta and Quebec explicitly aimed to give a greater place to citizens in various aspects of the governance of health care systems. In contrast, measures that have been taken in Ontario in this respect restricted citizens to a consultative role. The professional form of accountability is dominant in the three cases. However, in Alberta and Ontario, professionals have been increasingly co-opted into administration and hold senior posts within RHA and health care corporations. Development of this clinical leadership is expected to blur the traditional borders of professionalism and reduce the resistance of professionals to the introduction of new arrangements (see Table 7.1 for the main features of the accountability configuration in the three cases).

Bearing in mind what has already been said, a first conclusion that can be drawn from these case studies is that there is no one best way to frame accountability in health care systems. The four models presented in this chapter all claim to contribute to the improvement of specific aspects of accountability in health services delivery and they probably do. However, it is true that problems related to improvement of health care organisations are broad and complex. Agents in health care organisations have to face multiple expectations that are often contradictory (for example, better quality, greater access, increased participation of citizens, greater efficacy of the decision-making process, and so on). Different sources of power and control simultaneously operate to hold health care agents accountable and each source has its own legitimacy: ministry, local authorities, professional bodies, consumers, and managers. Domains for accounting are numerous and all seem relevant: professional competencies, utilisation of resources, quality of services, adherence to laws and administrative rules, responsiveness to community needs. The three case studies, and in particular the Ontario case, show strong competition between accountability for cost-containment and accountability for quality of services.

Table 7.1 Main features of accountability in the three case studies

Characteristics of accountability	Quebec	Alberta	Ontario
Main sources of control	Ministry Professional bodies	Ministry Senior managers Professional bodies	Ministry Senior managers Professional bodies
Primary domains for accountability	Budgetary process Professional competencies	Economic performance Heath care output and outcomes Professional competencies	Economic performance Productivity Professional competencies
Primary loci for accountability	Employer/employee Professional/peer	Purchaser/provider Professional/peer	Purchaser/provider Professional/peer
Main modalities for reporting	Verification of conformity Complaints management	Performance report Complaints management	Financial statements Client satisfaction measures Complaints management
Key mechanisms for performance management	Anti-deficit law	Performance review	Report card Measuring productivity
Frame of responsibility	Administrative rules Professional standards	Business plans Professional standards	Operating plans Professional standards

In Quebec, compliance to administrative rules competes with increasing calls for a management by results. While carrying out their tasks, professionals, managers, and political leaders have to accommodate divergent interests and fulfil multiple roles. Individual professionals, while giving primacy to the needs of their individual patients can no longer make abstraction of the financial context of the health service delivery. While accountability downwards to citizens and consumers and delegation of managerial responsibility to organisations outside the central government structure have been increasingly popular, the allocation of substantial funding from the centre, the scrutiny of the media and the potential political consequences of drawbacks related to health care have increased pressures for accountability upwards. Providers of health services need to pay attention both to care processes and results. As a consequence, it seems unrealistic to expect that one approach of accountability can meet all expectations, underscore both means and ends, make people accountable within all domains and ensure reporting to all legitimate instances. What we learned from the case studies is that accountability processes consistently draw from the multiple forms of accountability. Thus, interventions to enhance accountability may be most effective when they combine multiple approaches. Several forms operating together can contribute to reinforce accountability on a given aspect of health care services. This conclusion points out the need for comprehensive programmes that builds bridges between the different approaches. To address the multiple issues related to accountability in health care, we need the four pieces of the puzzle.

A second conclusion from these case studies is that overlapping accountability mechanisms may facilitate appropriate checks and balances in the health care system and prevent pathological complications that could result from the hypertrophy of a given form of accountability and the subsequent atrophy of the others. Health care is an arena in which contending parties compete for resources, territory and control in order to carry out their vision of the health care system and attain their goals. In light of the three case studies, a list of these parties should include, at the forefront, professionals, managers, central authorities in the ministries, citizens and consumers. Each of these groups relies on a specific form of accountability that sustains their power and keeps the other parties in check.

Self-regulation privileges ensure physicians the trust of their patients and deference from managers and politicians. Their expertise gives them sufficient legitimacy to check if politicians and managers, while running the health care system, make decisions that permit professionals to optimise treatments of patients. In a specific context where funding cutbacks were at the forefront of the agenda of all governments, this role assumed by professional groups may have ensured a good balance and tempered the drawbacks of the political programme.

Managerial procedures of accountability grant managers opportunities to shape the organisation and the economics of health care delivery by controlling the production process and by anticipating outcomes. Managerial procedures give them levers needed to check, as buyers, if professionals are utilising available resources in the best way. Calls for reviewing the status and the modalities of remuneration of physicians may be interpreted in this perspective. While the administrators in the health care organisations can take advantage of their employer status to balance the power of the different professional groups, physicians who are directly remunerated by the central government show strong independence vis-à-vis the health care organisations and resist any managerial control. Managerial expertise may also serve as a check on politics in surveying if resources allocated by political authorities are congruent with clients' needs.

Bureaucratic components of accountability oblige hierarchic authorities to protect the public and ensure the integrity of the administrative process. Health ministries vested with their hierarchical and legal power have the prerogative to check if professionals comply with the terms of self-regulation, that is, defining proper conduct for their members, promoting high practice standards, and establishing and enforcing both sanctions and incentives for professional excellence. They also have the legal prerogative to enforce compliance of all providers to government objectives and priorities.

Finally, political accountability bestows power to citizens and their governing representatives. It gives them the opportunity to question managers, professionals, politicians on how they are spending billions of taxpayers' dollars. It negates the perception that patients and citizens are unable to judge experts' actions, tackling what constitutes the irreducible core of professionalism.

This research highlights two features of accountability in health care systems. First, the coexistence of multiple forms of accountability is needed to have a fair balance between different interests, different sources of power and different visions of how health care should be. We observed that distinct stakeholders focus on distinct legitimate interests and domains for accounting. While reforms put emphasis on specific expectations, there is a risk of alienating some others. While reforms, as in the Ontario case, shift power towards the managerial elite, there is a risk of removing citizens from health care governance. To articulate different interests, to meet multiple expectations, it may be necessary to have good articulation of distinct forms of accountability. For example, articulation of professional accountability with political accountability promoted in the context of reforms in both Alberta and Quebec give citizens and/or customers opportunities to complain about low quality services but also to advocate for a better organisation of services and focus their input to that end. This necessity of articulating distinct forms of accountability reveals, as Ferlie et al.'s (1996) analysis of the organisational restructuring of British health care organisations suggests, a pattern of hybridisation of organisational forms in the health sector in which different forces that drive different and often conflicting logics may be brought together without letting any one preclude all others. Thus, the challenge for managers, professionals, political leaders is not to make a choice between different forms of accountability but to ensure their articulation and to take advantage of their potential benefits to address issues associated with a given context. Second, new arrangements of accountability inevitably generate tensions because they have to deal with a landscape of vested interests and their implementation depends upon the reaction of these interests. For instance, professionals may resist arrangements that reduce their privileges and threaten their influence. The case studies highlight different sensitive areas related to the renewal of the accountability process. While managers ask for a greater accountability of professionals, physicians are reluctant to accept any accountability arrangement that departs from the principles of self-regulation. While central authorities point out the stress on public finances and aim to purchase services at the lowest price, suppliers of services (namely, professionals and administrators) claim greater accountability for the quality of services. While professionals consider their primary accountability is for their competencies and to their individual clients, politicians and administrators call to extend this professional accountability to the utilisation of resources and a population perspective. Thus, reframing accountability in health care may require forceful negotiations and compromises between dominant stakeholders.

As a result of these dynamics of counterbalancing powers and interests, accountability in health care may be subjected to pathological complications when imbalances occur between the different forms of accountability, for example when components associated with a specific form hypertrophy and become overly dominant. Each one of the four approaches of accountability we have developed in this chapter, if independently examined in more detail, would show its own shortfalls. Each one carries germs of its proper pathology that may result in reducing the scope of the health care system, encouraging a schism between the different components of health care, diverting attention toward components not central to its assumptions, conferring a disproportionate influence to some stakeholders, carrying interests of particular stakeholders to extremes and denying all competitive interests. We have no intention in this chapter of providing a systematic review of the weaknesses of these four accountability models. Rather, in light of the case studies, we point out how the forms of accountability traditionally dominant in health care, namely the professional and bureaucratic forms, may hamper the introduction of new arrangements of accountability. Indeed, even if community participation, giving citizens the right to govern health care, and empowering consumers have been slogans constantly trumpeted in the context of the health care reforms, we observed that the reality of the accountability processes in the three provinces studied perpetuate the imbalance of power between bureaucratic and professional experts on the one hand and citizens or consumers on the other hand. Most of the time, citizen participation has been restrained to consultation while bureaucrats and professionals monopolise the real decision-making. With the dominance of the ideology of professionalism, health care systems have become clinically oriented and hyper-specialised systems with complex, fragmented services in which patients have a great deal to navigate. We also observed, in particular in Quebec, how the bureaucracy of health services forms a strong barrier to managerial components.

The renewal of accountability processes in health care organisation creates an urgent need to supplement both professionalism and bureaucratic processes, in articulating them with other forms of accountability. The challenge is important given the inertia of bureaucratic structures and the capacity of professionals to preserve the status quo through their structure. Each arrangement of accountability drives a different set of values. The shift from a given arrangement to another one presupposes the adherence of a majority of actors to this new set of values. Professional values and bureaucratic values are part of a larger set of social values (Emanuel, 1991). The legitimacy of professional and bureaucratic actions rests on their congruence vis-à-vis the societal values that are not static but changing and constantly in renegotiation between the different stakeholder groups. This implies professionalism as bureaucracy may be subjected to contestation if they can not fit new values largely adopted by the societal actors. This also implies organisational forms crystallising around competing modalities of managerial, political, bureaucratic and professional accountability require constant operational realignment induced by new values, new expectations, new demands, and new interests.

In conclusion, the three provinces studied face the same challenges and all three bank on the opportunities offered by accountability to improve their health services. In each case, new arrangements attempt to introduce new components in order to supplement the existing forms of accountability. While bureaucratic and professional forms of accountability have traditionally been dominant in the health care systems, there are attempts to introduce political and managerial components. The combinations resulting from the introduction of these new components are creating new dynamics by shifting the power relations, by promoting new interests or by focusing on specific expectations. To take advantage of the opportunities offered by accountability, reforms should ensure that the new arrangements are not generating imbalances in the health care system. It is important to keep in mind that the real stake is not to choose from among different models of accountability but to keep the best of each of them and to protect the system from the shortcomings inherent of each of them.

Acknowledgement

This chapter was supported by the Canadian Institute for Health Research and HealNet.

References

Clair, M. (2000), *Emerging Solutions – Report and Recommendations*, Québec: Commission d'étude sur les services de santé et les services sociaux.

Darby, M. (1998), 'Health Care Quality: From Data to Accountability', *Academic Medicine*, 73 (8), pp, 843–53.

Deleon, L. (1998), 'Accountability in a Reinvented Government', *Public Administration*, 76, pp. 539–58.

Emanuel, E. (1991), *The Ends of Human Life: Medical Ethics in a Liberal Polity*, Cambridge, MA: Harvard University Press.

Emanuel, E.J. and Emanuel, L.L. (1997), 'Preserving Community in Health Care', *Journal of Health Politics, Policy and Law*, 22 (1), pp. 147–83.

Ferlie, E., Ashburner, L., Fitzgerald, L. and Pettigrew, A. (1996), *The New Public Management in Action*, Oxford: Oxford University Press.

Fyke, K.J. (2001), *Caring for Medicare: Sustaining a Quality System*, Saskatchewan: The Commission on Medicare.

Hirschman, A.O. (1970), *Exit, Voice, and Loyalty : Responses to Decline in Firms, Organisations, and States*, Cambridge: Harvard University Press.

Mazankowski, D. (2001), 'A Framework for Reform', Report of Premier's Advisory Council on Health for Alberta, Alberta.

Romanow, R.J. (2002), *Shape the Future of Health Care*, Saskatoon: The Commission on the Future of Health Care in Canada.

Romzek, B. (1996), 'Enhancing Accountability', in J. Perry (ed.), *The Handbook of Public Administration*, San Francisco: Jossey-Bass.

Weber, E.P. (1999), 'The Question of Accountability in Historical Perspective: From Jackson to Contemporary Grassroots Ecosystem Management', *Administration and Society*, 31 (4), pp. 451–94.

Chapter 8

Building an Organisational Framework for Effective Clinical Governance

Elaine Moss and Peter Totterdill

Introduction

Clinical governance is well established in NHS acute hospital trusts, reflecting government priorities within the modernisation agenda including risk management, clinical effectiveness, patient involvement and enhanced professional competence. Its practice is largely defined by the controls with which government requires Trusts to regulate their activities. While its purpose reflects aspirations and standards widely accepted in the NHS community, this chapter argues that the regulation of hospital processes is not sufficient to ensure the organisational innovation required to sustain the reflexivity needed for safe, patient-focused care.

Indeed, policies for health service reform seem detached from wider European trends in work organisation. Recent surveys indicate that the introduction of new forms of work organisation such as empowered teamworking improves performance and innovation. An analysis of change in 1,000 Swedish workplaces (Gustavsen, 1996) shows a strong correlation with improved productivity. The same trend can be found in the 'Employee Participation and Organisational Change' survey of 6,000 workplaces in Europe, which confirms that direct employee participation and teamworking can have strong positive impacts on both productivity and quality of products or services (European Foundation, 1997). EU policy calls on employers to modernise work organisation as a means of enhancing innovation in products and services (Commission of the European Communities, 1997). This is echoed in successive policy statements and guidance issued by the Department of Trade and Industry – see for example the 1998 Competitiveness White Paper, 'Partnerships with People' (Department of Trade and Industry, 1997) and 'Living Innovation' (Department of Trade and Industry, 2000).

Surprisingly, work organisation achieves little recognition in the modernisation policy agenda even though the need for workplace change is recognised. 'Shifting the Balance of Power: Securing Delivery' (Department of Health, 2001a, p. 24) argues that:

> A real shift in the balance of power will not occur unless staff are empowered to make the necessary change ... Staff need to be involved in decisions which effect [*sic*] service delivery. Empowerment comes when staff own the policies and are able to bring about real change.

According to the NHS Confederation (2002), this implies a significant shift in management focus, one in which the delivery of targets is 'achieved as the by-product of wider and sustained improvements in service quality'. Such a shift from short-term target chasing to building the organisational competencies associated with adaptive, innovative organisations would represent a radical transformation of the NHS. However there is little evidence that the scope of such a transformation is adequately recognised or resourced within the modernisation policy agenda. 'Shifting the Balance of Power' has little to say on the hard realities of organisational innovation, of how to build effective workplace dialogue and participation, of job redesign and empowerment, of implementing and sustaining genuine teamworking, of creating a work environment which values reflection and creativity, of achieving convergence between quality of working life and performance. While these issues are recognised (see, for example, the 'Improving Working Lives' standard (Department of Health, 2001b), the 'NHS Taskforce on Staff Involvement' (Department of Health, 2000a) and the 'Managing Change in the NHS' initiative (Iles and Sutherland, 2001)) concrete interventions may prove to be poorly matched with the scale of the need.

Clinical governance has self-evidently become the foremost driver of innovation and change within the NHS. However its potential significance goes far beyond the current Modernisation agenda. The environment in which the NHS operates will face unprecedented change in the next decade, marked by rapid innovation in patterns of care and technology, a volatile political environment and more challenging social and cultural expectations (Giddens, 1998). To paraphrase Michael Porter (1985), quality, speed and cost-effectiveness will no longer be sufficient to ensure success: they will become entrance factors which must be met simply to stay in the game. However the fulfilment of short-term targets has become almost the sole preoccupation of politicians and health service managers with worrying consequences for the reflexive and innovative capacity of the NHS. Clinical governance must set itself a more strategic vision, laying the foundations for long-term learning and adaptation in an increasingly unpredictable and turbulent environment.

An approach to clinical governance in which health service organisations do indeed achieve external targets as a 'by-product' of their inherent organisational competence and values might be characterised as the 'high road'. The defining characteristics of the high road lie in the creation of organisational spaces and the liberation of the tacit knowledge, experience and talent of the entire workforce in ways which achieve a dynamic balance between service and process innovations. Crucially the high road seeks to reunite job satisfaction and patient satisfaction. In contrast the 'low road' – arguably the dominant mode of clinical governance for most NHS Trusts in the present environment – is driven by cost, performance measurement, punishment and reward. For NHS staff it frequently results in a deterioration in the quality of working life (Meadows et al., 2000) which remedial HR initiatives cannot redress. For Trusts this results in increasing problems with recruitment and retention (see, for example, Ball, Curtis and Kirkham, 2001).

This paper explores the origins, significance and problems of clinical governance for NHS acute hospital trusts. It examines the limitations and contradictions of the low road, analysing data from a recent cross-sectoral analysis of new forms of work organisation in European to identify the organisational choices and dilemmas implicit in the high road. Critically the paper argues for the integration of the regulatory perspective based on external performance measurement and the developmental perspective based on the enhancement of organisational competence.

The Implementation of Clinical Governance

By the mid-1990s doubts about quality and safety of patient care, underlined by certain high profile failures, raised serious questions about the effectiveness of existing quality improvement and assurance measures. Emerging problems included poor management of information, clinicians in management without relevant skills and target-driven quality initiatives achieving only limited improvement in care. Fair access, consistency ('postcode prescribing') and the apparent failure to share lessons also fuelled national debates on ensuring consistent high quality services.

'The New NHS: Modern, Dependable' White Paper (Department of Health, 1997) sought to combine efficiency and quality, broadening the scope of performance targets by placing quality of services on an equal footing with financial measures. The new focus on quality required 'every NHS Trust to embrace the concept of "clinical governance" so that quality is at the core'. National standards would be developed through National Service Frameworks and a National Institute of Clinical Excellence. At local levels clinical governance would become part of the Chief Executive's responsibility in every Trust. Other structural changes included the introduction of Trust Board subcommittee to monitor implementation and ensure that improvements to local services were achieved. Principal challenges included the need for greater consistency between Trusts and greater integration between the individual components of clinical governance. Effective communication, clarity of purpose, the reduction of professional demarcations and the active involvement of all professionals at ward and clinical levels were seen as crucial. Monitoring would be undertaken by the Commission for Health Improvement. Considerable emphasis would be placed on the assessment of structures and processes relating to patient involvement, risk management, clinical audit, staff development and information.

Implementation within Trusts

Clinical governance objectives are pursued through a series of measures implemented by Trusts:

- *accountability* – ultimate responsibility sits with the Chief Executive supported by a designated senior clinician to ensure that systems are in place and monitored;
- *quality improvement* – clinical audit, national confidential enquiries, staff development, implementation of the Caldicott Report on patient information and the monitoring of records;
- *risk management* – integration of clinical and organisational risks acknowledging that both affect patient care;
- *managing poor performance* – ensuring that incidents and complaints are reported and investigated, and that lessons are shared and lead to widespread improvements. The early identification of competency issues is also required. Support to staff involved in reporting concerns is seen as crucial.

National reporting requirements have grown substantially and, as well as Commission for Health Improvement reviews, organisations are required to collect and report data for many other assessments including performance ratings, clinical indicators and the Clinical Negligence Scheme for Trusts. In the early stages of clinical governance national assessments concentrated mainly on structures and processes. While it could be argued that their findings may have been useful in identifying areas for innovation, in practice the number and resource implications meant that outcomes were weighted toward quality assurance rather than quality improvement.

In most Trusts some components of clinical governance were already in place but with variable impact on quality of care. Even during the early stages the mixed reception which clinical governance received from many managers in NHS Trusts cast doubt on the prospects for substantial innovation and change. Evidence from meetings during 2000 at which the implementation of clinical governance was discussed showed that 'enthusiasts' began to implement the framework with little external guidance.[1] However there was also widespread scepticism or indifference, characterised by comments such as:

> More top down must do's that will take us away from patients.

> If we were just left alone to get on with it patient care would improve.

> This is just another fly by night initiative which will go away.

> We're already doing clinical audit – what more do you want?

> This is just policing – not improvement.

In short, commitment to the pre-existing components of clinical governance such as clinical audit and risk management was questionable. Moreover the new framework was being built on weak foundations, characterised by:

- poor levels of feedback to staff;
- a defensive approach to incidents, complaints and litigation;
- the belief by individual clinicians that they would be put at risk;
- the perceived risks to the organisation of transparency and scrutiny;
- the anticipation of excessive paperwork.

Practical Steps to Implementation

Many Trusts appointed clinical governance facilitators to support implementation. Teams within Trusts were also able to access programmes run nationally. The Clinical Governance Support Team (CGST) instigated a series of programmes which involve developing the skills of small groups of clinical staff who work together, enabling them to review their service and identify improvements. Further local and national level training is available on tools such as process mapping, problem solving and risk assessment.

Effective implementation, however, has to transcend some significant obstacles. Information from four Trusts received in response to inquiries during March 2002 identified a series of obstacles to implementation:

- limited feedback on the outcomes of complaints and incidents;
- staff involvement within several clinical areas and professional groups remains very limited: clinical governance continues to be seen principally as an issue for management;
- dominant voices distort decision-making processes;
- achieving national targets within very short timescales takes priority over real organisational and service innovation.

Compounding these difficulties Boards may lack the vision or capacity to establish values and strategic directions which enable Trusts to rise above imperatives imposed by the four hundred or so external performance targets. Targets also appear to induce reactive senior management cultures, stifling innovation and preventing the ability to deliver targets 'as the by-product of wider and sustained improvements in service quality'.

These conclusions are supported by findings from the Commission for Health Improvement's Clinical Governance Reviews (www.chi.nhs.uk). Ten recent reports were reviewed: in eight the Commission identified concerns about the ad hoc nature of clinical audit, research and/or risk management, highlighting an overall lack of strategic direction and multidisciplinary perspective.

Structures and standards alone are unlikely to produce the continual improvement needed for effective clinical governance:

> The basic components are a coherent approach to quality improvement, clear lines of accountability for clinical quality systems and effective processes for identifying and managing risk and addressing poor performance. Above all, though, clinical governance is about the culture of NHS organisations. A culture where openness and participation are encouraged, where education and research are properly valued, where people learn from failures and blame is the exception rather than the rule, and where good practice and new approaches are freely shared and willingly received (Professor Liam Donaldson, Chief Medical Officer, Department of Health, Clinical Governance, www.doh.gov.uk/clinicalgovernance/).

Likewise:

> Clinical Governance is about changing the way people work, demonstrating that effective teamwork is as important to high-quality care as risk management and clinical effectiveness (CGST website, www.cgsupport.org).

Critically this points to an organisational gap: considerable management resources are targeted at the need to achieve top-down performance targets while the potential capacity of front-line staff for continuous incremental improvement remains largely unharnessed. Clinical governance becomes defined as a managerial objective focused on compliance rather than service innovation: quality assurance without quality improvement. Indeed management practices to achieve compliance may undermine the conditions for bottom-up innovation, and many examples were found where local initiatives were abandoned because of national audit requirements.

At one level government policy does recognise that staff development and multi-disciplinary working practices play important roles in effective clinical governance. Yet traditional management attitudes, practices and work organisation constrain the extent to which current measures are sufficient to achieve and sustain quality improvement. The emphasis of policy remains firmly on the structures and processes required to measure performance and ensure compliance, with a relatively weak commitment to developing the underlying organisational competence of Trusts.

Organisational Dimensions of Clinical Governance

One of the key challenges is to ensure the end product is not quality assurance without quality improvement. This requires that a strong link is established between clinical governance and organisational innovation.

We have argued that measurement of performance against clinical governance indicators provides does not in itself permit assumptions to be made about the nature of effective practice at clinical team or management levels. It implies an highly mechanistic view of organisational behaviour, a 'black box' perspective in which outputs directly mirror commands. The pervasive cultural influence of F.W. Taylor's 'scientific management' (Taylor, 1911) is apparent: the hospital is a machine whose activities respond directly to the performance criteria against which it is measured.

Taylorism's origins lie in the emergence of mass production in the early twentieth century and are closely associated with Ford. Taylor himself proposed a management system which sought to eliminate inefficient variations in work procedures by prescribing the 'one best way' of carrying out individual tasks. However the division of tasks did not only relate to distinctions between different manual skills. Taylor advocated that: 'All possible brain work should be removed from the shopfloor and centred in the planning ... department' (Taylor, 1911).Workers would concentrate on manual tasks freeing up managers' capacity for intellectual activities, thus opening a deep chasm between the conception and planning of work on the one hand and its manual execution on the other. It fundamentally challenges the ability of employees to exercise control and autonomy in their working lives (Hague, 2000a); equally it denies organisations full access to employees' knowledge and experience.

While the NHS is far removed from an early twentieth century automobile factory, parallels are clear in terms of task separation, the division between conception and execution, and the unidirectional nature of target setting. In the wider world Tayloristic practices are increasingly recognised as a constraint on the adaptability and innovative capacity of organisations, especially in an increasingly uncertain (social, political, economic) environment. Less tangibly neo-Tayloristic thinking imposes intellectual constraints on governmental and managerial ability to reconfigure health service organisations.

Hospitals are complex organisations: day-to-day processes involve responding to non-standard problems in conditions of uncertainty. Moreover day-to-day problem solving and innovation has to recognise the often competing claims of multiple stakeholders. Effective clinical governance must therefore place a considerable premium on the ability of organisations to harness the tacit knowledge and creative potential of employees. This involves much more than the ability to recruit and retain staff with necessary competencies. The emphasis on developing individual competence needs to be matched by organisational competence-building an approach to work organisation which engages all levels of employee in planning, quality assurance, problem solving and innovation (Seely Brown and Duguid, 2000). Establishing this work environment involves a complex and contextualised process of dialogue, learning and organisational innovation based on interdependent processes which embrace workplace partnership, job design, teamworking, and quality of working life (Totterdill et al., 2002).

Work organisation must be seen as a reflexive process, not an end state. Data from the Hi-Res[2] project, a European research review and analysis of some 120 case studies of organisational innovation, were examined for relevance to the NHS. The Hi-Res findings suggest that workplace innovation cannot be defined in terms of the identification and implementation of a series of blueprints to change discrete aspects of an organisation. Although the traditional way to accomplish change is through the application of generalised concepts to specific problems according to a predetermined set of rules, it is now increasingly argued (see, for example, Fricke, 1997; Gustavsen, 1992) that this is a roadblock to real change. Rather it is important to understand the complex learning paths which characterise change in real situations. Pettigrew (1987) for example argues for greater focus on the internal and external contexts which drive, inform and constrain change. Such commentators criticise the common perception of change within management texts as rational and incremental, thereby supporting the use of normative change models. They argue instead that change is a dynamic and uncertain process which emerges through the interplay of many factors. Successful change always involves painstaking research, negotiation, experimentation, critical appraisal and redesign over many cycles (Totterdill et al., 2002).

Hi-Res recognises the importance of learning from case study experience but seeks to avoid prescription or the dubious claims of universality embodied in 'key learning points' (Hague, 2002b). Rather there is a need to understand the untidiness of real-life change processes embodied in the dilemmas, contradictions and choices faced by practitioners. Work organisation is essentially contested, reflecting complex interactions between internal and external drivers, influences and learning. In this analysis, organisational innovation struggles towards a virtuous circle in which reflexive practices capture employee knowledge and experiences to create a dynamic interaction between product or service innovation and organisational change. Hi-Res therefore identifies and explores the 'arenas' in which work processes are negotiated and tested.

The following section draws on the Hi-Res analysis to identify the specific organisational dimensions of clinical governance. Figure 8.1 identifies three principal high road arenas: knowledge as a resource for improvement and innovation; partnership and involvement; job design and multidisciplinary teamworking.

Arenas of Organisational Learning and Change

a) Knowledge as a resource for improvement and innovation As we argue in the previous section of this chapter, effective clinical governance places knowledge, innovation and learning close to the heart of the work process at all levels of the organisation. While clinical procedures are codified to minimise

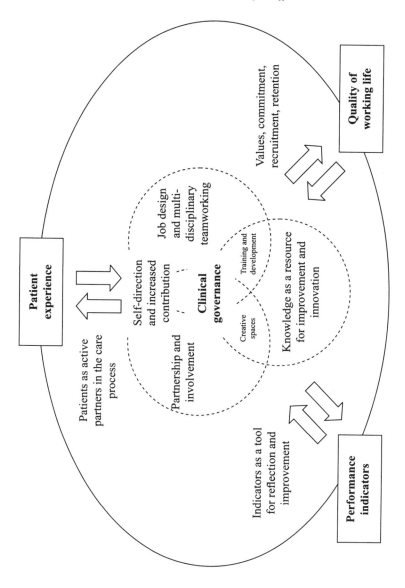

Figure 8.1 **Three principal high road 'arenas' in which work processes are negotiated and tested**

risk and maximise effectiveness, judgement and discretion are central to the day-to-day process of dealing with patients. Service improvement and risk management depend on the ability to capture learning and experience from practice, create spaces for reflection and innovation, and distribute knowledge as an organisation-wide resource. This goes far beyond the narrow 'learning from mistakes' approach within the NHS Organisation With a Memory (OWAM) initiative (Department of Health, 2000b).

Garvin (1993, p. 80) refers to the 'learning organisation' as 'an organisation skilled at creating, acquiring and transferring knowledge, and at modifying its behaviour to reflect new knowledge and insights'. At the most basic level, organisational learning can emanate from repeated tasks and activities which result in progressive adaptation and greater efficiency. At a higher level, however, the learning organisation progressively modifies its structures, technologies, practices and cultures to maximise and utilise the learning capabilities of its people (Shapiro, 1999; Stalk et al., 1992). Critically:

> Although organisational learning occurs through individuals, it would be a mistake to conclude that organisational learning is nothing but the cumulative result of their member's learning. Organisations do not have brains, but they have cognitive systems and memories (Hedberg, 1981, p. 3).

This re-emphasises the importance of the distinction between individual and organisational learning. Argyris (1977) distinguishes between single-loop learning (in which the need for improvement is identified by individuals but where the objectives and policies of the organisation remain essentially unchanged) and double loop learning in which the organisation has the capacity to reflect on itself and to develop appropriately adaptive behaviour. Double-loop learning can be identified with the reflexivity characteristic of the high road of clinical governance, creating a collective knowledge resource to support the dynamic balance between organisational innovation and service innovation. However the bridge between single loop and double loop learning can be seriously impeded in the hospital context by professional demarcations and organisational divisions. Recent illustrations can be found in the Kennedy (2001) Report into children's heart surgery at the Bristol Royal Infirmary, and the Toft (2001) Report into a death at the Queen's Medical Centre, Nottingham.

Organisational structures, technologies, practices and cultures either help or hinder organisational learning and improvement. The Hi-Res study identifies several cases where new approaches to work organisation have been introduced to overcome identified obstacles to learning and improvement, ranging from the introduction of semi-autonomous teamworking to the physical integration of R&D and production functions.

While these concepts are acknowledged within the NHS modernisation agenda, the capture, analysis and distribution of knowledge in the hospital context is not simply about the creation of centralised 'good practice' databases. Rather it focuses on two dimensions of work organisation: the establishment of workplace practices conducive to partnership and dialogue between management and employees, and the establishment of effective multidisciplinary teamworking.

b) Partnership, involvement and participation In many Trusts forms of workplace partnership have become established to deal proactively with industrial relations issues, ensuring early consultation on pay and conditions, employment changes and organisational restructuring. However emergent thinking moves partnership away from a specific focus on industrial relations, recasting it as a potentially important driver of, and resource for, organisational innovation (Dawson et al., 2002). In Ireland, for example, social partners and government identify workplace partnership as central to the modernisation of work organisation. In particular it is seen as a vehicle for initiating change, ensuring its widespread 'ownership' by employees thereby enhancing effectiveness and reducing risk of innovation decay (Savage, 1999; Sharpe and Totterdill, 1999). In the Health Service this is recognised by the Report of the NHS Taskforce on Staff Involvement (Department of Health, 2000a) which argues that opportunities for active participation in the workplace help staff to 'feel valued and make a better contribution to service delivery'. However the resulting Action Plan reveals only limited measures to support implementation at Trust level (Department of Health, 2000c).

Employees increasingly expect rewarding work and a high quality of working life, a key component of which is the ability to influence their own work environment (Knell, 2001; Hague et al., 2002). Meaningful work has always offered the NHS an important advantage in attracting and retaining employees, even where quality of working life is problematic (Meadows et al., 2000; Nottingham City Hospital NHS Trust, 2002). 'Health service values' have always been one of the Health Service's most important intangible assets, though one which can no longer be taken for granted without more explicit staff recognition, involvement and self direction.

Partnership in its fuller sense has to permeate all levels of the organisation. Representative measures (such as partnership agreements, management/staff side panels or employee directorships) may play an important role in anchoring partnership firmly within the practice and culture of an organisation. However they do not ensure opportunities for direct employee involvement which, in clinical governance terms, can enable the full knowledge and experience of staff to be utilised in identifying risks and opportunities for improvement. In part such direct employee involvement is a product of effective job design and teamworking (see below) but in complex organisations such as hospitals 'dialogue structures' which cut across and by-pass line management channels could become an important mechanism for challenging established practice and promoting innovation. Dialogue structures can include organisation-wide events such as Change Conferences designed to inform corporate strategy, ad hoc project groups or inter-team forums. In each case they need to be governed by agreed procedures designed to ensure full participation by all levels of employee, thereby enabling the force of the better argument to prevail (Gustavsen, 1992). Above all there needs to be an acceptance by management that lean, cost-driven organisations are not innovative organisations: people need slack to be creative together.

Employee involvement and participation challenges senior and middle management prerogative, exposing decisions and styles to much greater scrutiny. At a minimum this requires the acquisition of new competencies by many mangers, and in many cases the resign of the management function within organisational structures (for a radical example in health care of the elderly, see Sherrin, 2002).

'Bottom up' approaches to organisational and service innovation require careful preparation and resourcing, using evidence-based tools to promote dialogue, trust and the transformation of traditional management practices. This, as yet, is scarcely recognised in the government's approach to staff involvement.

c) Job design and teamworking Traditional approaches to job design and work organisation are no longer sustainable in a hospital context which demands greater responsiveness to patient needs. As recent CHI audits illustrate (www.chi.nhs.uk) professional demarcations, poor inter-professional communication and lack of autonomy in non-medical staff roles are obstacles to the delivery of safe, effective and patient-focused care.

Teamworking has been one of the defining characteristics of new forms of work organisation, with deep roots in European thinking about management and organisation dating back to the 1940s (Sherrin and Procter, 2002). The current interest in teamworking dates back to its rediscovery in the North

American manufacturing sector in the mid-1980s, since when the concept has spread widely into other areas of work. However the term is increasingly used to describe such a diverse range of workplace situations that arguably it has become meaningless. Mueller and Purcell (1992) attempt to clarify the modern conception of teamworking by drawing on the definition used in GM/Opel:

- the team works on a common task;
- its work is spatially concentrated and it has a recognisable territory;
- the allocation of tasks is largely organised by the team;
- the team encourage and organises the acquisition of multiple skills;
- it has decision-making power over time and appropriate means;
- there is team spokesman/leader;
- the team has some influence on who will join it.

What distinguishes a team in the sense used here from a collection of workers who merely work in the same department is the degree of autonomy it enjoys in relation to formal line management structures. However – and this is particularly pertinent to the health service context – it is also necessary to consider the quality of dialogue and innovation which takes place inside the team. If teams are to be more than decentralised units for the production of a given service, all team members must have the potential for a high level of reflexivity unconstrained by internal demarcations and privileges (Gustavsen, 1992).

Within the NHS progress has been made in certain areas of job design, notably the expansion of nursing roles into areas of practice traditionally reserved exclusively for doctors. However the nature of clinical work organisation remains largely neglected and considerable variations in practice exist even within individual hospital Trusts.

At a clinical level, the distinction between team-based and non team-based approaches to patient care was clarified in a study of five paediatric renal units in different European countries (Centre for Work and Technology, 1995). Although each of the units described themselves colloquially as 'teams', two broad organisational approaches could be distinguished:

- in the more traditional model patients and their families are seen by the medical consultant, who decides whether they should then be referred to other professionals such as dieticians, clinical psychologists or social workers. These referrals could involve patients and their families in multiple visits to the hospital, often with significant gaps. Eventually the consultant will receive reports on the patient from the other professionals and will use them to make a diagnosis and prescribe treatment on the basis of his or her own judgement. In many cases the consultant and the other professionals will be located in different parts of the hospital or even on different sites and will meet only rarely. Separate patient notes will be kept by each professional so there is no integrated case history;

- in the much rarer team-based model (only found at one hospital in the paediatric renal study) each professional group is located within a common area, at least on relevant clinic days. Depending on the case history all the relevant professionals will be present at the consultation, or will be available for referral shortly afterwards. The different professionals will confer on the spot and ensure that the patient leaves with the benefit of an integrated diagnosis and treatment plan. Clinic sessions are followed by case meetings at which both the medical and psychosocial aspects of each patient's condition will be considered. Diagnosis and prescription are therefore a continuously negotiated process based on high levels of mutual trust and understanding between the different professions. For patients and carers this provides a relatively seamless route through the different aspects of care. The different professional groups (including doctors) involved in the team-based model each reported enhanced levels of job satisfaction compared with their previous experience of more traditional approaches. In part this reflected improved clinical results generated by the more effective pooling of expertise; in part it grew from a sense of mutual support and sharing between team members. Nurses and other professionals commented on their ability to use competencies to the full in a team setting, enjoying higher levels of discretion and respect. Interaction between professionals in a team environment also generates high levels of innovation in terms of service improvement and team development. The team was also a potential (though largely untapped) resource as a 'dialogue structure' to promote wider employee engagement with corporate strategy.

Significantly although the team-based model demonstrated tangible patient benefits, there was no hospital-wide strategy to adopt the approach as the norm for clinical work organisation. Indeed the wider organisational environment in which the paediatric renal unit existed acted as a significant constraint on teamworking, particularly because of:

- limited control over budgets;
- tension between vertical line management based on professional groups and team accountability;
- limited ability to recruit its own membership (team members were often recruited by line managers without wider involvement);
- the lack of corresponding team practices in related parts of the hospital (for example, ward staff) leading to broken lines of communication;
- poor information technology support, preventing the creation of integrated, multi-professional case notes.

At corporate level the hospital's understanding of team principles was limited and there was little evidence of central support to develop the team further or to avoid innovation decay. Stronger support was required for non-medical staff in developing teamwork competencies including facilitation skills; arguably this should eventually lead to a separation in roles between medical leadership and team leadership in order to reinforce open dialogue and extended participation.

Teamworking should not be restricted to the point of service delivery (a wider conclusion drawn from the Hi-Res research) but needs to become a defining characteristic of all aspects of work, both routine and developmental, at all levels of the organisation. In this sense teamworking emerges not as a formulaic model but as an approach to work organisation which broadens job design and challenges both hierarchical and horizontal demarcations in order to optimise levels of agility and innovation. It also provides the day-to-day context for enhancing quality of working life.

Clinical Governance as a Reflexive Process

In summary, the arenas of organisational learning and innovation described above offer the scope to shift clinical governance from emphasis on compliance to improvement and innovation. If the current focus on performance management implies a mechanistic view of hospital organisations, the high road in contrast emphasises their organic nature and their potential for learning, risk-taking and innovation. Indeed it offers a profound challenge to the Tayloristic separation of planning and delivery which lies at the heart of current policy.

Conclusion

This paper argues that distortions in the implementation of clinical governance result in quality assurance without quality improvement. While there is recognition of the importance of staff in achieving effective clinical governance, there is little practical understanding at Trust level of how to achieve this by reuniting patient satisfaction and quality of working life.

Likewise there is little evidence that Trusts recognise the need to strengthen the basic, interdependent building blocks of post-Taylorist work organisation: knowledge creation and distribution, partnership and involvement, and multidisciplinary teamworking. The prioritisation and resources given to enhancing these building blocks simply do not match the obstacles encountered in attempting to change traditional forms of work organisation and management practice.

Acute hospital Trusts need to formulate a more strategic role for Boards, to value staff involvement and participation as a core strategic value, to build team-based practice throughout their organisations, to redefine the roles and competencies of managers, and to build the skills required to make new forms of work organisation successful. Few Trusts can achieve this on their own. The question is whether government can develop modes of policy intervention capable of animating and resourcing such widespread organisational innovation.

Acknowledgements

The authors are grateful for help received from other members of the Hi-Res project team at The Work Institute, especially Jeremy Hague, Annette Sharpe and Jessica Sherrin. Thanks also to Gilly Shapiro (CENTRIM, University of Brighton).

Notes

1   Author's personal notes from meetings involving different Trusts.
2   'Hi-Res: Defining the *Hig*h Road of Work Organisation as a *Reso*urce for Policy Makers and Social Partners', project undertaken for the European Commission by a consortium of partners from six member states led by The Work Institute at Nottingham Business School. See Totterdill et al., 2002.

References

Argyris, C. (1977), 'Double Loop Learning in Organizations', *Harvard Business Review*, September–October, pp 115–25.

Ball, L., Curtis, P. and Kirkham, M. (2001), 'Why do Midwives Leave?', RCM Report for the DTI Partnership Fund, London: Royal College of Midwives.

Centre for Work and Technology (1995), 'Women and Teamworking in the Health Services of Europe Project Report', Nottingham Trent University.

Commission of the European Communities (1997), 'Partnership for a New Organisation of Work', Green Paper, Brussels.

Dawson, S., Hague, J., Knell, J. and Totterdill, P. (2002), 'Partnerships for Workplace Innovation?', a UK WON Dialogue Report UK Work Organisation Network, Woking.

Department of Health (1997), 'The New NHS: Modern, Dependable', London: HMSO.

Department of Health (2000a), 'NHS Taskforce on Staff Involvement', London: DoH.

Department of Health (2000b), 'An Organisation with a Memory', London: DoH.

Department of Health (2000c), 'NHS Taskforce on Staff Involvement', London: DoH.

Department of Health (2001a), 'Shifting the Balance of Power: Securing Delivery', London: DoH.

Department of Health (2001b), 'Improving Working Lives', London: DoH.

Department of Trade and Industry (1997), 'Partnerships with People', London: DTI.

Department of Trade and Industry (1998), Competitiveness White Paper, London: HMSO.

Department of Trade and Industry (2000), 'Living Innovation,' London: DTI.

European Foundation for the Improvement of Living and Working Conditions (1997), 'New Forms of Work Organisation – Can Europe Realise its Potential?', Luxembourg: Office for Official Publications of the European Community.

Fricke, W. (1997), 'Evaluation of the German Work and Technology Programme from an Action Research Point of View', in T. Alasoini, K. Kyllönen and A. Kasvio (eds), *Workplace Innovation: A Way of Promoting Competitiveness, Welfare and Employment*, Helsinki: National Workplace Development Programme.

Garvin, D. (1993), 'Building a Learning Organisation', *Harvard Business Review*, July–August, pp. 78–91.

Giddens, A. (1998), *The Third Way*, Cambridge Polity Press.

Gustavsen, B. (1992), *Dialogue and Development*, Stockholm: Center for Swedish Working Life; Assen: Van Gorcum.

Gustavsen, B. (1996), 'Action Research, Democratic Dialogue and the Issue of "Critical Mass" in Change', *Qualitative Inquiry*, 2 (1).

Hague, J. (2000), 'Work Organisation: New Wine in Old Bottles?', Innoflex Working Paper, Nottingham Trent University.

Hague, J. (2002), 'Arenas of Change Hi-Res', Working Paper, Nottingham Trent University.

Hague, J., Huzzard, T., den Hertog, F. and Totterdill, P. (2002), 'Better Rich and Healthy than Poor and Sick', Innoflex Project Report, Nottingham Trent University.

Hedberg, B. (1981), 'How can Organizations Learn and Unlearn?', in P. Nystrom and W. Starbuck (eds), *Handbook of Organizational Design*, Vol. 1, Oxford: Oxford University Press.

Iles, V. and Sutherland, K. (2001), *Organisational Change: A Review for Managers, Professionals and Researchers*, London: NCC SDO.

Kennedy, I. (2001), 'Report of the Public Inquiry into Children's Heart Surgery at the Bristol

Royal Infirmary 1984–1995', London: DoH.

Knell, J. (2001), *The Quiet Birth of the Free Worker*, London: Industrial Society.

Meadows, S., Levenson, R. and Baeza, J. (2000), *The Last Straw: Explaining the NHS Nursing Shortage*, London: King's Fund.

Mueller, F. and Purcell, J. (1992), 'The Drive for Higher Productivity', *Personnel Management*, pp. 28–33.

NHS Confederation (2002), Update August.

Pettigrew, A.M. (1987), 'Context and Action in the Transformation of the Firm', *Journal of Management Studies*, 24 (6), pp. 649–70.

Porter, M.E. (1985), *Competitive Advantage*, New York: The Free Press.

Savage, P. (1999), *New Work Organisation in Ireland*, Dublin: Irish Productivity Centre.

Seely Brown, J. and Duguid, P. (2000), *The Social Life of Information*, Boston: Harvard Business School Press.

Shapiro, G. (1999), 'Inter-project Knowledge Capture and Transfer: An Overview of Definitions, Tools and Practices', CENTRIM Working Paper, University of Brighton.

Sharpe, A. and Totterdill, P. (1999), *An Evaluation of the New Work Organisation in Ireland Programme*, Dublin: Irish Productivity Centre.

Sherrin, J. (2002), 'Arboga Case Study', available at www.ukwon.net.

Sherrin, J. and Procter, S. (2002), 'The Team-Based Organisation', Hi-Res Working Paper, Nottingham Trent University.

Stalk, G., Evans, P. and Schulman, L. (1992), 'Competing on Capabilities: The New Rules of Corporate Strategy', *Harvard Business Review* (70), pp. 57–69.

Taylor, F.W. (1947 [1911]), *The Principles of Scientific Management*, New York: Harper.

Toft, B. (2001), 'External Inquiry into the Adverse Incidents that Occurred at Queen's Medical Centre', Nottingham, 4 January, London: DoH.

Totterdill, P., Dhondt, S. and Milsome, S., (2002) 'Partners at Work? A Report to Europe's Policy Makers and Social Partners', The Work Institute, Nottingham.

SECTION III
INTERNATIONAL POLICY
INNOVATION

Chapter 9

Roemer's Law: Does it Apply in Greece?

Natasa V. Daniilidou, Kyriakos Souliotis and John Kyriopoulos

Introduction

In 1961 Roemer examined the relation between the supply of hospital beds and hospital admission rates, which resulted in the formulation of his well-known law: 'A built bed is a filled bed' (Shain and Roemer, 1961). This statement suggests that there is a positive effect of bed supply and bed availability on hospital utilisation and consequently on hospital costs. The mix of particular activities selected by a hospital to undertake, the mix of the inputs it chooses to produce that mix of outputs, and the cost of those inputs, all come together to form 'the costs' of the hospital (Phelps, 1997).

The number of hospital days is considered to be the hospital's output and it is the product of the number of admissions multiplied by the mean hospitalisation stay (Feldstein, 1970). But are more hospital services being provided than are really necessary? Is there a chance that individuals remain in hospital for more days than they need to? Are useless laboratory tests and possibly harmful operations being performed?

Other factors known to influence admission rates include the number of doctors and the number of pharmacies, from the supply side (Folland et al., 1997), and from the demand side health care need indicators, demographic factors and socioeconomic factors – health status, ageing of population, income, and so on (Folland et al., 1997; Benzeval and Judge, 1994). The research question in this paper is whether Roemer's Law applies in the Greek health care system, as examined over a period of 30 years (1970–2000), and particularly what is the correlation of hospital utilisation rates and factors of supply and demand.

Background

The Greek health care system had been traditionally based on the Bismarck model, as it was partly financed by social health insurance. In 1983 a major reform led to the establishment of the National Health System (NHS), which attempted to increase the share of state financing of the health system. Today, the major characteristics – at least on paper – are the extensive insurance coverage, free access to zero cost state health services and equity in health care provision.

Primary health care is provided by the state through rural health centres, by social insurance funds through insurance funds polyclinics, and by practitioners in private practice, either with or without contracts with the social insurance funds (Tragakes, 1999). The primary health care sector is weak, poorly organised and seriously understaffed, mainly because the medical specialty of general practice does not attract medical students. Due to the lack of general practitioners, continuity of care is lacking. Greater continuity of primary care is associated with higher quality of care (Christakis et al., 2002) and a close out-patient relationship between patients and physician can reduce the number of non-urgent consultations at emergency rooms (Stein et al., 2002). Primary care professionals take a holistic approach to health care, provide continuing personal care and are able to understand illness in the context of patients' daily lives.

Secondary and tertiary care are officially provided by the state. There is also a significant private sector in primary and secondary care provision.

Following the 1983 reforms, there is high population coverage, especially for secondary health services, which reaches 94 per cent (Kyriopoulos et al. 2003), access to health services is improved and benefit packages offered by health insurance funds are increased (Tragakes, 1999). However, under-the-table payments to doctors are high (16.9 per cent of total spending in 1994) and may affect admission rates, as the real cost of health services becomes greater. In any case, high under-the-table payments compose the main reason for people's low satisfaction from the public health care system (Kyriopoulos et al., 1998).

Data from the National Statistical Service of Greece (NSSG) show that in 1997 there were 144 public hospitals in Greece (excluding military hospitals and beds therein), accommodating a total of 37,340 beds, of which 5,269 were psychiatric beds. In comparison, there were 206 private hospitals with 15,134 beds, of which 3,602 were psychiatric beds (NSSG, 2001a). Considering the number of beds for all medical specialties, the public sector prevails with 71 per cent of the total beds.

In terms of health professionals, Greece has a high ratio of physicians to population (one for 233 in 1997). According to the OECD, in 2001 the Greek ratio of physicians to population was the highest among Australia, Canada,

Japan, the United States and many European countries except Italy, to name but a few (OECD, 2001). On the contrary, there is a shortage of nursing staff (one for 249 in 1997) (NSSG, 2001a; NSSG, 2001b), with Greece having the lowest ratio of nursing staff to population among most European countries. According to the World Health Organisation (WHO) the highest ratio belongs to Norway, with one nurse for 73 people in 1994 (WHO, 1994). The high number of physicians in Greece can be partly explained by the lack of medical resource planning, and has led to higher levels of unemployment among physicians (Saltman and Figueras, 1997). Specialised physicians are not willing to work as general practitioners, mainly because specialised doctors consider general practitioners as unspecialised, thus they believe that their role is limited. In addition, general practitioners support that only specialised general practitioners are able to perform their duties.

During the 1990s, and despite economic recession and austerity measures, health expenditures increased at an accelerated annual rate of growth, of about 6.8 per cent per year (Kyriopoulos and Levett, 1999). Total health expenditure, including out-of-pocket payments and side-payments, was 8.2 per cent of the gross domestic product in 1996, according to official data (OECD, 1998), which are considered to underestimate particularly private expenditure (Kyriopoulos, 1994). In 2000 total health expenditure was 9.1 per cent of the gross domestic product, according to recent research (Souliotis, 2001). Private health spending reaches 3.9 per cent of GDP and is ever growing, probably being one of the highest among European countries (Kyriopoulos and Levett, 1999).

Health policy remains in a transitional state, implementation of major reforms is still problematic and the health sector is characterised by the gap between the rhetoric of reform and the reality of non-implementation (Levett, 1996). Greece faces the same health problems as most European countries: rising health care costs, changing disease patterns (in part due to migration from neighbouring countries) and an aging population. Health reforms have been taking place over the last 20 years but the outcome has not lived up to expectations and there is still lack of clear measures regulating the demand and supply sides.

The Greek health care system, and the hospital sector in particular, is undergoing changes, with the introduction of hospital managers, the reduction of hospital beds, the unification of health funds and so on. The development of primary health care is a top priority in the recent health care legislation of 2001, which reinforces the system of family doctors and the establishment of primary care networks.

Data and Method of Analysis

In this study, data were collected on a national level, mainly from the National Statistical Service of Greece, and also from OECD databases. Due to the structure of the Greek health care system, previously described, the level of services offered to the Greek population is considered to be fairly homogeneous, mainly through the National Health System, which has been operating throughout the country for the last 20 years. For this reason the analysis was carried out at a national level.

For the analysis of factors influencing hospital admission rates a model was set up, including both supply and demand indicators. The statistical analysis used was multiple regression, in which the dependent variable was the number of outgoing patients. The independent variables of the model possibly influencing hospital admission rates included both demand and supply factors:

1   demand:
    a) people over 65 years of age (as a percentage of total population);
    b) gross domestic product (GDP).
2   supply:
    a) number of beds (excluding psychiatric beds);
    b) number of doctors;
    c) number of pharmacies;
    d) mean hospitalisation stay per admission (excluding patients with mental disorders).

Results

The coefficient of determination R^2, which shows the degree of variability in y explained by the variables x included in the model, is 97.7 per cent, which means that this model has very satisfactory explanatory power.

Hospital bed supply and the number of doctors proved to be the key factors affecting hospital admission rates, as given by the number of outgoing patients. Variables excluded were GDP, the number of people over 65, mean hospitalisation stay and number of pharmacies, as they failed to enter the regression model at the 95 per cent level of significance.

The fact that R-square and adjusted R-square are almost the same numbers means that the model is a strong one. The variables are positively correlated with the number of outgoing patients. More specifically, when one more doctor

Table 9.1   Results of multiple regression analysis

Outgoing patients	B-coefficient	P-value
Number of doctors	19.976	0.000
Number of beds	8.684	0.007
Constant	221,094.9	0.137

R = 0.989
R-square = 0.979
Adjusted R-square = 0.977

is employed, 19.976 more patients exit the hospital. When one extra bed is provided 8.684 more patients exit the hospital. In conclusion, the model is as follows: *outgoing patients* = 221,094.9 + 19.976 (number of doctors) + 8.684 (number of beds).

In order to establish the model's credibility the residuals were checked. They were checked for normality according to Kolmogorov Smirnov test (Lilliefors correction), which gave $p = 0.188 > 0.05$, so the residuals are normally distributed. They were also checked for homoscedasticity according to Levene test, which gave $p = 0.130 > 0.05$, which means that the residuals are homoscedastic. Finally they were checked for independency according to Runs test, because the model refers to a period of 30 years, which gave $p = 0.261 > 0.05$, which means that the residuals are independent. In conclusion, the standards for accepting the model are met.

Limitations of the Study

The main limitation of the present study derives from the lack of data concerning the contribution of primary health care services to hospital use. It is well known that primary health care can form a substitute and a gatekeeper to hospital admission rates. However, the number of GPs in Greece is very low (1.1/10,000 people) and primary health care is generally underdeveloped (Gregory et al., 2002), at least as it is provided by the public sector. For this reason, it is suggested that the exclusion of this kind of data from the present study does not play a major role. Besides, the nonexistence of a clear relationship between the use of hospital services and the degree of the development of general medical services is mentioned in the literature (Bevan and Charlton, 1987).

The second limitation of this study is due to the inability to discriminate between first-time hospital admissions and re-admissions for the same cause in other hospitals, which would lead to a false increase in the number of outgoing patients. An electronic system that would register the patients according to cause of admission would facilitate the creation of an outgoing patients database and would lead to the avoidance of double counting of an unquantified number of patients.

Furthermore, as mentioned before, this model refers to a period of 30 years. Changes in the provision of medical services and the development and widespread use of biomedical technology when studied in long-term period, but especially during recent years, affect the system of hospital admissions and treatment of patients. However, the influence of this factor cannot be measured separately.

Discussion

The supply of hospital beds has generally been considered to have a critical role in the variation of hospital admission rates. A review of the literature in the late 1980s pointed to this conclusion (Sanders et al., 1988) and various studies in the 1990s suggested that the more hospital beds provided the more would be used (van der Zee and Groenewegen, 1987; Clark, 1990; Kirkup and Forster, 1990; van Noordt et al., 1992). However, in the 1980s, most OECD countries tried to control health expenditures by introducing major changes in health systems, including the reduction of beds. The association of hospital admission rates and hospital beds was somewhat questioned and it was suggested to be dependent on time and place (van Noordt et al., 1992). It has also been suggested that a positive effect of bed supply exists on length of hospital stay but not on admission rates (van Doorslaer and van Vliet, 1989).

According to the results of the present study, Roemer's Law applies in the Greek health care system, as the number of outgoing patients is positively correlated with the number of doctors and beds. The social context may influence doctors' behaviour in their daily practice (Westert and Groenewegen, 1999) and they may induce demand in an effort to achieve a desired income (Evans, 1974), especially considering that the number of doctors in Greece is still increasing. It is suggested that the increase of providers can increase demand for health care services (Folland et al., 1997). The combination of important structural factors, such as the availability of hospital resources, the way the doctor is reimbursed and the way the hospital is financed lead to variations in the doctors' decision behaviour (Westert and Groenewegen, 1999). Besides, other factors such as professional uncertainty (ibid.), lack of confidence in their diagnostic skills, and being unaware of the problem of rising health care costs may also lead to induced demand. From the patient's point of view, increased number of beds and doctors may cater for the non-satisfied demand, as it is manifested through waiting lists.

The positive correlation of GDP with the number of outgoing patients has been suggested elsewhere. More specifically, the utilisation of specialist visits was found to be greater for those in higher socioeconomic groups (Dunlop et al., 2000) since the increase of GDP leads to improved living conditions and qualitative and quantitative increase in health services demand. The relationship among per capita real income and per capita real health care expenditure exists in different health systems as well (Okunad and Murthy, 2002). However, in the present study no relation was found to exist between GDP and the dependent variable. It could be suggested that the existence of almost universal insurance coverage of the population for health services is the main reason why hospital utilisation, as expressed by the number of outgoing patients, remains almost stable even when available income increases.

The number of pharmacies does not seem to influence the number of outgoing patients, even though it has been suggested that increased drug consumption may facilitate patients to exit the hospital sooner and that they may partly substitute hospital utilisation. Mean hospitalisation stay is also not correlated with the dependent variable, even though improved medical technology and better patient management allow patients to exit the hospital sooner (Van den Heuvel et al., 1997).

The paradoxical finding of this study, namely the absence of a correlation of people over 65 with the number of outgoing patients, may be partly explained by the existence of alternative forms of health care, mainly home care, and the provision of health services from local authorities. Traditionally in Greece the family takes care of its older members if need be. In Europe in general, hospitals have long been losing ground to other forms of health care, such as institutions providing pre- and post-hospital treatment (Plaff and Nagel, 1986). This trend could perhaps be also applied to the Greek health care sector, since the need for more caring rather for curing patterns of service has started to manifest itself. Even more important, however, seems to be the increase in drug consumption. It is generally easier and much cheaper for older people to obtain medication rather than to be admitted to hospital, especially when the high under-the-table payments in hospitals are taken into account. In the literature, van Noordt et al. (1992) did not find the number of older people to have a statistically significant effect on number of outgoing patients and Wennberg (1987) suggested that age and morbidity rates explain only a small part of the variation in hospital admission rates in the USA.

Conclusions

As growth of services push expenses up, the reduction of hospital beds, and consequently admission rates with simultaneous increase in the participation of primary care, as is the case in Europe, is considered to be the solution for hospital cost containment. The same trend has applied to the Greek health care sector since the mid 1980s. The findings show that supply factors need to be controlled if hospital admissions rates are to be rationalised. The expected development of the primary health care sector, according to the legislation recently passed, may have a strong negative influence on hospital admission rates, mainly because of the counterbalance effect the primary health sector has over the hospital sector, as happened in other European countries' health systems almost a decade ago (van der Zee et al., 1990). As the Greek health care sector faces financing problems, the use of these findings in the context of the health care reform, which currently is taking place in the country, could contribute to the effective use of scarce resources.

Acknowledgements

We express our grateful thanks to Dimitrios Zavras, Research Fellow in the Department of Health Economics in the National School of Public Health and to Athanassios Zavras, Assistant Professor of Health Policy and Epidemiology in Harvard University, for their valuable contribution in the statistical analysis of the results.

References

Benzeval, M. and Judge, K. (1994), 'The Determinants of Hospital Utilisation: Implications for Resource Allocation in England', *Health Economics*, 3 (2), pp. 105–16.
Bevan, G. and Charlton, C. (1987), 'Making Access to Health Care more Equal: The Role of General Medical Services', *British Medical Journal*, 295, pp. 764–6.

Christakis, D.A., Wright J.A., Zimmerman, F.J., Bassett, A.L. and Connell, F.A. (2002), 'Continuity of Care is Associated with High-quality Care by Parental Report', *Pediatrics*, 109 (4): e54.

Clark, D.J. (1990), 'Variation in Michigan Hospital Use Rates: Do Physician and Hospital Characteristics provide the Explanation?', *Social Science and Medicine*, 1 (30), pp. 67–82.

Dunlop, S., Coyte, P.C. and McIsaac, W. (2000), 'Socio-economic Status and the Utilisation of Physicians' Services: Results from the Canadian National Population Health Survey', *Social Science and Medicine*, 51 (1), pp. 123–33.

Evans, R.G. (1974), 'Supplier Induced Demand: Some Empirical Evidence and Implications', in M. Perlman (ed.), *The Economics of Health and Medical Care*, London: Macmillan.

Feldstein, M.S. (1970), 'The Rising Cost of Hospital Care', Harvard Institute of Economic Research, Discussion Paper No. 129.

Folland, S., Goodman, A. and Stano, M. (1997), *The Economics of Health and Health Care*, New Jersey: Prentice Hall.

Gregory, S., Liatsou, M. and Kyriopoulos, J. (2002), 'The Number of Specialized Doctors and General Practitioners Required in Greece: Delphi Panel Research', *Iatriki*, 82 (1), pp. 65–71.

Kirkup, B. and Forster, D. (1990), 'How will Health Needs be Measured in Districts? Implications of Variations in Hospital Use', *Journal of Public Health Medicine*, 1 (12), pp. 45–50.

Kyriopoulos, J. (1994), 'Health Care Cost Containment Policies: The Greek Paradox', in P. Kekki (ed.), *Understanding and orienting national health systems*, Helsinki: University of Helsinki.

Kyriopoulos, J., Geitona, M. and Karalis, G. (1998), 'Hidden Economy, Private Spending and Informal Copayment in Health Care: The Role of Medical Power in Greece', in T. Beazoglou, D. Heffley and J. Kyriopoulos (eds), *Human Resources Supply and Cost Containment in the Health Systems*, Exandas, Athens: FICOSSER.

Kyriopoulos, J. and Levett, J. (1999), 'Health Care Reform in Greece', in A. Ritsatakis, J. Levett and J. Kyriopoulos (eds), *Neighbours in the Balkans: Initiating a Dialogue for Health*, Athens, Greece: WHO-Europe, National School of Public Health.

Kyriopoulos, J. Gregory, S. and Economou, Ch. (2003), *Health and Health Services in the Greek Population*, Athens: Papazisis (in Greek).

Levett, J. (1996), 'Health Policy Reform in Greece', *Eurohealth*, 2 (1), pp. 33–4.

National Statistical Service of Greece (2001a), *Social Welfare and Health Statistics, 1997*.

National Statistical Service of Greece (2001b), *Statistical Tables of Greece, 2000*.

OECD (1998), *Health Data File*, Paris.

OECD (2001), *Health Data File – Definitions, Sources and Methods*, Paris.

Okunad, A.A. and Murthy, V.N. (2002), 'Technology as a "Major Driver" of Health Care Costs: A Cointegration Analysis of the Newhouse Conjecture', *Journal of Health Economics*, 21 (1), pp. 147–59.

Phelps, C.E. (1997), *Health Economics*, Cambridge, MA: Addison-Wesley.

Plaff, M. and Nagel, F. (1986), 'Consequences for Hospitals Resulting from demographic, Social and Morbidity Changes: A European Perspective', *International Journal of Health Planning and Management*, 1 (5), pp. 311–33.

Saltman, R.B. and Figueras, J. (1997), 'European Health Care Reform. Analysis of Current Strategies', WHO Regional Publications, European Series, No. 72, Copenhagen.

Sanders, D., Coulter, A. and McPherson, K. (1988), *Variations in Hospital Admissions Rates: A Review of the Literature*, Oxford University, Department of Community Medicine and General Practice.

Shain, M. and Roemer, M.I. (1961), 'Hospital Costs Relate to the Supply of Beds', *The Modern Hospital*, 4 (92), pp. 71–4.

Souliotis, K. (2001), 'Health Expenditure Analysis in Greece 1989–1998', in J. Kyriopoulos and K. Souliotis (eds), *Health Expenditures in Greece, Estimating Problems and the Impact in Health Policies*, Athens: Papazisis (in Greek).

Stein, A.T., Harzheim, E., Costa, M., Busnello, E. and Rodrigues, L.C. (2002), 'The Relevance of Continuity of Care: A Solution for the Chaos in the Emergency Services', *Family Practice*, 19 (2), pp. 207–10.

Tragakes, E. (1999), 'Health Care Reforms in Countries of the Balkans: Implications for Public Health', in A. Ritsatakis, J. Levett and J. Kyriopoulos (eds), *Neighbours in the Balkans: Initiating a Dialogue for Health*, Athens, Greece: WHO-Europe, National School of Public Health.

Van den Heuvel, W.J., Wieringh, R. and van den Heuvel, L.P. (1997), 'Utilization of Medical Technology Assessment in Health Policy', *Health Policy*, 42, pp. 211–22.

Van der Zee, J. and Groenewegen, P.P. (1987), 'General and Specific Factors in the Explanation of Regional Variation of Hospital Admission Rates: Policy Consequences for Belgium and the Netherlands', *Health Policy*, 8 (1), pp. 77–93.

Van der Zee, J., Groenewegen, P.P., Gloerich, A.B.M., Lebrun, Th., Sailly, J.C., Verhasselt, M. and Leroy, X. (1990), 'Determinants of Regional Variation in Hospital Admission Rates: The Case of the Low Countries and the North of France', *International Journal of Health Services*, 4 (1), pp. 257–70.

Van Doorslaer, E.K.A. and van Vliet, R.C.J.A. (1989), 'A Built Bed is a Filled Bed?: An Empirical Re-examination', *Social Science and Medicine*, 28, pp. 155–64.

Van Noordt, M., Groenewegen, P.P. and van der Zee, J. (1992), 'Regional Variation in Hospital Admission Rates in the Netherlands, Belgium, Northern France and Nordrhein-Westfalen', *Das Gesundheitswesen*, 54, pp. 173–8.

Wennberg, J.E. (1987), 'Population Illness Rates do not Explain Population Hospitalisation Rates', *Medical Care*, 25, pp. 354–9.

Westert, G.P. and Groenewegen, P.P. (1999), 'Medical Practice Variations: Changing the Theoretical Approach', *Scandinavian Journal of Public Health*, 27 (3), pp. 173–80.

World Health Organisation (1994), Regional Office for Europe, *Health for All* Database.

Chapter 10

Reflections of Globalisation on Public Health

Nesrin Çilingiroğlu and Hilal Özcebe

Globalization is just like electricity. If you put your finger in a socket, it's bad. But if you use it to plug in things that improve your well-being, it's wonderful (Dr David Heymann, Head of WHO's communicable disease activities).

Globalisation: Is it Hope or Apprehension?

The greatest improvements in people's health have resulted not from health services but from social and economic changes and there remain high opportunities to do even better. In fact, the recent experience shows that health must be seen as a central factor not only in social development, but also in countries' ability to compete on the global economic stage and achieve sustainable economic progress. This means that there is a reciprocal relationship between health and economic issues. Therefore, health is a necessary investment for the human capital (World Bank, 1993; Çilingiroğlu, 1998).

There is no precise, widely agreed definition on the globalisation phenomenon. 'I see globalisation as a morally neutral but nonetheless inevitable force that poses both opportunities and threats', says Dr Nils Daulaire, president of the Global Health Council. It is possible to say that; globalisation is a source of both hope and of apprehension. It refers to various processes that take place globally. It is an accelerating factor in flow of information, technology, capital, transportation, goods and services as well as production means.

The experience in the historical context shows that globalisation somewhat conflictingly characterised by rapid economic transformation, new trade regimes and a growing increase of the poverty gap along with revolutionary electronic communications and transportation means and the hope held out by the new transnational social and political movements. However, these trends offer both possibilities and problems for public's health. Although this concept of globalisation is comparatively new, but its effects are not. For example, on the American continent the indigenous peoples have suffered severe health consequences of the European invasion of their lands 500 years ago. The recent examples of this argument can be observed in developing world. For example, Tanzania ranks as one of the world's poorest countries according to World Bank figures. But, its commercial centre, Dar es Salaam, is one of the most expensive cities in the world in which to live because expatriates on developed world salaries have helped to increase living costs. An even greater irony is that for Tanzania and many developing nations net flows of wealth remain, as in colonial days, from poor to rich. Far more is spent on servicing national debt than on services such as health or education. These are perhaps some of the less expected features of globalisation of the world economy. On the other hand, Western tobacco and arms companies seek to support their profits through selling more to low-income countries. Since 1945, the vast majority of the deaths directly or indirectly due to armed conflict have been among the world's poor. Besides, efforts within low income countries to implement rational drug policies through lists of essential drugs have met with resistance from multinational pharmaceutical companies (Unwin et al., 1998).

These are some examples of economic globalisation that implies an unfair selection on behalf of developing world. However, globalisation is both inevitable and usually desirable and contains advantageous and disadvantageous issues. Interfering with the free movement of capital hinders the advantages that will bring better standards of living and health for all. On the other hand, what it is observed is at the moment is very far from 'free trade', but a world economy increasingly dominated by a small number of multinational giants able to dictate the conditions of trade. Whatever the point of view, the last decade has undoubtedly seen an increase in the inequality gap between the world's rich and poor (World Bank, 2000).

On the other hand, the literature have suggested (Chen and Ravallion, 2000) two proximate causes of the low overall rate of poverty reduction in the 1990s, despite aggregate economic growth in the developing world. Firstly, too little of that economic growth was in the poorest countries. Secondly, persistent inequalities (in both income and non-income dimensions) within those countries and elsewhere prevented the poor from participating fully in the growth that did occur.

Therefore, it is possible to quote that globalisation creates challenges for the governance of global health, including the need to construct international regimes capable of responding to global threats to public health. It also refers to the process of increasing interconnectedness between societies such that events in one part of the world increasingly have effects on peoples and societies far away (Yusuf, 2001; World Bank, 2002, http://www.worldbank.org/poverty). However, the direct and indirect effects of globalisation process are varying according to the level of development, growth capacity and wealth distribution of a country.

Common Effects of Globalisation on Public's Health

Today's commentators argue that the facilitating factors accounting for globalisation, such as greater openness, flow of information and technology, rapid transportation, free trade and the flow of capital, increased pollution, changes in diet produced by genetically modified foods, increase in the tobacco market, increasing inequality and more cultural contacts undermine the state's control over what happens in its territory. In fact it is possible to analyse the common effects of globalisation within many contexts (Cornia, 2001).

In the modern world, bacteria and viruses travel almost as fast as money. With globalisation, a single microbial sea washes all of humankind. Because, millions of people cross international borders every single day: almost a tenth of humanity each year. It is not only the infectious diseases that spread with globalisation. Changes in lifestyle and diet can prompt an increase in heart disease, diabetes mellitus and cancer. More than anything, tobacco is sweeping the globe as it is criss-crossed by market forces (Brutland, 2001).

In order to argue the effects and reflections of globalisation on public's health it is useful to build a framework that covers the harmful, beneficial or mixed effects of this process. However this is not an easy work since one effect can be beneficial for one county while the same one can be harmful for the others. Within this context, for example, Woodward and his friends developed a conceptual framework for assessment of the linkages between globalisation and health. This framework is not approaching this topic in terms of beneficial or harmful effects but it includes both the indirect effects of globalisation on health, operating through the national economy, household economies and health-related sectors such as water, sanitation and education, as well as more direct effects on population-level and individual risk factors for health and on the health care system (Woodward et al., 2001).

It is recognised that fundamental changes are currently taking place in health. Some of these are caused by developments within the health sector, including new discoveries and treatments in health care and a greater awareness of the effects of the environment on population health. Some are caused by developments outside the health sector, such as globalisation and the growth of the telemedicine and Internet. These changes are likely to increase in the coming years and new developments will take place. Within this climate there is a need for policy to become more informed about the context in which it operates and to take a long-term, strategic view of developing countries health.

There is no consensus either on the pathways and mechanisms through which globalisation affect the health of populations. Health is one of the facets of globalisation that has complex relations. Its effects are mediated by income growth and distribution, economic instability, the availability of health, education and other social services, life-style such as stress and other factors, a review of which has recently appeared. Some health impacts of globalisation can be defined as positive such as telemedicine that could help in the provision of services in remote areas. But, telemedicine also requires substantial investment in equipment, communications infrastructure, and training of personnel, which can be counted as negative economic and health effect. Telemedicine presents mixed effects.

In summary, globalisation has advantages as well as disadvantages for public's health. Inequalities within country define the positive or negative health effects of globalisation. For example, globalisation increases the accessibility to health information, health services or new treatment regimes of rich people, while these opportunities are not attainable for poor, more disadvantages groups. Therefore, when discussing the reciprocal relationship between globalisation and health it is necessary to take into account some issues such as poverty, inequalities, and free trade.

Poverty, Inequalities and Health

It is agreed that there is a reciprocal relation between poverty and health. There is a growing concern that globalisation increases marginalisation of the world's poorest. This issue is argued by many commentators. Globalisation will be the most important risk factor to enlarge the gap between the rich and poor. The existence of inequalities enlarges the adverse effects of globalisation on health. As it is indicated in the 1999 UN Human Development report, the income size of the top fifth of the world's people living in the richest countries was compared with that of fifth in the poorest. The ratio had changed from 30 to 1 in 1960, to 60 to 1 in 1990 and to 74 to 1 in 1997 (UNDP, 1999). The World Development Reports and Indicators emphasises the disadvantages of globalisation on poverty (World Bank, 2002, http://www.worldbank.org/poverty; World Bank, 2001):

The Effects of Globalisation on Health

1 Speed and spread of diseases (as a result of the movement of people and environmental changes)
   - Importation of infectious diseases and possible epidemics (HIV/AIDS, STDs, influenza, tuberculosis and others)
   - Spreading of increased non-communicable diseases (for example, increased number of coronary heart diseases, obesity, asthma, depression, hypertension and others)
2 Standardisation of medical education
   - An establishment of a common curriculum and acceptable professional standards (medical professionals) among countries
   - Requirement of licensing for cross-border medical practice
   - Harmonising accreditation standards
   - The development and improvement of skills of health providers through access to new technologies
3 Availability of dangerous products
   - Movement of legal and illegal drugs that pose as a health risk
   - Increased trafficking (modern slavery, organ trafficking, prostitution)
   - Smuggling (human, arm, and others)
4 Changes in health systems
   - Creation more flexible health insurance for portability
   - Reconstruction health systems and more privatisation in health sector
   - Reduced public health funding
   - Not enough attention for equity and access to health care services as resources shift from public to the private sector
   - Limited resources (financial, human and technological) in the public sector to provide efficient health care services in developing countries
5 New rules for cross border flows
   - Movement of medical technology
   - Capital flows
   - Movement of production means
   - Difficulty in attracting foreign and domestic investors in developing countries
   - Brain drain from developing countries
6 Increased inequalities within and among countries which increases health risks
   - Skewed income distribution (poor people have worse health)
   - Ignorance high-risk groups by health authorities
   - Expanded trade in the health sector driven by economics without consideration to the social and health aspects
   - Increased health inequalities cause extra economic and social burden

1   *poor people have worse health* – for example, in several Sub-Saharan African countries, as many as 173 out of every 1000 children born will die before their fifth birthday, while in Sweden; by contrast, under five mortality rate is 3 per 1,000 live births (UNICEF, 2003);

2   *ill health is a dimension of poverty as well as it generates poverty* – closing inter- and intra-country gaps between rich and poor, by securing greater proportional improvements amongst poorer groups is not only a poverty issue, it is also a question of social justice and equity;

3   *inequalities* – for example, as it was indicated by Bezruchka, the health of the population of the United States is poor compared to other rich countries. In terms of life expectancy in 1997, the US stood twenty-fifth, behind all the other rich countries, even a few poor ones. The country that has longest life expectancy every year since 1977, Japan, has the highest smoking prevalence in the world. However, the Japanese do not die of smoking-related diseases to the extent that Americans do. Therefore, it can be said that the health of population in rich countries is determined primarily not by the sophisticated and expensive health care system or by individual risk factors such as smoking but rather, by the gap between the rich and poor. Many recent studies show that populations with a greater income hierarchy are less healthy and specifically have shorter lives, then populations that are more equitable (Bezruchka, 2000). This situation is more crucial in developing countries. Therefore, in order to tackle this problem, it is necessary to analyse the power relationships that lie behind the poverty.

Liberalisation in Trade and Health:

The benefits from growing exchange of health related goods and services between countries were decided to be channelled in order to improve the health status and decrease the inequalities by General Agreement of Trade in Services (GATS). GATS was the outcome of the multilateral negotiations of recent Uruguay Round since there was a need to regulate the growing trade activities according to the same principles underlying all agreements under the umbrella of the World Trade Organisation (Adams and Kinnon, 1997).

The intellectual property rights and access to essential medicines in the poor countries is an ongoing debate. This is very clearly the case with HIV/AIDS in Africa where the growth of the epidemic is formidable and the pricing policies of multi-national pharmaceutical companies mean treatment choices are very limited for those living in poor countries (Baum, 2001).

Free trade could offer risks that can be harmful effect on health by promoting, marketing and trading *hazardous products* such as tobacco. Although the global reach of the transnational tobacco companies that has been enhanced by a recent wave of liberalisation, they have also taken advantage of more direct forms of market penetration via direct foreign investment, either by licensing arrangements with a domestic monopoly, joint ventures, or direct acquisition of a domestic company (Bettcher et al., 2000).

Some modes of trade – namely, *cross-border trade, movement of consumers, foreign commercial presence, movement of personnel* – can be taken into account to examine the trade liberalisation effects of globalisation on health from the standpoint of health systems in developing countries (Adams and Kinnon, 1997).

Cross-border trade, which involves in particular telemedicine, together with certain support services, is not yet widespread in developing countries. Although it could help in the provision of services in remote areas, it requires substantial investment in equipment, communications infrastructure, and training of personnel.

Movement of consumers involves both patients seeking treatment abroad and students receiving foreign training. Flows are usually from developing to industrialised countries, but movement in the opposite direction is also occurring as developed country patients seek good quality treatment at lower prices abroad. Health authorities would need to ensure that any upgrading of services for foreign patients extends equally to domestic patients, and that these are not excluded from the services offered to foreigners. Foreign education can help to upgrade the skills of personnel, provided that students return home, and the training they receive matches needs in the home country. Much attention has been given to designing incentives to encourage trainees to return, and to finding other solutions, such as setting up regional training facilities.

Foreign commercial presence in the health sector so far is limited in developing countries, and its growth will depend on the size and value of the target market. It will be a sensitive area for health authorities to handle as it involves both foreign direct investment and private sector supply of services. Such investment may not match with national health policy objectives, or may cause a dual system, with a different quality of service for the wealthy and for the needy. Competition among providers may also induce health facilities increasingly to invest in expensive high-technology equipment.

The *movement of personnel* to provide health services abroad has been a longstanding problem for developing countries. Better working conditions and higher remuneration often attract their trained staff elsewhere. This can produce shortages of staff in the home country, which might have to be compensated by an inflow of foreign health personnel. The home country has to support the cost of training without receiving the benefits, although this expenditure may be offset to some extent by the remittances sent home by workers abroad.

Besides these, *reduced public health funding* is another possible effect that may threaten the developing countries: The emergence of the global market where trading of products is highly competitive and 'survival of the fittest' is the dictum has prompted developing economies to reduce national expenditures for low priority programs like public health. Thus, reduction in public health expenses in these countries has slowed down public health surveillance efforts.

However, to make a preliminary appraisal of the potential impact of this trade, three health policy objectives can be taken into account: equity of access, quality of services and efficient use of resources. Therefore, health authorities of developing countries will need in particular to strengthen their regulatory framework in order to ensure that national health systems derive maximum benefit from trade in health services in terms of equity, quality and efficiency, while reducing potential social cost to a minimum.

Some Examples from the Literature on the Dark Side of Globalisation

Recent literature on globalisation, development, poverty and health status of low and middle-income countries' brought the facts into the open. Some examples are given below.

1   In a World Bank briefing paper (Weisbrot et al., 2001) it was indicated that for economic growth and almost all of the other indicators, the last 20 years have shown a very clear decline in progress as compared with the previous two decades. The authors proved their argument by using some indicators derived from World Development Reports. For each indicator, countries were divided into five roughly equal groups, according to what level the countries had achieved by the start of the period; 1960 or 1980. They analyse the adverse effects of globalisation in developing countries under below given headings:
    *   *growth: the fall in economic growth rates was most pronounced and across the board for all groups or countries.* The poorest group went from a per capita GDP growth rate of 1.9 per cent annually in 1960–80, to a decline of 0.5 per cent per year (1980–2000). For the

middle group (which includes mostly poor countries), there was a sharp decline from an annual per capita growth rate of 3.6 per cent to just less than 1 per cent. Over a 20-year period, this represents the difference between doubling income per person, versus increasing it by just 21 per cent. The other groups also showed substantial declines in growth rates (Figure 10.1).

• *Life expectancy: progress in life expectancy was also reduced* for 4 out of the five groups of countries, with the exception of the highest group (life expectancy 69–76 years). The sharpest slowdown was in the second to worst group (life expectancy between 44–53 years). Reduced progress in life expectancy and other health outcomes cannot be explained by the AIDS pandemic (Figure 10.2).

• *Infant and child mortality: progress in reducing infant mortality was also considerably slower during the period of globalisation* (1980–98) than over the previous two decades. The biggest declines in progress were for the middle to worst performing groups. Progress in reducing child mortality (under 5) was also slower for the middle to worst performing groups of countries (Figures 10.3 and 10.4).

• *Education and literacy: progress in education also slowed during the period of globalisation.* The rate of growth of primary, secondary, and tertiary (postsecondary) school enrolment was slower for most groups of countries. There are some exceptions, but these tend to be concentrated among the better performing groups of countries. By almost every measure of education, including literacy rates, the middle and poorer performing groups saw less rapid progress in the period of globalisation than in the prior two decades. The rate of growth of public spending on education, as a share of GDP, also slowed across all groups of countries (Figures 10.5 and 10.6).

2 Cornia (2001) argues that with slow growth and frequent rises in inequality, health improvements during the era of deregulation and globalisation decelerated perceptibly, especially during the 1990s. The author indicates that in many parts of Africa and countries of the former Soviet Union there was total stagnation or a sharp regression. The infant mortality rate, a key indicator of overall health in developing countries, fell more slowly over the period 1960–98 than in previous decades (Table 10.1), despite the massive increase in the coverage of low-cost, lifesaving public health programmes (vaccination coverage rose from an average of 25 per cent to 70 per cent between 1980 and the end of the 1990s) and the spread of knowledge about health, nutrition, and hygiene among parents.

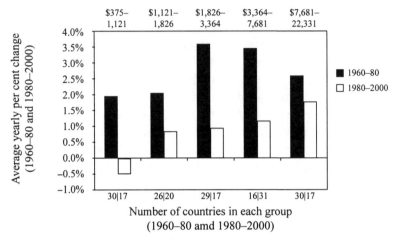

Figure 10.1   Average yearly change in real per capita GDP

Source: Weisbrot et al., 2001.

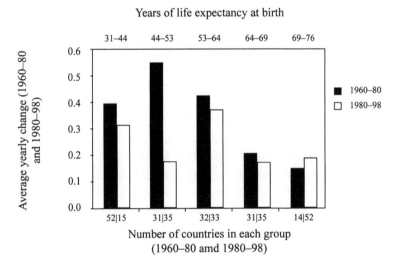

Figure 10.2   Average yearly change in total life expectancy

Note: total (male and female combined) life expectancy at birth is the number of years a newborn
infant would live if prevailing patterns of mortality at the time of its birth were to stay
the same throughout its life.

Source: Weisbrot et al., 2001.

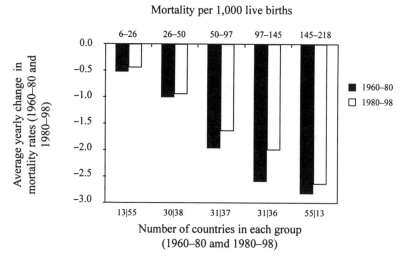

Figure 10.3   Average yearly change in infant mortality rate

Source: Weisbrot et al., 2001.

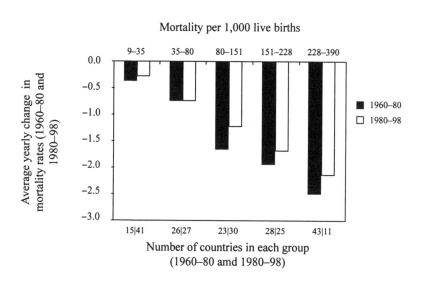

Figure 10.4   Average yearly change in mortality rate of children under five years of age

Source: Weisbrot et al., 2001.

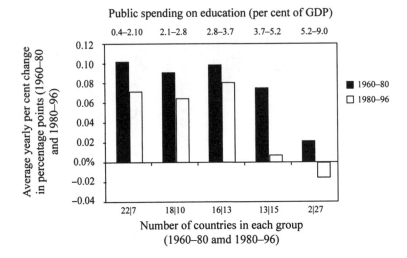

Figure 10.5　Average yearly change in total public spending on education

Source: Weisbrot et al., 2001.

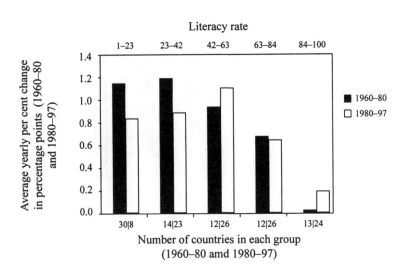

Figure 10.6　Average yearly change in literacy rates

Source: Weisbrot et al., 2001.

**Table 10.1   Trends in average regional annual decline in infant
mortality rate: 1960–98[1]**

Years	1960–70	1970–80	1980–90	1990–98	1960–80	1980–98
World	–2.6	–2.0	–2.7	–1.3	–2.3	–2.1
High-income countries	–3.9	–5.3	–3.8	–4.0	–4.6	–3.9
Low-and middle income countries	–2.8	–2.1	–2.8	–1.3	–2.4	–2.1
Eastern Europe and Central Asia	–	–	–3.9	–3.1	–	–3.5
Sub-Saharan Africa	–1.8	–1.7	–1.3	–1.2	–1.8	–1.2

1   Rates are compounded and weighted by population size.

Source: Cornia, 2001.

3   In his report, Yusuf (2001) indicates that globalisation is not a panacea.
Under some circumstances it can increase the susceptibility of countries
to shocks. The experience of the preceding century, which is still fresh in
our minds, teaches us that erecting barriers to the flow of goods, factors,
information and ideas, was injurious to welfare and entailed a loss of
freedom. Reversing globalisation, even if it could be done, would be
an enormous setback. Slowing international integration, while it might
temporarily protect some groups from competition will often be purchased
at high long-term costs for the majority. Frequently the delay in opening the
economy does not lead to reforms that strengthen vulnerable sectors or to
the creation of safety nets to protect low-income groups. Generally reforms
are compelled and implemented by having to face a challenge head on.

4   Another World Bank report (Solimano, 1999) showed that global business
cycles give rise to considerable macro economic volatility at the national
level that has become more acute in late twentieth century globalisation.
In particular, the scope and severity of the crisis of the 1990s, say in
Mexico (1994–95), Asia (1997), Russia (1998), Brazil (1999), Argentina
(2001–02), Turkey (2001–02) is evidence that we are facing severe
financial vulnerability. This is a very serious problem of globalisation as
highly integrated financial markets transmit, very quickly, across countries,
financial shocks and change in confidence levels that affect exchange rates
interest rates, asset prices and ultimately output and employment with
adverse social effects.

Some Evidence from Turkey

In Turkey, due to the continuous, consistent and reliable data deficiencies it is sometimes hard to compare and analyse the reciprocal relations between health, social, demographic and economic variables. But nevertheless the available data indicates that Turkey is affected from the merits and demerits of global trends, especially economic crises.

As it will be seen from Tables 10.2 and 10.3, there is considerable income and quality of life variations and the gap is widening with time. The degree of inequality within the country is strongly associated with an increase in social problems. Turkey has one of the more complex health care systems in the world. A wide array of health care providers, financiers, and organisation arrangements has resulted in an inefficient system, which increasingly fails to effectively meet the health needs of the country's 64 million population. Poor health status of the population relative to the country's income level, inequitable access to health care, an unsustainable public insurance system, inefficient use of resources make health care reform activities imperative (Çilingiroğlu, 1999). As an OECD member and as an EU accession candidate, Turkey is seeking ever-closer ties with Western Europe and the EU. Yet, equity in the health sector is one of the important stumbling blocks that the country must address in order to achieve social peace. While Turkey is the world's seventeenth most industrialised nation, it ranks only eighty-second out of 180 countries as measured in the 2000 UNDP Human Development Index, far behind most middle income countries, most notably the middle income countries in Latin America such as Argentina (34), Chile (39), and Mexico (51). Factors contributing to this low ranking are the nearly 17 per cent adult illiteracy rate and poor health outcomes (UNDP, 2001). Global economic crises are affecting the whole population. The effect of the recent one (2001) will show itself on the health status and this will be seen by 2003 Turkish Demographic and Health Survey.

Global Problems vs Global Solutions

Globalisation is sometimes used in a much broader economic sense, as another name for capitalism or neo-colonisation or the market economy. Today, almost two billion of people live in deep poverty in this world. And the world has the resources, technology and knowledge to improve their health as well as of all humankind. The solution is in the hands of owners of these resources.

Table 10.2 Percentage distribution of income by regions in Turkey: 1968–94

Regions	1968		1973		1987		1994	
	Household	*Income*	*Household*	*Income*	*Household*	*Income*	*Household*	*Income*
West	30.7	39.3	33.7	37.7	37.0	45.0	42.3	52.5
South	15.3	11.4	15.2	13.2	13.4	10.7	12.5	11.0
Central	22.5	23.1	21.9	23.4	24.3	21.5	17.9	15.4
North	17.7	14.7	14.5	15.8	10.6	8.9	12.8	10.9
East	13.8	11.5	14.7	9.9	14.7	13.9	14.5	10.2

Source: SPO, 1997.

Table 10.3 Health-related indicators in Turkey: 1960–2001

Years	GNP growth (%)	Rural population (%)	Life expectancy (years)	Infant mortality rate (000)	Total fertility rate		Literate population (%)
1960	3.4	67.6	43	206	(1960)	6.2	39.5
1980	-2.8	57.9	61	111	(1983)	4.05	67.5
1990	6.8	46.6	66	65	(1993)	2.7	80.5
2001	- 8.5	29.4	69.4	33.9	(1998)	2.6	na

Source: Cerit, 1989; Shorter, 1969; DPT, 1997; DPT, 2001, HIPS, 1987.

But it is not clear that whether the developed world really want to pay the opportunity cost of their welfare.

The countries that have been excluded from the benefits of the global market should create a ground in strengthening their human resource bases, infrastructures and macroeconomic balance. For many countries, some components of globalisation, such as trade liberalisation and technology transfer, could, in principle, increase efficiency, welfare and health. Under the present restrictive rules of access to the international market, further liberalisation and globalisation would help these countries to improve their market position, economic efficiency and health status. Uncontrolled globalisation in these countries could be expected to immediately generate considerable costs in efficiency and social affairs that would worsen growth performance and health outcomes. Particularly for these countries, a gradual and selective integration into the world economy and to the creation of new democratic institutions of global governance is highly preferable to instant globalisation.

The role of the state is changing. Governments should constitute strong national health policies, regulations, programmes and institutions in order to protect public's health from the negative effects of globalisation. Strategies, which maintain and create equity in health status, should be an integral part of sustainable social, economic and human development policies. Within the context of health reforms every country should be supported by global health promotion programs in order to create rational and effective health policies. Also, the public health workers should be equipped with the knowledge and skills to engage partners across sectors and across borders to achieve health and social goals.

International bodies such as WHO, UNDP and the World Bank should continue to function as an independent provider of knowledge and evidence. International and national public health movements need the power of strong public and non-governmental organisations' support. People should raise their voices in order to establish advocacy against the growing power of multinationals and increasing inequalities.

As a result, global problems can be solved by global efforts. The recent United Nations Millennium Declaration contains an integrated and comprehensive overview of the current situation and searches solutions. It outlines potential strategies for action that are designed to meet the goals and commitments made by the 147 heads of state and government, and 189 member states in total, who adopted the Millennium Declaration. The Declaration suggests paths to follow and shares information on 'best practices'. It draws on the work of governments, the entire United Nations system, including the Bretton Woods institutions and the World Trade Organisation, intergovernmental organisations, international organisations, regional organisations and civil society (UN, 2000).

Positive and negative health effects of globalisation should be investigated by developing and implementing research agenda at national and international level. The governmental and non-governmental bodies should carry this responsibility. The outputs of the researches can be utilised to create more rational policies, practices and evaluations.

References

Adams, D. and Kinnon, C. (1997), *Measuring Trade Liberalization against Public Health Objectives: The Case of Health Services*, WHO Task Force on Health Economics, WHO/TFHE/TBN/97.2.

Baum, F. (2001), 'Health, Equity, Justice and Globalisation: Some Lessons from the People's Health Assembly', *Journal of Epidemiological Community Health*, 55, pp. 613–16.

Bettcher, D.W., Yach, D. and Guindon, E. (2000), 'Global Trade and Health: Key Linkages and Future Challenges', *Bulletin of the World Health Organization*, 78 (4), pp. 521–34.

Bezruchka, S. (2000), 'Is Globalization Dangerous to Our Health?', *Western Journal of Medicine*, 172 (5), pp. 332–4.

Brutland, G.H. (2001), 'Globalization as a Force for Better Health', lecture, London School of Economics, 16 March.

Cerit, S. (1989), *Population, Fertility, Mortality in Turkey*, Ankara (in Turkish).

Chen, S. and Ravallion, M. (2000), 'How did the World's Poorest Fare in the 1990s?', The Development Research Group, World Bank.

Çilingiroğlu, N. (1998), 'Human Capital and Development', *The Turkish Journal of Population Studies*, 21, pp. 39–50 (in Turkish).

Çilingiroğlu, N. (1999), 'The Need for Change: Health Reforms in Turkey', in H.T.O. Davies, M. Tavakoli, M. Malek and A. Neilson (eds), *Controlling Costs: Strategic Issues in Health Care Management*, Aldershot: Ashgate, pp. 15–32.

Cornia, G.A. (2001), 'Globalization and Health: Results and Options', *Bulletin of World Health Organization*, 79 (9), pp. 834–41.

Hacettepe Institute of Population Studies (1987), *1983 Turkish Population and Health Survey*, Ankara: Semih Ofset.

Shorter, F.C. (1969), 'Information on Fertility, Mortality and Population Growth in Turkey', *Turkish Demography: Proceeding of A Conference*, Ankara, p. 31.

Solimano, A. (1999), 'Globalization and National Development at the End of 20th Century', World Bank Policy Research Working Paper.

State Planning Organization (1998), *Basic Socio-economic Indicators: 1950–1997*, Ankara: DPT Matbaası.

UN (2000), 'United Nations Millennium Declaration', http://www.un.org/millennium/summit.htm.

UNDP (2001), *Human Development Report 2001: Making New Technologies Work for Human Development*, Oxford: Oxford University Press.

UNDP (1999), *Human Development Report 1999: Globalization with a Human Face*, Oxford: Oxford University Press.

UNICEF (2003), *The State of the Worlds Children 2003*, New York.

Unwin, N., Alberti, G., Aspray, T., Edwards, R., Mbanya, J.-C., Sobngwi, E., Mugusi, F., Rashid, S., Setel, P. and Whiting, D. (1998), 'Economic Globalisation and its Effect on Health', *British Medical Journal*, 316 (7142), pp. 1401–2.

Weisbrot, M., Baker, D., Kraev, E. and Chen, J. (2001), 'The Scorecard on Globalization 1980–2000: Twenty Years of Diminished Progress: A Briefing Paper', *The Center for Economic and Policy Research*, World Bank.

Woodward, D., Drager, N., Beaglehole, R. and Lipson, D. (2001), 'Globalization and Health: a Framework for Analysis and Action', *Bulletin of World Health Organization*, 79 (9), pp. 875–81.

World Bank (1993), *World Development Report: Investing in Health*, Oxford: World Bank/ Oxford University Press.

World Bank (2002), 'Inequality, Poverty and Socio-economic Performance', http:// www.worldbank.org/poverty/.

World Bank (2001), *World Development Report 2000/2001: Attacking Poverty*, Oxford: Oxford University Press, http://www.worldbank.org/poverty/wdrpoverty/.

World Bank (2000), *Global Economic Prospects and the Developing Countries*, Oxford: Oxford University Press.

Yusuf, S. (2001), *Globalization and the Challenge for Developing Countries*, New York: Development Research Group, World Bank.

Chapter 11

Opportunity Knocks: Ten Years of Health Care Reform, Strategic Policy Implementation and Maori Health Development in New Zealand

Lynette Stewart, Louise Kuraia and Karleen Everitt

The title of this chapter contains a passing reference to a popular television game show from the 1970s. A cynical view is that the game show analogy seems a fitting one for the New Zealand health sector of the 1990s – opportunistic competition within a contrived setting, a system of few winners and many losers. While not wholly in disagreement with this view; we will examine innovative *Maori* (the indigenous people of New Zealand) health developments during the 1990s in New Zealand that challenge the stereotypical conception of 'indigenous' development as ad hoc and inferior to 'mainstream' health development.

The New Zealand public health sector underwent ten years of dramatic change, with four wholesale structural changes and a myriad of functional and organisational changes in that time. A fair amount of negative analysis has been written about the impact of the reforms (Cheyne et al., 1997; Durie, 1998a; Fleras and Spoonley, 1999), and conventional political wisdom would have it that the 'market-driven' health system approach of the 1990s was an abject failure.

Less well-canvassed is our contention that the environment of constant change and liberal pluralism (Fleras and Spoonley, 1999) enabled highly innovative and opportunistic Maori health policy and health care service development to flourish during the 1990s. Our assertion is that Maori health policy makers and service providers trail-blazed the concept of integrating health care in New Zealand, particularly public health and primary care services during this time.

In this chapter we will explore, through experiential historical analysis, effective and transportable Maori health development models unique to the northernmost region of the North Island of New Zealand, and examine the successes achieved.

A Decade of Political Change

The 1990s dawned in New Zealand in quite spectacular fashion. Auckland, our largest and most cosmopolitan city, hosted the 1990 Commonwealth Games with splendid success. 1990 was also New Zealand's sesquicentennial year – 150 years since the signing of *Te Tiriti O Waitangi* (The Treaty of Waitangi, our nation's founding document) by Lieutenant Governor William Hobson as agent for Queen Victoria and 512 'Chiefs of New Zealand'.

Maori commemoration, such as the events organised by the Maori Standing Committee of the New Zealand 1990 Commission for the period leading up to and including Waitangi Day (6 February) were on a grand scale. In particular, the denouement of the *Kaupapa Waka* project was a breathtaking celebration of Maori achievement, ability and pride – past, present and future. A majestic fleet of more than two dozen ceremonial *waka* (canoes) came from all over *Aotearoa* (New Zealand) and assembled at Waitangi, the site of the Treaty signing. The mammoth gathering of both Maori and *Pakeha* (New Zealanders of European descent) attested to the possibilities for *kotahitanga* (unity) within the nation that had not occurred at Waitangi since 1840.

However, *Kaupapa Waka*, for all its laudable aims of bringing Maori and Pakeha together, was more the exception rather than the rule. In many ways, the 150 year anniversary of the 'birth of our nation' barely registered for the majority of New Zealanders. The largely desultory way in which we celebrated our sesquicentennial was indicative of our immaturity as a country to come to grips with both the concept and the reality of our nationhood being founded on *Te Tiriti O Waitangi*. Indeed, the simple premise of two peoples living harmoniously together in one land is yet to be fully realised.

In October 1990 the Labour government, which had held power for much of the 1980s, was defeated at the polls by a National Party intent on reinforcing the Right in New Zealand politics. The newly elected government not only maintained the momentum of social and economic reform of its Labour predecessors, but substantially 'upped the ante', in the colloquially referenced 'Mother of All Budgets' in 1991, which slashed social spending and firmly entrenched the New Right ideologies that were to dominate the rest of the decade (Fleras and Spoonley, 1999).

The early 1990s also saw a fundamental change in New Zealand's electoral system. Two electoral reform referenda were held in 1992 and 1993, culminating in the introduction of the mixed member proportional representation system (MMP), replacing the first past the post system.

Nineteen ninety-six was a watershed year in New Zealand politics – a year of many notable 'firsts'. The first general election under MMP was held, and whilst it was one of the highest voter turnouts in history, particularly of Maori (Durie, 1998a); on election night there was no outright winner. With no clear majority held by any party, the first coalition government was eventually formed between National and New Zealand First. But perhaps the most surprising 'first' of all, certainly for mainstream political commentators was that for the first time in New Zealand's political history, Maori were undoubtedly the most visible force in mainstream politics. For all intents and purposes it was Maori parliamentarians and through them, Maori voters who held the balance of power. A total of 15 Maori Members of Parliament (MPs) were elected from across the political spectrum heralding as one renowned Maori academic observed, a 'new dawn' of Maori political might (Durie, 1998a).

New Zealand First Maori politicians, who, in another historic 'first' in 1996 made a clean sweep of all five Maori electorate seats breaking the Labour stranglehold of some 40 years, came under intense scrutiny during the early months of the new coalition government. A seemingly orchestrated series of media attacks, largely without foundation or sound supporting evidence of wrong doing, painted these five men as 'arrogant warriors' who could not be trusted (Durie, 1998a). Nor was there ever any attempt by the mainstream media to bring some sense of relativity into its analysis (Stewart et al., 2001).

Yet for all their media 'mishaps', the New Zealand First 'tight five' (a rugby-referenced tag they wore with some pride), along with their charismatic and politically perspicacious Maori leader the Rt Hon. Winston Peters, appeared to raise Maori political power to levels not previously seen in mainstream politics. That was until the politically tempestuous events of 1998, which saw the incumbent National prime minister rolled and replaced by New Zealand's first woman prime minister, quickly followed by the acrimonious split within New Zealand First. The split, on its surface at least, between Peters and four of the 'tight five', ultimately led to the collapse of the first coalition government, almost the complete demise of New Zealand First, and a return to power for Labour in 1999.

From a Maori political perspective the 1990s was a decade of compelling change. The Maori voice in mainstream politics was never more vocal, and at the same time, 'grassroots' Maori leadership vigorously upheld the paramouncy of *Te Tiriti O Waitangi* as the cornerstone of Maori-Crown relationships. The influence of Maori political participation in the 1990s shaped the policy environment that gave rise to Maori development opportunity on an unprecedented scale.

Maori Policy in the 1990s

The state sector's response to Maori during the 1990s was an often confusing and almost always politically charged business. The macro-political shift to the Right was reflected in the 'downsizing' of state mechanisms of administration, and 'mainstreaming' of Maori social policy.

Two themes consistently appeared in Maori social policy during the 1990s: biculturalism and institutional responsiveness (Fleras and Spoonley, 1999). Biculturalism in policy and practice emphasised a 'treaty-driven framework', and included the following concepts as outlined by one of the authors of the National government's 1991 *Ka Awatea* Maori Policy:

*   a partnership between two founding nations;
*   Maori self-determination;
*   bilateral decision-making;
*   the devolution of services to Maori tribal authorities;
*   increased responsiveness to Maori values, needs and aspirations;
*   a willingness to rely on Maori structures and culture as a basis for renewal and reform (Henare, 1995).

Institutional responsiveness focused on encouraging mainstream institutions and state sector agencies to actively incur Maori participation in the design and implementation of policy, practices and programmes (Fleras and Spoonley, 1999).

Linked to the state sector's responsiveness focus, increased numbers of Maori policy makers notably influenced the strategic direction of Maori development, particularly in health. Maori policy makers ingeniously potentiated the open-ended policy environment to push the boundaries of mainstream complacency, creating a platform for Maori participation and inclusion at levels not experienced before.

The decade ended with the election of a new Labour-led coalition government, who carefully trod the centre line with their Maori policy *He*

Putahitanga Hou: Labour on Maori Development (New Zealand Labour Party, 1999). Labour had the Maori electorate seats handed back to them on a platter in 1999 due to the disintegration of New Zealand First. Yet, for all that, they also knew that they could no longer simply take the Maori vote for granted, so they ensured they implied fulfilment of Maori aspirations for *tino rangatiratanga* (self-determination) through the forging of 'new and stronger partnership relationships between Maori and the Crown' (New Zealand Labour Party, 1999). *He Putahitanga Hou* re-emphasised the importance of *Iwi* (tribal authorities) as the primary service delivery mechanism for Maori development and promised to deliver resources into Maori hands through legislation if required.

To date, implementation of Labour's Maori policy has been in a manner reminiscent of Labour's 'devolution' policies of the 1980s. In effect, state control is maintained through the auspices of devolution, which provides for the transfer of responsibility for service delivery to Maori through state-sanctioned *Iwi* authorities, yet stops short of sanctioning full Maori autonomy (Durie, 1998a; Fleras and Spoonley, 1999).

Health Reforms, Restructuring and Transformations

The New Zealand health sector in the early 1990s, like that of most other Western industrialised nations at the time, was faced with the converging challenges of ever-increasing demand for high-cost new technologies, economic recession and an aging population (Cheyne et al., 1997). The National government's response was to catapult New Zealand's health system into the uncharted waters of the 'free market', with the key drivers being efficiency, effectiveness and cost containment through managed competition.

On 1 July 1993 the Health and Disability Services Act took effect and the new health sector structures supporting the purchaser/provider split become operational. Semi-elected area health boards, (primarily centred on public hospitals) were disestablished, with functions, assets and personnel transitioning into:

- Crown Health Enterprises (CHEs) – crown companies, providers of secondary care/ hospital-based services who were legislatively required to return a dividend to the government;
- Regional Health Authorities (RHAs) – four government purchasers of health services for the populations of their respective regions (Northern, Midland, Central and Southern);

- Public Health Commission – quasi-independent government purchaser of 'non-clinical' public health services; disestablished in 1995;
- Ministry of Health (MOH) – largely confined to policy guidelines development, accountability monitoring of the 'sector' and public health regulatory functions, with no role in directly purchasing or administering health services.

A change of political system and government in 1996 saw a 'softening' and 're-centering' of the health reforms through the implementation of the *New Zealand First and National Coalition Agreement* (New Zealand Government, 1996). In practical terms this also triggered two more years of major structural change and concomitant loss of institutional knowledge, as the focus of the sector moved from competition to cooperation, and from sector reform to transformation. CHEs become hospitals (and health services or HHSs) again and the four regional purchasers (eventually) become one national funder (Transitional Health Authority in 1997, followed by the Health Funding Authority or HFA in 1998).

In November 1999, the newly elected Labour-Alliance Coalition government announced plans to immediately implement Labour's pre-election promise to put the 'public' back into the 'public health system'. The funder/provider split was plastered over by the establishment of partially elected District Health Boards (DHBs), created from the no-longer profit-focused HHSs, and the HFA was abolished with a correlative explosive growth in the MOH to avoid wholesale redundancies.

Eight years after the New Zealand's foray into the 'free market', the health sector effectively turned full circle when 21 Crown-owned DHBs become fully operational in July 2001. DHBs are responsible for improving the health of the population of their districts through the funding of primary and community services and the delivery of secondary and (in some cases) tertiary services.

The super-sized MOH has been busy producing new policy frameworks to guide the sector, central to which is the *New Zealand Health Strategy* (Ministry of Health, 2000a). Also important in this era of national frameworks, local implementation are: *The Primary Care Strategy* (Ministry of Health, 2001a); the *New Zealand Disability Strategy* (Ministry of Health, 2000b); and *He Korowai Oranga: Maori Health Strategy Discussion Document* (Ministry of Health, 2001b).

Opportunity Knocks: Maori Health Development

The health reforms of the early to mid-1990s had their basis in New Right ideologies and the entire decade was dominated by significant structural change, yet within this ever-changing context Maori health development came into its own.

Maori health development in the 1990s was a unique marriage of ideas and aspirations, policy and practical solutions. On the one hand, there was the holistic, 'indigenous socialism' of *Te Ao Maori* (the Maori worldview), as exemplified in *oranga* (health) by *Nga Whare Tapa Wha*, or the four cornerstones of good health – *hinengaro* (mind), *tinana* (body), *whanau* (family), *wairua* (spirituality) (Stewart et al., 2001). By contrast, the laissez faire philosophies behind the National government's health reforms, focusing on individualism, choice, the free market and entrepreneurship could have been seen as an anathema to Maori aspirations for development. Instead, these ideas were creatively adapted to suit Maori development ends, and Maori became the biggest collective 'player' in health's burgeoning 'third sector' during the 1990s (Stewart et al., 2001).

The Te Tai Tokerau Experience

There are two major strands that weave through out the tapestry of Maori health development in *Te Tai Tokerau* (Northland) during the 1990s – identification of Maori need and recognition of Maori rights to develop.

Addressing Maori Need

Te Tai Tokerau, the Maori place-name for Northland, is, as its Pakeha name suggests, the northernmost region of the North Island of New Zealand. Te Tai Tokerau has a population base of approximately 140,000; of that 30 per cent are Maori, although the population makeup of individual communities can be up to 90 per cent Maori, particularly in the very far north.

It is like most other areas of provincial New Zealand – a collection of predominantly small rural communities dotted around the region, heavily reliant on primary industry – farming and forestry particularly. The demise of primary industry protectionism in the 1980s hit the region hard and those who relied on the primary industry for employment and income suffered. Freezing Works (meat-processing plants) and dairy factories, the major employers in Te

Tai Tokerau closed or substantially scaled back activity, soon followed by post offices, banks and the service industry as the economic recession intensified and unemployment skyrocketed in the early 1990s.

Te Tai Tokerau's Maori population bore the brunt of the economic policies of the 1980s and 1990s. Two recent health needs assessment reports confirm that Maori in Te Tai Tokerau continue to occupy all the worst echelons of the deprivation indices – collectively Maori are the least educated, least employable, least healthy, least wealthy, least free population group in this region (Northland District Health Board, 2001; Te Tai Tokerau MAPO, 2001). It is this evident need that has prefaced the development of robust Maori health organisations as a means to combat the inequalities in health and socio-economic status of Maori.

Maori Rights to Develop

The bicultural policy frameworks developed in the public sector in the 1990s were created by Maori and policy-makers intent on securing Maori rights to develop through acknowledging the paramouncy of *Te Tiriti O Waitangi* as the basis for state (Crown) and Maori interaction.

The Northern Regional Health Authority ('North Health') led the way in Maori health policy and strategic development in the mid-1990s with its Maori 'Co-Purchasing' Strategy, premised on:

* operationalising the good faith partnership between Maori and the Crown inferred by Te Tiriti O Waitangi;
* ensuring greater Maori participation at all levels of the health sector through Maori decision-making and provider and workforce development; and
* actively seeking to protect the physical, spiritual and economic interests of Maori to achieve Maori health gain.

A full explanation and exploration of the Maori 'Co-Purchasing' Strategy and its application is contained in the paper 'Strategic Health Care Policy and Development for Maori, the Indigenous People of New Zealand' (Stewart et al., 2001). Maori health development in Te Tai Tokerau has its genesis in this highly innovative and unique strategy.

Success Breeds Success

Key to the success of Maori health development in Te Tai Tokerau is the leadership provided to the sector by Te Tai Tokerau MAPO Trust (TTTM). TTTM are one of three 'Maori Co-Purchasing Organisations' (MAPO) established by North Health in partnership with the *Iwi* of Tainui (based south of Auckland), Ngati Whatua (based in the greater Auckland region) and the collective *Iwi* of Te Tai Tokerau (based in Northland) in the mid-1990s. The primary role of the MAPO is to advocate for and secure equitable funding to support and strategically develop Maori and mainstream health organisations to deliver effective and appropriate health services targeted at reducing inequalities in health status between Maori and non-Maori.

TTTM has consolidated its position in the Te Tai Tokerau sector through successive contractual relationships which operationalise Treaty-based partnerships with each of the government purchasers/funders since 1996. Current partnership arrangements operate at a national level with the Ministry of Health, and at a local level with the Northland District Health Board.

Over the last seven years, TTTM has significantly contributed to numerous successful health developments in Te Tai Tokerau.

Since 1996 TTTM and it's government health funding partners have established, managed and facilitated the ongoing growth and development of six *Iwi*-governed Maori health providers, two community-governed health providers and three provider-governed rural health training consortia.

Prior to 1995 there was one small Maori health provider contracted to North Health, operating in the mid-north with fewer than ten staff on the ground. Today there are six Maori health providers operating throughout the Te Tai Tokerau region, employing upwards of 350 staff and contractors and all significantly contributing to the health, social and economic development of their respective communities.

Concomitant with Maori provider development has been the substantial growth in health funding contracts with Maori health organisations which can be directly attributed to the advocacy of TTTM. In 1996, Maori health funding equated to less than NZ$900,000. Today, the figure is in excess of NZ$15 million representing an average percentage growth of 275 per cent per annum over six years.

TTTM is a founding Director of the Te Tai Tokerau Rural Maori Health Training Consortium, which coordinates health training and higher education for Maori health personnel working within Maori providers. Since 1996, more than 400 Maori health workers have availed themselves of further educational opportunities in numerous health fields, including:

- medicine;
- dentistry;
- nursing (diploma and degree levels);
- mental health and alcohol and drug;
- disability support services;
- health management.

The past six years have also seen positive growth in mainstream services providing Maori-focused programmes. Northland Health, the provider arm of the Northland District Health Board has been the major mainstream recipient of increased funding for sector enhancement programmes in recent years, particularly in the areas of health promotion and education, mental health and alcohol and drug services.

In 1999 *Te Poutokomanawa*, the Maori Health Directorate of Northland Health was formed. The Directorate's establishment was the culmination of several years of internal change management and development coupled with external championing by TTTM, Maori providers and key Maori community figures. The Directorate provides an all important link between Maori and community providers and Northland Health as the largest mainstream provider of health services in the north.

TTTM has also had considerable influence in the development of two community-governed health trusts that play a major part in the delivery of services to Maori in their respective areas. Both are based in remote coastal regions of *Te Tai Tokerau* and have high Maori utilisation rates due to the predominantly Maori populations living in their service areas.

The sustainable development of Maori Providers in Te Tai Tokerau through the strategic deployment of human, technological and financial resources by TTTM is acknowledged locally, regionally and nationally as one of the great Maori development success stories.

A Strategic Response to Change – Te Tai Tokerau Maori Health Alliance

In May 2000, TTTM facilitated the formation of a strategic alliance of nine Maori and mainstream health organisations, in order to consolidate the developments of the previous five years and further the goal of increasing and improving Maori health gain in Te Tai Tokerau. This Te Tai Tokerau Maori Health Alliance ('the Alliance') developed a five-year *Maori Health Strategic Operational Plan* (Te Tai Tokerau Maori Health Alliance, 2000) as its collective pathway to achieve the same, and is currently into year two of actioning the Plan.

The Plan is based upon implementing *Te Tiriti O Waitangi* in the Te Tai Tokerau health sector and prioritising the needs of Maori *whanau, hapu* and *Iwi* (immediate family, extended kinship group and tribal group). The Alliance provides dynamic Maori leadership and has pioneered relationships and partnerships across health and other sectors in order to address Maori disparities. The Alliance Plan prioritises the development, consolidation and implementation of *Kaupapa Maori* (Maori-based philosophy) models and solutions for Maori health gain and development focusing on best practice and quality of care in both the clinical and cultural contexts.

The Alliance's Plan foreshadowed the collaboration and cooperation expected of the New Zealand Health sector as a whole in later published government strategies (Ministry of Health, 2000a and b, 2001a and b), drawing heavily upon the substantial practical, professional and personal experience amongst the Alliance members. Consultation with governance and operational staff of the membership, local communities, health providers and government stakeholders prior to the Plan's launch and during the various stages of strategic implementation has ensured a high degree of support for the Alliance and its collective activity. The Alliance's Plan has been acknowledged by the local funder in its five-year District Strategic Plan (Northland District Health Board, 2002) with a commitment by the Northland District Health Board to prioritise Maori health gain and reduce inequalities through supporting the implementation of the Alliance's strategies for Maori Health.

In August 2001 the Alliance shared its vision with the rest of New Zealand through its organisation and promotion of a National Symposium on 'Maori Leadership, Strategic Partnerships and Alliances in the 21st Century', known as *Ka Oho Ake Nga Korero – Still the Conversation Lives.* The Alliance co-hosted this event with the University of Auckland Business School – the arrangement itself a testament to successful intersectoral partnerships. The programme attracted over 170 participants from throughout the country to hear national and international speakers on indigenous development; the Renaissance of Maori; and building New Zealand's Knowledge Economy; and to learn from leading-edge Maori academics, business people, clinicians, political leaders, media experts and sporting personalities.

Ka Oho Ake Nga Korero wonderfully showcased Maori success and achievement in all sectors - health, education, business, the arts – while also recognising that individual Maori success is premised on open opportunities for *whanau, hapu* and *Iwi* growth and development. It is the reciprocity of those who have 'made it' giving back to those who have supported them to make it that is the key to the future for Maori.

Building Forward – Maori Primary Health Organisations

In February 2001 the Minister of Health released *The Primary Health Care Strategy* (Ministry of Health, 2001a), a 5–10 year vision for primary health care. The strategy clearly signals the present government's intent to integrate primary and community health care as the 'heart' of the health sector. This will occur through the direction of new and eventual redeployment of existing resources to the 'top of the cliff' primary health care services and a greater emphasis on population health promotion and prevention services. The strategy envisages systemic, structural and attitudinal change, with the development of Primary Health Organisations (PHOs) as the vehicles to achieve local health goals.

The strategy outlines the following key points about PHOs:

- PHOs will be funded by District Health Boards for the provision of a set of essential primary health care services to those people who are enrolled.
- at a minimum, these services will include approaches directed towards improving and maintaining the health of the population, as well as first-line services to restore people's health when they are unwell;
- PHOs will be expected to involve their communities in their governing processes;
- all providers and practitioners must be involved in the PHO's decision-making, rather than one group being dominant;
- PHOs will be not-for-profit bodies and will be required to be fully and openly accountable for all public funds that they receive;
- while primary health care practitioners will be encouraged to join PHOs, membership will be voluntary (Ministry of Health, 2001a).

Maori providers, under the leadership of TTTM, immediately took to implementing the primary care strategy. They have always been at the cutting-edge of integrating primary medical and community health services under a uniquely Maori philosophy of service delivery. Their existing way of working already meets all the key points noted above, so the philosophical and conceptual leap from an informal alliance to a collective PHO model was not a difficult one to make.

However, Maori PHO development has met with resistance from some quarters, particularly general practitioners (GPs) who consider the PHOs to be a threat to their largely unchecked domination of the primary health care sector to this point. This resistance has been met by Maori with a solid stance of openness and inclusiveness which has slowly but determinedly chipped away at the barriers to change thrown up by others in the sector. Also, not all GPs fall into that 'resistant to change' mode, and in Te Tai Tokerau there are sufficient groups of practitioners who are willing to open their minds and hearts to the opportunities offered by the PHO model of collaboration.

While PHO development is still very much in its infancy, and potentially as subject to the vagaries of political change as the rest of the health sector, there would appear to be sufficient good will and strategic intent for progress to continue cautiously but constructively.

Looking Back – Moving Forward

The determination and passion that has driven Maori health development to obtain its current successes is irrefutable. Looking back over the past six years it is clear to see that the successes which have occurred are as a result of innovative and provocative strategic thinking and more importantly, indomitable commitment to inspired implementation.

Maori co-purchasing in health provided the opportunity for the dawning of a new day, in which Maori could rise above the slough of health disparity and turn despondency into dynamic action for Maori health gain.

References

Cheyne, C., O'Brien, M. and Belgrave, M. (1997), *Social Policy in Aotearoa New Zealand: A Critical Introduction*, Auckland: Oxford University Press.

Durie, M. (1998a), *Te Mana, Te Kawanatanga: The Politics of Maori Self-Determination*, Auckland: Oxford University Press.

Durie, M. (1998b), *Whaiora: Maori Health Development*, 2nd edn, Auckland: Oxford University Press.

Fleras, A. and Spoonley, P. (1999), *Recalling Aotearoa: Indigenous Politics and Ethnic Relations in New Zealand*, Auckland: Oxford University Press.

Henare, D. (1995), 'The Ka Awatea Report: Reflections on its Process and Vision', in M. Wilson and A. Yeatman (eds), *Justice & Identity: Antipodean Practices*, Wellington: Bridget Williams Books.

Ministry of Health (2000a), *The New Zealand Health Strategy*, Wellington: Ministry of Health.

Ministry of Health (2000b), *The New Zealand Disability Strategy*, Wellington: Ministry of Health.

Ministry of Health (2001a), *The Primary Health Care Strategy*, Wellington: Ministry of Health.

Ministry of Health (2001b), *He Korowai Oranga: Maori Health Strategy Discussion Document*, Wellington: Ministry of Health.

New Zealand Government (1996), *New Zealand First and National Coalition Agreement*, Wellington.

Northland District Health Board (2001), *An Assessment of the Health Needs in the Northland District Health Board Region: Te Tirohanga Hauora O Te Tai Tokerau*, Northland District Health Board, Whangarei.

Northland District Health Board (2002), *District Strategic Plan 2002-07*, Northland District Health Board, Whangarei.

Stewart, L., Davis, L. and Shea, S. (1991), 'Strategic Health Care Policy and Development for Maori, the Indigenous People of New Zealand', in H.T.O. Davies, M. Tavakoli and M. Malek (eds), *Quality in Health Care: Strategic Issues in Health Care Management*, Aldershot: Ashgate.

Upton, S. (1991), *Your Health and the Public Health*, Wellington: New Zealand Government.

Te Tai Tokerau Maori Health Alliance (2000), *Te Tai Tokerau Maori Health Strategic Operational Plan 2000–0*, Whangarei: Te Tai Tokerau MAPO.

Walker, R. (2001), *Profile and Health Status of the People in Te Tai Tokerau* (unpublished report), Whangarei: Te Tai Tokerau MAPO.

Chapter 12

Reorganising Health Care Delivery in Hospitals: Structure and Processes to Serve Quality

Federico Lega

Why the Prevalence of Functional Organisational Design in Hospitals in the Past?

In the last 50 years, most hospitals in developed countries have grown-up adopting a functional-like organisational structure, built around a discipline-based specialisation (Shortell and Kaluzny, 2000).[1] As Mintzberg pointed out, they assumed the form of *professional bureaucracies*, characterised by the search for standardisation of procedures and products through the so-called *pigeonholing* process: the organisation seeks to match predetermined contingency to a standardised programme, and so organise itself around the skills and knowledge of its professionals who are in charge of categorising or 'diagnosing' the client's (patient) need and then apply, or execute, the matching programme or procedure (Mintzberg, 1983). Organisation around skills is what determines a functional design (Duncan, 1979).

From an organisational perspective, the trend that led to the extensive adoption of functional designs in hospitals, thus acting as professional bureaucracies, can be explained both by rational and 'irrational' reasons. On the rational side, in fact, functional discipline-based design was helpful in supporting and fostering the knowledge development required by medical and hospital progress. This explains the developing structural patterns in a hospital, where, for example, as its physicians developed specific skills and competencies, different specialties, such as nephrology, gastroenterology, geriatrics, neurology, and so on, progressively emerged from an initial general medicine unit, leading to other specialised medicine units (Figure 12.1). Such a pattern was ultimately coherent with the hospital's main organisational need: focusing on the development of expertise and on economies. Moreover, at the same time it responded to the need to keep a 'feasible' span of control, since it was clear that managing, organising and supervising large units (in terms of beds and personnel) was a difficult task. However, if we consider that this is something that did not necessarily require a design based on a functional structure, since it could be achieved with other schemes of organisational power distribution, it is in the search for better skills and knowledge through specialisation that we can trace the rational reasons for hospitals' functional structural design.

On the other side, from an organisational point of view we recognise also some irrational reasons, although they seem perfectly rational from a 'human relations' perspective:

- the need to reward, with a senior position, the previous 'loyal' and valid vice-manager. In this case, from the division of an internal medicine unit two similar units were created: Medicine I, managed by the previous manager of the original medicine unit, and Medicine II, managed by the previous vice-manager of the original medicine unit;
- in public sector contexts structure is often used instrumentally to bypass limits of other 'underdeveloped' support systems, in particular those of the rewarding system. In those sectors, in fact, civil servants' wages are in general linked exclusively to organisational position (same position, same wage), and the only means to reward the people is by having them advance in the hierarchy, that is to say, the organisational structure. This means that because the organisation would like to pay more to one of its employees, it is forced to create a new unit that he/she can manage as a precondition to increasing his/her wage.

As things are 'favourably' changing (reform of civil servants' employment, new rewarding tools, differentiation of professional and managerial career paths, and so on), and environmental turbulence is increasing (citizens' pressure, cost containment need, quality, evidence-based medicine, and so on), hospitals can no longer sustain the rational/irrational oversizing and overspecialisation due to hyperfunctional design choices, but need to rethink their actual structure of responsibilities to improve future developing patterns.

In other words, hospitals must find new and more appropriate answers to the traditional issue of organisational design: the labour division. In fact, we must not forget that organisations, and so also hospitals, as they grow more complex in a more unstable environment, always face the problem of coping simultaneously with the need both to differentiate (as with the identification of functional discipline-based units) and to integrate work (Charnes and

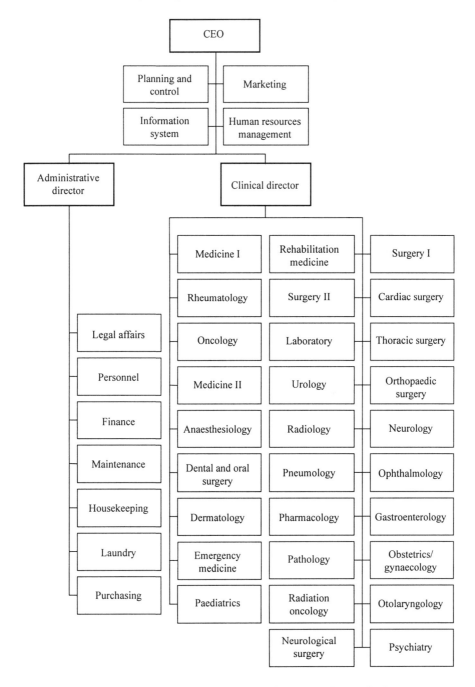

Figure 12.1   A typical functional (discipline-based) hospital structure

Smith-Tewksbury, 1993). Where to position them and how to face this issue in modern hospitals is the subject of this chapter.

Do Hospitals Still Need Functional Design?

Hospitals' traditional functional (disciplines-based) design is now struggling to respond to emerging organisational needs in the medical field. In fact, functional designs are most appropriate when an organisation operates in a relatively simple and stable environment. Clearly, this becomes unsuitable when the organisation grows and begins to diversify its services, mainly because inter-unit coordination tends to be poor and decisions pile up at the top or are taken independently, their consequences affecting the rest of the organisation. Not surprisingly, beginning in the early 1990s, there was a period of intense change in the health sectors of most countries, a period in which the environment had become more hostile, unpredictable and competitive after years of tranquillity and stability in which most hospitals had grown too much, and were therefore often oversized (Nauert, 1995). Most countries had shifted the focus from productivity towards cost and quality issues. So, after various reforms and changes that took place in almost all the health systems of developed countries, with the introduction of the principle of managed care, diagnosis-related groups (DRGs) and/or capitation financing schemes by third party payers, hospitals are now facing the difficult task of delivering high quality services with a cost-conscious approach: in other words, cost-effective services. Cost-effective services require a good understanding and managing of delivering processes, in order to combine a cost-conscious approach with an appropriate clinical approach. But a cost-conscious environment cannot ignore the fact that some sort of simplification of the structure is required: hyperspecialisation of units creates expensive and unproductive duplication of resources and transaction costs due to increasing coordination needs. The more the delivery processes are fragmented in sequentially, reciprocal or mutually interdependent specialised actors (the units), the more costly will be the effort to coordinate these processes (Thompson, 1967).

It is in this new environment that functional design is not only inadequate, but seems to be an impediment to any potential improvement in hospital activities. Let's see why taking as an example a simple but common and exhaustive case: lung cancer (Figure 12.2). In a general hospital organised with a functional structure the treatment requires the intervention of different units: pneumology, where the diagnosis might take place; oncology, whose consultancy might be required by the pneumology unit or where the patient might be transferred to complete the diagnosis process; dietary, in charge of giving advice along the entire treatment pathway on patient diet prescription; laboratory and imaging unit, where the examinationss take place; thoracic surgery and radiotherapy, where the patient might go on to complete the treatment (with different patterns); respiratory rehabilitation, where the patient completes his/her recovery before being discharged if everything has gone well. This complex scheme is further complicated by the fact that the same clinical problem (lung cancer) in a similar patient might be tackled with a (possibly radically) different approach by different physicians of the same unit or by different units where the patient is admitted (the diagnosis process might differ consistently between the pneumology and the oncology unit). If we all agree that clinical judgment should be mostly free from a predetermined and engineered scheme, on the other side, decisions based predominantly on a physician's personal experience (which does not mean necessarily patient-tailored solutions) might result in different cure/care pathways with final different costs, outputs and patient health outcomes. Is this sustainable under both perspectives, cost and outcome? To what point? With such a framework, some critical aspects arise: who is responsible for patient's length of stay, number and type of exams, drugs therapy variation and overall pathway cost? Is it correct to allow large variability in treatment between different physicians and/or units? It is correct to have different units treating the same cases, or should we define better reciprocal vocation (for example, which patients' pathologies should be referred to the pneumology, and which to the oncology? Should the diagnosis of lung cancer be performed by both units? Or preferably by one of them? How can we improve patient experience, avoiding its peregrination among different units, streamlining the cure processes and continually improving the clinical quality?

As Willcocks (1998) suggests in his studies, since the typical organisation of acute specialties might be a potential barrier to a more managerial approach, it may be necessary to encourage a shift in organisational emphasis in some specialties away from hierarchy, centralisation and individual autonomy and move towards a team-based structure which facilitates communication, ownership and empowerment. How can we do that?

Should we Simply Modify Functional Design ...?

In order to tackle some of the problems created by the functional organisation

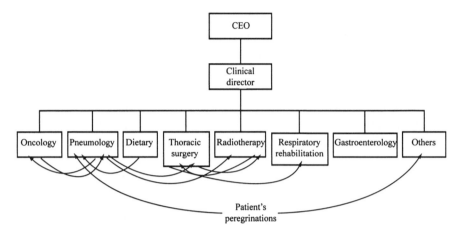

Figure 12.2   Coordination needs arising among different discipline-based units in curing a patient with lung cancer

discussed in the previous paragraph, a first step could be its fine-tuning based on the introduction of integration/coordination roles with specific responsibilities over economic and clinical performances of production processes.[2] This choice would lead to a modified functional structure.

   In organisational theory we distinguish between functional models modified by:

1) product/market manager: a permanent role of integration among different units, with no hierarchical authority over them.[3] The product manager is responsible for product line results, and in order to achieve his/her goals he/she must use leadership skills, persuasion and cooperation abilities, information availability and transmission;

2) project manager: a temporary role of coordination of a specific set of resources over which he/she has hierarchical authority with the aim of completing the project assigned within a specific amount of time.

While the latter type of role might be more appropriate when a new service has to be developed and launched, at least for the time needed to consolidate the organisation skills and the client's demand, the first one might be a helpful mechanism to facilitate the management of situations in which cooperation and coordination needs arise frequently, if not continually. Obviously, the organisation needs the 'right' manager for that position.[4]

A simple example of a product manager's role in a hospital can be traced to the introduction of managers to take an overview of workgroups in charge of studying, developing and 'engineering' clinical problems (pathologies): the group manager is the coordinator of a multidisciplinary and multiprofessional workgroup, and his/her goal is to facilitate the production and implementation of clinical pathways as hospital's routines (Figure 12.3). Consequently, the workgroup should be formed by physicians and other professionals belonging to the units were the pathologies object of study were usually treated. Clinical pathways should combine evidence-based medicine (EBM) with a cost-conscious approach, in order to provide the highest clinical quality with a sound rational utilisation of resource. Obviously, pathways should represent only a reference guideline, and case managers do not have the authority to enforce their implementation. But, nonetheless, the group manager should use his/her leadership to assure a good use of the pathways, and it is reasonable to think that the work done by the workgroup might influence naturally the behaviour of its participants towards a diffuse use of the pathways, so facilitating the case manager's job (Schriefer, 1994, 1995). A diffuse pathways implementation offers the opportunity for reducing the variability in treatment of similar patient-pathology. Finally, the pathway should define the unit in charge of treating the different clinical problems. Consequently, when a patient is admitted to one of the units, the physicians and nurses involved in the workgroup and belonging to that unit are then potential case managers in charge of 'guaranteeing' that the appropriate clinical pathway is delivered to the patient. So, for any patient admitted, one of the members of the group – and it will be a group or hospital decision to define if it must be a physician or a nurse or both – should take formal responsibility for monitoring the patient's treatment through the pathway.

To conclude, key success factors for this functional design modified by product (group) managers responsibilities include (Leatt et al, 1994):

- a strong management information systems that links clinical, financial and volume data by product line, that is to say by process;
- a strong budgeting-financial system that can disaggregate costs and revenues so that accountability can be appropriately assigned to group managers;
- reward systems to encourage innovation in group practice finalised to foster continuous improvement cycle in pathways study and implementation.

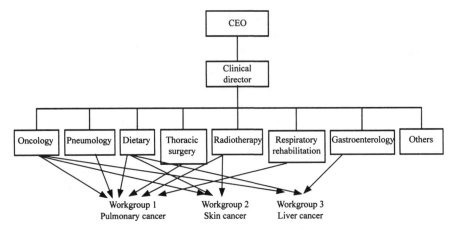

Each group is multidisciplinary and multiprofessional, being made up of physicians, surgeons and specialised nurses.

Figure 12.3   Functional disciplines-based structure modified with product (group) managers

... or Should we Redesign Structure and Processes to Serve Quality Better?

Introducing product line (group) managers is certainly an option that should be evaluated accurately. Favourable circumstances (managers' attitude and personality, physicians' involvement, and so on) can produce excellent results even in a still monolithic functional structure, and in any case it represents the preferred mechanism to stimulate the studying and improvement of clinical pathways. But it has its limits, and after all it does not tackle one of the main critical aspects of the functional organisation: cost and quality pressures make it necessary to look not only at better management of delivering processes, but, as we said earlier, also at scale or scope economies. This might be realised through a reaggregation of fragmented specialties into larger units, such as departments or divisions. In the case of a hospital, clinical integration could be achieved initially through workgroups, but logistical and organisational integration require more structured solution, such as a different design. It is in this framework that departments or divisions,[5] as design solutions grouping together different hospital units and their responsibilities, might (and should) enable better use of fixed resources (beds, technologies, personnel and so on), from which follow improvements in productivity and savings in costs. That is the concept behind the quest for scale and scope economies.[6]

Divisionalisation and Departmentalisation

Given the issues so far discussed, the first step to a fitter hospital's design seems to be moving toward divisional/departmental structure (Figure 12.4).[7]

In general terms, hospital units' aggregation of divisions or departments makes sense when grouped specialties horizontal overlap each other in services delivered (for example, pneumology, medicine, geriatrics, oncology, which partially produce the same outcome or cure the same pathologies) or integrate vertically along a production process (cardiology, cardiac surgery, cardiologic rehabilitation – three units which take charge at different but sequential stages of the same cure process).

Examples of these aggregation criteria that may coexist and apply to different units in the same hospital are:

1 horizontal overlapping through the creation of department-based on macro-areas of specialties (general medicine, general surgery, specialist medicine, diagnostic imaging) grouping similar units;
2 vertical integration through units grouped on a product basis, such as body organs/parts (heart, head-neck, liver, and so on – grouping units cooperating at different stages of the same care/cure processes), on homogeneous medical areas (oncology, digestive apparatus, muscle-skeleton – grouping units cooperating either at the same time or at different stages on the same care/cure processes) or on the age of patients basis (elderly, maternal, paediatric departments).

It is important to note that, in order to fulfil its expectations, the division/department should present some characteristics. First of all, a 'strong' management role must be played by the department's clinical director (Willcocks and Conway, 1998; Willcocks, 1998). As hospital organisational design evolves, a more managerial role is required. Burgoyne and Lorbiecki (1993) point out that the clinicians' role had indeed moved away from conventional management tasks, which looks inward at the needs of a clinical specialty, to one which steps outside and incorporates the need for a sense of vision and leadership for the direction of the unit as a whole. Nevertheless, some findings show that the road is still difficult, as it is possible that, while some clinical directors were supportive of clinical management (radiology, pathology, psychiatry, and so on) from the beginning, because of their traditional involvement in the managerial process of their own work, others, and in particular the more glamorous and powerful surgical,

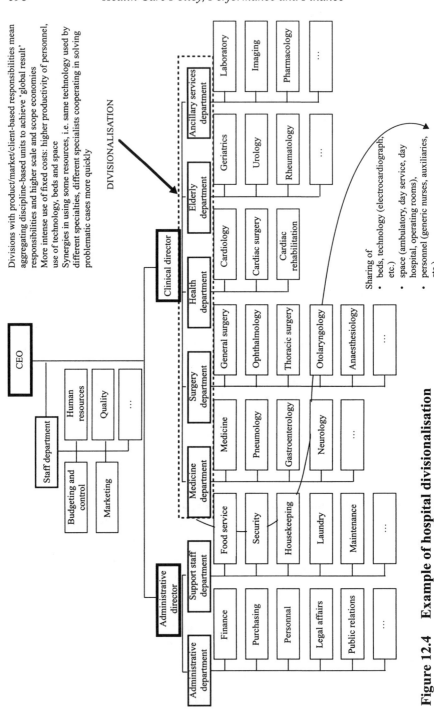

Figure 12.4   Example of hospital divisionalisation

medical, paediatrics and obstetrics/gynaecology specialties, were more likely to emphasise the clinical and professional aspects of their role (Willcocks, 1998). It is also true that a variety of aspects might influence the way the introduction of clinical management of a department/division takes place, such as historical background, cultural heritage, nature of work, technology and organisation, power differentials between specialties and individual factors, for example motivation, training, awareness, attitudes to management, and so on (Pettigrew et al., 1992; Willcocks, 1998).

In any case, organisational development in hospitals promoted through divisionalisation requires a new class of manager, able to integrate the clinical competencies needed for driving strategic repositioning and development of the department, with the managerial skills needed to reorganise and improve resources utilisation in the department. In both cases, in the professional context of the hospital, a 'strong' department management means the ability to exercise a strong leadership.

A second requirement concerns the logistical design of the division/ department. It is preferable to reorganise the specialties into logistically integrated departments, sharing the same space. In fact, it is in this situation that becomes possible to implement the most comprehensive policies of resource pooling, in order to exploit scale and scope economies.

Finally, a third requirement refers to the need to refocus the main organisational support system (planning and control, human resource, and so on) on the department level. Such support systems reinforce and clarify the game rules, helping in defining the departments as the organisational level that really counts in the organisation dynamics (such as strategy formulation, decision-making processes, and so on). In other words, budget process, reward system, doctors' career paths, strategic planning, information systems, and so on, should be developed and managed accordingly to the departments' needs. Departments are then responsible for a global financial budget negotiated with the top management, and for products/services results (productivity and quality of the different units grouped). In this sense, is important to notice that, from the hierarchical perspective, each specialty must belong to one department.

If the aforementioned aspects are implemented by the divisionalisation of the hospital we might expect effective common use of scarce resources, the basis for achieving scale and scope economies.

And then? How do we generate greater clinical coordination along care processes? How can we effectively tackle inefficiency and ineffectiveness due to high variability, high diffusion and low quality of care processes? Formally pooling and sharing resources is just the half way mark. We have redefined the organisational skeleton and its nerves, and now we need to reallocate internal organs in the most appropriate and functional way. Why not try to rethink labour organisation, starting from the processes themselves?

Adding the Workgroups ... and Creating Internal Quasi-markets

Rethinking labour organisation starting from a process management logic means reintroducing the clinical, multi-professional, multi-disciplinarian workgroups. But, in this case, they are not just a simple coordination mechanism. They become the backbone on and around which is organised the structure of the departments' responsibilities. The vertebrae are represented by the delivery areas organised by the intensity of care required: outpatients, ambulatories, day-service, day hospital and/or day surgery, ordinary beds, semi-intensive and intensive care beds, emergency beds.[8] Each of these delivery areas is managed by a physician on a part-time basis. For a part of the time they manage the logistical area they supervise, for the rest of the time, they act as clinician in the workgroups to which they belong. In this framework, delivery area managers are providers of productive factors that must be negotiated and fully exploited by workgroups, once assigned to them. That is the idea of the internal market. Delivery area managers are in charge of guaranteeing best allocation and maximum utilisation of pooled 'scarce' resources (beds, technologies, nurses and other personnel), while workgroups' leaders should concentrate on developing the best cost-conscious and efficacious care pathways. The latter are responsible for an operative budget, in term of productivity (mix and volume) and cost consumption, while the former are in charge of a budget related to the full utilisation of the resources they manage. For example, the delivery area manager is responsible for achieving maximum occupation of all the beds of his or her area, which are allocated to different workgroups who at the same time have the goal of exploiting them optimally. If a workgroup does not guarantee fully appropriate occupation of its allocated bed, the delivery area manager is authorised to reallocate the underutilised beds to other workgroups. Also, to increase flexibility in resource utilisation, the area manager might keep a few beds in reserve, so that in case of need these might be allocated day-by-day to different workgroups that require them to face justified emergencies or variances in planned activities.

Basically, delivery sites could be organised on the basis of patient needs. As already discussed, a simple case would be a specialisation of wards between day-services, such as day hospitals and day surgery, and ordinary, semi-intensive and intensive care. A more sophisticated example could be found in the Mount Sinai Hospital of New York, where, during a re-engineering process in 1995, the Department of Medicine decided to reorganise its ward and the nursing staff around four categories of patients (covering 80 per cent of the typical case mix):

1 patients in 'mental states', such as kidney failures, Alzheimer's and any other diseases or illness in which the patient lost their faculty to reason and needed to be watched all the time;
2 patients who were not breathing independently, due to asthma, hearth attack, and so on, typically on respirators;
3 patients with complicated IVs, such as oncology and dialysis patients, since the key factor in caring for these patients was to manage the IV systems that they were being treated with;
4 patients needing more tests and who were frequently 'off the floor', since the Department of Medicine was the typical destination for the emergency room patient who had not yet been diagnosed specifically; these patients typically missed meals, waited endlessly for transportation to other pavilions, and so on.

The idea was that this formula would enable the department to do better staffing, better monitoring and better diagnosing of its patients, and it has proven to be successful (Stein et al., 1996).

Going back to the example discussed in Figure 12.2 relating to a patient with lung cancer, a reorganisation of the functional structure toward divisional logic would be then represented by the creation of a cancer treatment department, aggregating the discipline-based units most involved in cancer diagnosis and treatment (Figure 12.5). Other units would remain out of this department and aggregated in other departments, but they might have to collaborate with the patients' diagnosis and care pathways through their representatives in the workgroup.

Organisation by workgroup should stimulate effective clinical integration in the department, addressing aforementioned problems such as variability, diffusion, quality, and so on (Spath, 1994). Physicians or surgeons and highly specialised nurses are then reorganised in the workgroups, each physician or surgeon belonging to two to three groups in order not to specialise their skills excessively and to maintain an overall competence in their specialty. Each workgroup takes charge of several care processes, and therefore its members represent potential case managers for any patients admitted in the department with a suspect or diagnosis relative to those care processes.

The heads of the specialties grouped in the department play a techno-structure role,[9] being in charge of defining innovation policies, validating workgroups' clinical guidelines and pathways, training and developing the physicians' professional skills, while the department management (with its staff) must assure to groups the best possible work condition in terms of logistic (organising and managing the delivery areas targeting cure intensity), patients' comfort, technologies and resource availability (consumption goods, pharmaceuticals, and so on). Beds, technology, spaces, part of the nursing staff and the rest of the department staff are assigned to delivery areas under the supervision of its manager, in order to facilitate their utilisation at maximum productivity level (that is, bed occupation rate) and their exploitation of possible scale and scope economies. This reorganisation in areas with different intensity of care means greater attention to patients' needs, on the premise that patients admitted to those different areas have common care (but not necessarily cure) needs, and their identification and 'segregation' in specific wards should allow, as explained in the beginning of this paragraph, for better staffing, higher 'hotel' quality, and maximum productivity.

Given the department's role, the department chief will no longer need to be a physician, but it could be any person with a managerial background. In this case, he/she might be supported by a clinical director for what concerns the evaluation and development of operation plans. In this sense, it might be something similar to the organisation of some large American academic medical centres (AMC), where the head of a department is more a financial director than a clinical one, but is supported by a clinical consultant (Shortell and Kalunzny, 2000). Obviously, it will depend on the hospital nature (for profit vs. non profit) and on the financing scheme adopted by its third party payers if the department might work as a true 'industrial' division,[10] with its own profit goals and total autonomy in its development and management policies. Basically, the departments should have large autonomy in using its financial budget to provide its workgroups with the best possible environment to practice, to foster innovation and to develop people skills and career, but this autonomy should be exercised coherently with the mission and values of the hospital. In non-profit hospitals, entrepreneurship of departments should be governed by the top management according to the hospital mission statement and health needs of the population served.[11]

In any case, the department should take charge of the following aspects:

- budgeting with the hospital top management on one side, and with the workgroups and delivery areas manager on the other;

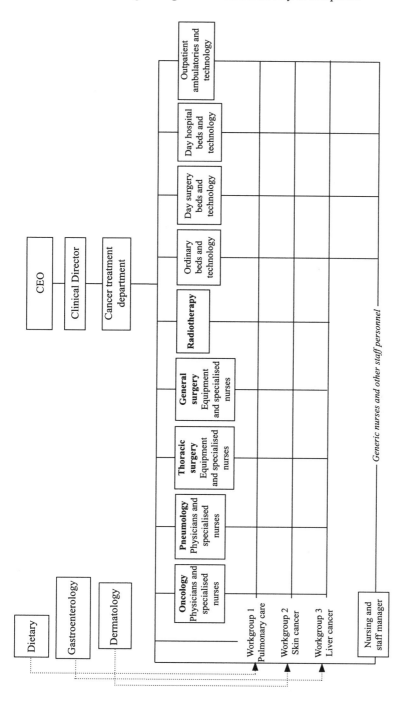

Figure 12.5 Reorganising the department on the basis of patients' needs

- fundraising, to provide the department with extra resources needed for investments in infrastructure, technology, people, and so on;
- human resource management, defining according to the hospital scheme for rewards, training and career policies;
- innovation, stimulating head of specialties to develop a strategic long-term vision able to sustain the hospital and the department's competitive advantage.

Support systems should be centred on the departments and workgroups, that is to say the delivery areas and the production processes. In particular, the department will need a budgeting and controlling system with that focus.

What Design for the Hospital of the Near Future?

As Bergman (1993) states, it might be true that the design, services, name and location of hospitals will undergo a major transformation by the first decade of the twenty-first century. Most health care procedures will be dispersed to alternative sites, and, therefore, while the hospital will no longer exist in its present form, something resembling a hospital will continue to be needed for emergency services, intensive care, and some diagnostic work. Other services can be mobile or housed in satellite locations, such as travelling MRIs and radiology clinics located in shopping malls. Hospitals will take on a totally new role and became data centres. Patients will be treated at home through interactive television, while specialists and 'super specialists' back at the hospital work with and manipulate the system to treat them. The hospital will not be a place you go to, but something that comes to you. This is a possibility, but surely not in the near future, and not in the first decade of the twenty-first century, and not everywhere at the same speed. What seems to be happening, instead, is a progressive specialisation of the general hospitals, as they join a network with other general hospitals and develop strategies of refocusing their services to minimise risks of internal disruptive competition and better exploit potential scale and know-how economies (Blecher, 1998; HCAB, 1995; Kassirer, 1995). It is in these 'new hospitals', as they become focused factories, that the department design proposed might find its best implementation, leading to a situation in which hospitalisation patterns can be more easily controlled by the departments, thanks to a limited and filtered demand and a focus on elective procedures. But, knowing that those processes of refocus towards a deeper specialisation will take time and might not interest all the hospitals, and in particular the academic medical centres and the metropolitan large hospitals, in the meantime we must find the best possible solution for running better those and the rest of our 'typical' general hospitals, experimenting, when necessary, with new organisational designs. In fact, for discipline-based structured hospital, in this first decade of the twenty-first century it would be a major transformation just to introduce some kind of flexibility in resource utilisation and having the physicians working in teams, collaborating, discussing critical cases and enhancing patient compliance in the cure processes. Repositioning patients and their needs at the centre of the hospital design should be the target, making this choice profitable from an economic perspective too. An appropriate, cost-conscious, high quality approach: that is the issue. In this chapter we have discussed some design choices that might be evaluated by hospitals in search of possible answers: we analysed functional modified structures based on workgroups and product managers, divisional structures and matrix structures with internal quasi-market mechanism. They are not 'the answers', but suggestions that will hopefully lead and contribute, at best, to pragmatic and effective hospital redesign, and at worst, feed a debate that seems to have been inadequately addressed in recent years.

Notes

1   In general terms, a functional design refers to a structure in which labour is divided into units specialised by functional area. It enables decisions to be made on a centralised, hierarchical basis. Unit managers are usually promoted from within the organisation and have a depth of technical knowledge in the functional area.

2   Obviously, each unit has responsibility over a budget, but in a context of large professional autonomy the budget is linked to past results, results incorporating inefficiency and ineffectiveness not clearly visible in 'consolidated numbers' produced by the management control system and easily defendable on a professional basis). That is why we need to rebuild responsibilities along the production processes and on what happens in those processes.

3   Obviously, this clear definition is again a little blurred in reality, where organisations tend to give a mixed hierarchical authority over some units or decisions to the product manager (as, for example, product pricing and promotion).

4   The selection and training of the product manager is particularly important. Individuals must be identified who have good technical knowledge of the product line and good analytical and interpersonal skills. In particular, they must be innovative, feel comfortable with ambiguity and complexity, and be able to work with more than one manager (the functional units manager).

5   We will assume the terms 'divisions' and 'departments' as synonyms.

6   Basically, we can define scale economies those reduction in services' unitary costs that depends on the greater utilisation of a fixed cost – a bed, an equipment, an ambulatory – due

to its sharing. Obviously, part of the economies relate also to the reduction in duplicated resources thanks to the sharing. When the sharing is due to a interdependence in working activities we define the economies as scope economies.

7   Many hospitals have already adopted a divisional structure, grouping different specialties by department. Nonetheless, in many cases, as we point out later, the incoherence of the support system (planning, budgeting and controlling, and human resources management), still 'tailored' around and for specialties' managers, the logistical impediments and the poor and weak leadership of department chiefs, make unproductive the new organisational divisional structure and keep alive the traditional specialties-based hospital functioning.

8   The more the department is able to segregate emergency activity frem elective activity, the more the delivery area managers and workgroups will be able to concentrate on the latter, finding the maximum appropriate productivity. This implies that either the hospital should segregate its emergency area – with dedicated personnel, ward and resources – or each department should try to do so, implementing among its delivery areas one dedicated to the emergency.

9   We refer to Mintzberg's (1983) idea of technostructure, made of a group of people, the analysts, that plan and control formally the work of others.

10   In the sense proposed by Robert Duncan (1979). In the purest form, a division/department should represent a profit centre treated as a minicompany, run by a departmental manager who is responsible for planning, marketing and controlling service delivery (Wodinsky and Egan, 1988; MacStravic, 1989). Theoretically, the manager has a great deal of autonomy over both clinical and financial operations: in reality, though, the manager typically works with upper administration on price-setting, contracting and negotiating with third-party payers (Nackel and Kues, 1986).

11   It is necessary in particular given the problems related to the supply-induced demand typical of the health sector, where very aggressive supply policies might be very profitable but do not satisfy population's needs.

References

American Hospital Association (AHA) (1992), *Hospital Mergers and Consolidations, 1980–1991*, Chicago: AHA.

Bergman, R.L. (1993), '2013: The Hospital is not a Place', *Hospitals and Health Networks*, 67 (19), p. 29.

Blecher, M.B. (1998), 'Size does Matter', *Hospital and Health Networks*, 20 June, pp. 29–36.

Burgoyne, J.C. and Lorbiecki, A. (1993), 'Clinicians into Management, an Experience in Context', *Health Services Management Research*, 6 (4), pp. 248–58.

Charnes, M. and Smith-Tewksbury, L.J. (1993), *Collaborative Management in Health Care*, San Francisco: Jossey-Bass.

Duncan, R. (1979), 'What is the Right Organization Structure? Decision Tree Analysis provides the Answer', *Organizational Dynamics*, Winter.

Health Care Advisory Board (HCAB) (1995), *Network Advantage*, Washington, DC: The Advisory Board.

Herzlinger R.E. (1997), *Market-driven Health Care*, Reading, MA:Addison-Wesley.

Kassirer, J.P. (1995), 'The Next Transformation in the Delivery of Health Care', *The New England Journal of Medicine*, 5 January, pp. 52–4.

Leatt, P. Lemieux-Charles, L. and Aird, C. (1994), *Program Manager and Beyond: Management Innovations in Ontario Hospitals*, Ottawa: CCHSE.

MacStravic, S. (1989), 'Market Administration in Healthcare Delivery', *Health Care Management Review*, 14 (1), Winter, pp. 41–8.

Mintzberg, H. (1983), *Structuring in Fives: Designing Effective Organization*, Englewood Cliffs, NJ: Prentice-Hall.

Nackel, J.G. and Kues, I.W. (1986), 'Product-line Management: Systems and Strategies', *Hospital and Health Services Administration*, March/April, pp. 109–23.

Nauert, R.C. (1995), 'Academic Medical Centers and the Fight for Survival in the New Era of Managed Care', *Journal of Health Care Finance*, 21 (4), pp. 47–59.

Pettigrew, A., Ferlie, E. and McKee, L. (1992), *Shaping Strategic Change: Making Change in Large Organizations*, London: Sage.

Raffel, M. and Raffel, N. (1994), *The US Health System: Origins and Functions*, New York: Delmar Publishers Inc.

Schriefer, J. (1994), 'The Synergy of Pathways and Algorithms: Two Tools Work better than One', *Journal on Quality Improvement*, 20 (9), pp. 485–99.

Schriefer, J. (1995), 'Managing Critical Pathways Variances', *Quality Management in Health Care*, 3 (2), pp. 30–42.

Scott L. (1996), 'Will we like Tomorrow's Giants?', *Modern Healthcare*, 5 August.

Shortell, S.M. and Kalunzny, A.D. (2000), *Health Care Management: Organization Design and Behavior*, 3rd edn, New York: Delmar Publishers Inc.

Skinner W. (1974), 'The Focused Factory', *Harvard Business Review*, May–June, pp. 113–22.

Spath, P.L. (1994), *Clinical Paths: Tools for Outcomes Management*, Chicago: AHA.

Stein, J.E. Kruger, K.F. and Siegel, P.W. (1996), 'The Role of Human Resources in Supporting Reengineering', *Health Care Supervisor*, 15 December, pp. 8–16.

Sullivan C.B. and Rice T. (1991), 'The Health Insurance Picture in 1990', *Health Affairs*, Summer, pp. 104–15.

Thompson, J.D. (1967), *Organizations in Action*, New York: McGraw-Hill.

WHO (1992), *World Health Statistics Annual.*

Willcocks, S. (1998), 'The Development of Clinical Management at an NHS Trust Hospital', *Journal of Management in Medicine*, 12 (3), pp. 168–77.

Willcocks, S. and Conway, T. (1998), 'Strategic Marketing and Clinical Management in Health Care: A Possible Way Forward', *Journal of Management in Medicine*, 12 (2), pp. 120–34.

Wodinsky, H.B. and Egan, D. (1988), 'Product Line Management in Oncology: A Canadian Experience', *Hospital and Health Services Administration*, Summer, pp. 221–36.

Chapter 13

Access to Pharmaceuticals in Transition Countries

Maria M. Hofmarcher and Christine Lietz

Introduction

Individuals who consume drugs generally base their consumer decisions on their confidence in the safety and effectiveness of the medicine. Uncertainties regarding the quality of drugs concern not only patients but also doctors. As the majority of drugs in industrial nations are paid for from public funds there is no other sector in the health service that is as greatly affected by the mix of public consumption and private production as is the drug market. Furthermore, the research-based pharmaceutical industry is very concentrated. Ten firms dominate half of the world drug market. The role of regulation in drug markets is complex, as in most countries health policy and industrial policy goals coexist.

Innovations in the drug sector depend heavily on the establishment of suitable incentives to efficiently remunerate research and development in this sector and to promote future innovations. The role of the state or the health insurance organisation as payer and in regulating prices makes the public sector an important protagonist when it comes to creating these incentives.

Research and development are financed to a large extent by contributions or taxes. The share of public expenditure on drugs as a percentage of total expenditure on drugs in the EU is around 60 per cent. This proportion varies between approximately 50 per cent in Denmark and Finland and 84 per cent in Ireland; in Austria around 60 per cent of total expenditure on drugs is paid for by the public sector (OECD Health Data, 2000).

The safety and effectiveness of drugs is basically evaluated through clinical studies. The rigorous use of scientific methods in the development of new drugs only became established in the 1960s and is greatly influenced by the regulation environment. As a result of the increasing number of necessary clinical tests the average development time for drugs has doubled over the last 30 years (Scherer, 2000). Following the 'Contergan Crisis', intensified testing was introduced in the United States in the 1960s. While an average of 4.7 years were required in the 1960s to bring a drug onto the market, in the 1990s the development period was already 9.1 years. Test costs thus increased substantially. One reason for the increasing test requirements was to limit the number of licenses for imitation products (me too products) (Scherer, 2000). While up to 50 licenses were registered per year in the 1960s at present the US Food and Drug Administration (FDA) grants an average of 3.6 new drug licenses per year. It can be assumed that the stemming of licenses for imitation products encouraged the trend towards concentration in the world drug market (Scherer, 2000). However, the technical revolution in the process of testing may have also contributed to substantial cost increases in the development of new products (Jacobzone, 2000). On the other hand, it is occasionally unclear what should be considered as basic research costs; there are indications that the share of marketing costs have grown more over the last 10 to 15 years than pure research expenditure (ibid.). Equally unclear is the question of to what extent basic research in the public sector contributes to total research and development outlays.

As risk is involved in the development of drugs, patent laws are asserted on new chemical entities. As a result of the extension of average testing times, the effective patent protection has decreased over the last few years.

The patenting of new chemical substances is a central factor for the profit expectations in the industry. The development of new drugs is mainly established in industrial nations. At present around 50 per cent of drug innovations come from the USA and 25 per cent from Germany, France, Sweden and the UK (ibid.). Patent protection did not originally extend to 'developing countries': the enforcement of patenting in transition economies or developing countries was only established at the beginning of the 1990s during the negotiating rounds of the World Trade Organisation (WTO) as a result of successful lobbying above all by the US pharmaceutical industry. Consequently the importing of modern and effective drugs became more expensive for those countries. As a result of the HIV/AIDS and/or tuberculosis crisis in many developing countries, the pharmaceutical industry's policy of patent protection led to worldwide protests and in part to drastic falls in the prices of patented products (Rosenberg, 2001).

The market for patented drugs in many ways has the features of a bilateral monopoly. In a monopoly it is difficult for the state or health insurance organisation to set prices in the area of conflict between production costs and private monopoly rents. The regulation and the fixing of prices for patented products therefore necessitate a balancing act. Health policy goals are mostly aimed at making drugs with high therapeutic quality available as quickly as possible at the lowest possible prices. In contrast maintaining profits in order that innovation is encouraged in the longer term is also a goal to be pursued.

To enable countries to design a national drug policy WHO has began to develop means to assist member states and published guidelines in 1988 which were updated in 1998 (WHO, 1998). WHO's Mission in Essential Drugs and Medicines Policy includes four main objectives:

1 policy: ensure commitment by all stakeholders to national drugs policies, to coordinated implementation, and to monitoring policy impacts;
2 access: ensure equitable availability and affordability of essential drugs, with an emphasis on priority health problems and poor populations;
3 quality and safety: ensure the quality, safety and efficacy of all medicines by strengthening and putting into practice regulatory and quality assurance standards;
4 rational use: ensure therapeutically sound and cost-effective use of drugs by health professionals and consumers.

Countries joining the World Trade Organisation (WTO) have to adhere to Trade-Related Aspects of Intellectual Property Rights (TRIPS), which creates an international obligation among its members, the most important of which is full patent protection. TRIPS is expected to have the greatest impact on the pharmaceutical sector. Thus, the WHO objectives must be seen in the light of the TRIPS agreement, which also includes safeguards to protect public health (WHO, 2001a).

The Drug Market is not Well Behaved; It is Unique

Drugs are very special goods. Used correctly they preserve and prolong life or improve health. Cost savings increasingly accompanies this improvement in health because many modern drugs have the potential to reduce or avoid inpatient stays (Noonan, 2000). Without clinical effectiveness, however, drugs can even lead to death.

Persons who consume drugs generally base their consumer decisions on their confidence that the medicine is safe and effective. The special feature of the drug market is that demand-side features or uncertainties interact with the monopolistic structure of the industry and often of the drug distribution system as well. As the majority of drugs in industrial nations are paid for from public funds, no other sector of the health service is as greatly affected as the drug market by the public/private mix, which, in addition, has a global dimension.

The role of regulation of drug markets is complex, as in the most part health policy and industrial policy goals coexist. The health policy goals are to provide safe and effective medicines economically and in suitable volumes, to ensure access to drugs independent of the ability to pay. In contrast, the industrial policy goals promote growth, innovation and competition in a national economy. This is under the constraint that public expenditure for drugs is limited. Figure 13.1 shows the basic relationship between the key players in the drug market, differentiated according to flows of money, services and regulations. Patients pay contributions to insurers who, for their part, remunerate the service providers; in addition, patients pay taxes to the state, which pays contributions for public employees (or in some cases pays subsidies to the health insurers). Furthermore, co-payments and out-of-pocket payments exist in most countries. In all industrial nations the majority of drugs can only be obtained with a doctor's prescription. In addition, the purchase of drugs is in many cases only possible in licensed pharmacies.

Because the majority of patients are unable to assess the quality, safety and effectiveness of a medicine, an information deficit emerges that is compensated for by the establishment of public or quasi-public institutions (for example, authorisation authorities). The drug market policy in all countries is therefore usually based on the principle of making pharmaceutical products with high quality, safety and effectiveness available to the population. In many countries this goal is accompanied by the economic policy goal of regulating drug prices in order to resolve the price-information problem between patients and suppliers (trade, doctors). Taking on the role of complementary agents, the state, and/or health insurance organisations accompany the agent roles of doctors (Breyer and Zweifel, 1997). The state as a complementary agent also helps to minimise the uncertainty and the lack of information about the safety and effectiveness of drugs on the part of doctors.

When patients or others who pay for drugs make a purchase they are charged a price that is made up of the price for the manufacturer and the various profit margins. Profit margins can account for up to 50 per cent of the market price of drugs; in addition they vary across countries considerably. Various degrees of price regulation can often be found at all pricing stages and these likewise vary greatly between countries (Rosian et al., 2001).

Prices at the manufacturing level and also in the wholesale market are influenced by the world market and by price decision at company level. When

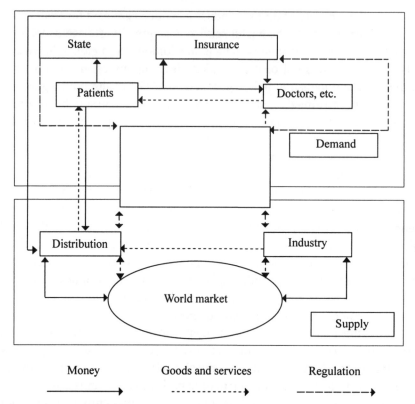

Figure 13.1   Key players in the drug market

Source: IHS-HealthEcon, 2001.

a product is brought onto the market the prices charged at the manufacturer's level consist of costs for research and development and for production. According to US data, basic research in the pharmaceutical industry consumes around 16 per cent of the research and development budget. In contrast to this the average cost in other research-intensive industries is around 6 per cent (Scherer, 2000).

Ten Firms make up Half of the World Drug Market

The manufacturing of pharmaceutical products is dominated by multinational firms, which in the last few years have grown increasingly, mostly as a result of company takeovers. The turnovers of the ten largest pharmaceutical companies have increased sixfold since 1981 and reached US$145,000 million in the year 2000 (at current prices). This turnover volume is higher than the combined gross domestic product of Hungary (US$50,000 million), the Czech Republic (US$54,000 million) and Slovakia (US$20,000 million); it is slightly below Poland's GDP (US$153,000 million) and equal to around 70 per cent of Austria's GDP (US$209,000 million). The turnovers of the world's largest pharmaceutical companies were around eight times as high as Austrian health expenditure (US$17,000 million).

The multinational character of the leading manufacturers has also increased greatly as a result of takeovers over the last 20 years. The world market share of the leading ten firms has doubled since 1981 and is now 45 per cent. Motives for this concentration in the industry lie in the intention to pool research and development funds, optimise the transfer of knowledge and insure against the risk that arises when new products are developed (Scherer, 2000). Concentration of a comparable extent also took place worldwide in the wholesale sector.

The Provision of Drugs in Transition Countries: A Large Pill to Swallow

Drug expenditure in transition countries is sometimes around twice as high as in industrial nations. While the weighted average expenditure on drugs in the EU is around 16 per cent of total health expenditure, the share in transition countries totals up to 30 per cent and higher (see Figure 13.2).

Import liberalisation at the beginning of the 1990s led in most transition countries to increased demand for drugs from industrial nations. At the same time a downturn in economic growth was recorded everywhere. Apart from Slovakia, which in 1999 exceeded its 1989 GDP level, none of the countries have as yet been able to catch up in terms of their pre-transition economic performance level. The recession in the Ukraine and Georgia is particularly sustained; in 1999 both countries reached only 35 per cent of their 1989 economic performance level (Kolodko, 2000).

Distorted Allocation

In the 1990s recession, declining resources for the health sector and rising demand for safe and effective drugs in all transition countries caused a distorted allocation of the budget for the health sector in comparison to industrial

Table 13.1 Pharmaceutical companies, arranged in order of turnover and world market shares

	1981			2000	
	Turnover in 1,000 million $	Market share in %		Turnover in 1,000 million $	Market share in %
Höchst	2.56	3.7	Pfizer	23.15	7.3
Ciba-Geigy*	2.10	3.0	GlaxoSmithKline	22.04	6.9
Merck	2.06	2.9	Merck	16.49	5.2
Roche	1.48	2.1	AstraZeneca	14.29	4.5
Pfizer	1.45	2.1	Bristol-Myers Squibb	13.28	4.2
American Home Products	1.42	2.1	Novartis	12.41	3.9
Sandoz*	1.42	2.1	Johnson & Johnson	12.36	3.9
Eli Lilly	1.36	1.9	Aventis	11.31	3.6
Bayer	1.22	1.8	Pharmacia	10.25	3.2
SmithKline Beckman	1.22	1.7	American Homeproducts	9.57	3.0
Total	**16.29**	**23.4**		**45.15**	**45.7**

* Became Novartis in 1996.

Source: Financial Times, 8 May 2001, p. 15.

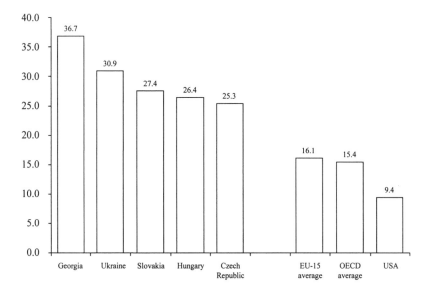

Figure 13.2   Drug expenditure in per cent of total health expenditure, 1999

Source: The World Bank, IMF, TACIS, OECD, IHS-HealthEcon calculations, 2001.

nations. As health services are consumed at a price level specific to a nation but drugs are imported at 'world market prices', transition countries have to spend relatively more on drug provision.

Creating a general strain on the public sectors and the societies, the dramatic decline in national income accompanied by inflation and exchange rate crises aggravated the decline in resources for the health sector significantly; furthermore, in many EU candidate nations the various sectors of the health service were budgeted without suitable adjustments for inflation. Thus, for example, the Hungarian health insurance's real expenditure declined by around 20 per cent between 1994 and 1999 (Hofmarcher and Orosz, 2001). Real public per capita health expenditure in the Ukraine in 2000 only reached around 70 per cent of its 1996 level (Hofmarcher, 2001a).

In accordance with the different income levels of the countries shown in Table 13.2, per capita expenditure for drugs varies between US$14 in Georgia and the Ukraine and US$344 in the USA. However, from a certain income level, drug consumption apparently only grows at a less than proportionate rate to income. While, for example, the average per capita income in the EU

Table 13.2 Drug expenditure in selected transition countries, 1999

	Drug expenditure			Gross domestic product				Consumption in packages	
	In % of GDP	In % of total health expenditure	Per capita, US$	Per capita, at const. 1995 US$	Index 1999 1989 = 100	Index 1999 1995 = 100	Av. annual growth rate, % (1995–99)	Index 1999 1995=100	Av. annual growth rate, %
	(a)	(b)	(c)	(d)	(e)	(f)	(g)	(h)	(i)
Hungary	1.8	26.4	65[1]	2,315	99	–	–	–	–
Czech Rep.	1.8	25.3	96[1]	5,122	95	–	–	–	–
Slovakia	1.6	27.4	60[1]	3,892	102	121	4.8	132	6,9
Ukraine	1.6[2]	30.9[2]	14[3]	2,250[7]	36	95[9]	–1.3[10]	84[10]	–5.8[10]
Georgia	2.3[2]	27.4–46.0[2]	14[3]	434	34	–	–	–	–
OECD average [4]	1.2	15.4	240[4]	–	165[8]	121[8]	–	–	–
EU-15 average[5]	1.4	16.1	267	22,090[7]	164[8]	113[8]	–	–	–
USA	1.4	9.4	344[6]	31,935[7]	166[8]	124[8]	–	–	–

Notes

1 1999, at 1995 prices and in constant 1995 US$.
2 Estimates for 2000.
3 2000, Ukraine: at 1996 prices and in constant 1996 US$; Georgia: at 1997 prices and in constant 1997 US$.
4 1996 without the Czech Republic, Hungary, Korea, Mexico, Poland and Turkey; Spain and Japan are not included in the unweighted per capita average.
5 1997, weighted averages; expenditure per capita in US$ purchasing power parity.
6 At constant 1996 US$.
7 In US$ purchasing power adjusted.
8 In US$ purchasing power adjusted, averages are weighted by population.
9 1996 = 100.
10 At constant 1996 US$.

Sources: The World Bank, IMF, TACIS, OECD, EIU, IHS-HealthEcon calculations, 2001.

is around nine times higher than the Hungarian per capita income, average per capita expenditure on drugs was only four times as high as in Hungary.

Income Elasticity

The empirical literature concerning the question of whether and how price changes for patients (additional payments, and so on) lead to a change in drug consumption, come to mixed results (Jacobzone, 2000). With the data available we can merely make the observation that a change in income is accompanied by a greater than proportional change in drug consumption; i.e. drug consumption seems to react elastically to changes in income. This is depicted in Table 13.2. Between 1995 and 1999, drug consumption in Slovakia as measured in packets records are stronger annual growth (+6.9 per cent) than the national economy (+4.8 per cent) and the decline in drug consumption in the Ukraine (-5.8 per cent) is greater than the decline in income (-1.3 per cent).[1]

The different institutional and regulatory environments in Slovakia and the Ukraine are perhaps reasons for this development. While the share of publicly financed drugs is around 24 per cent of the estimated market volume in the Ukraine, the majority of drugs in Slovakia are at least partially reimbursable. Thus the consumption of drugs in Slovakia is less dependent on the ability of households to pay. Access to drugs in the Ukraine depends mainly however on current income, which at present is on average only around 50 per cent of its 1991 level. Although the total availability (packets produced nationally and internationally) of drugs in the Ukraine increased by around 7 per cent between 1996 and 2000, consumption in 1999 was 16 per cent lower than in 1996 and declined on average by 5.8 per cent annually. In Slovakia the annual average growth in consumption exceeded the rate of real growth in income by around 2 percentage points.

Increased Co-payments and Out-of-pocket Payments

Increased co- and out-of-pocket payments impede the access to safe and effective drugs. The increase in reimbursable drugs in Slovakia was accompanied by increased co-payments by patients because the share of products, which were then only partially reimbursable, increased greatly at the same time. As a result, private households pay increasingly more from current income for the purchase of drugs. Currently, the co-payment rate in Slovakia is about 20 per cent and thus high compared to EU countries like Germany (1997: 6.1 per cent) Italy (1997: 7.2 per cent) and United Kingdom (1997:

5.8 per cent) (Hofmarcher, 2000). Further, as a proportion of total private expenditure on health in Hungary, drug consumption almost doubled between 1992 and 1999 (European Observatory on Health Care Systems, 1999).

In countries like the Ukraine and Georgia the access to drugs is very limited, as almost all medicines must be paid for from current income, which moreover is not increasing. Falling or non-increasing income combined with increased co- and out-of-pocket payments intensifies the consequences of an unequal distribution of income. Furthermore, impeded access to drugs can lead to deterioration in the state of health or in its distribution.

According to surveys, the share of household expenditure that is spent on drugs in Eastern European and Central Asian countries ranges between 2.6 per cent in Russia and 28.6 per cent in Kirghisia. Life expectancy in this region has continuously declined and in 1999 was only around 95 per cent of its 1990 level. Although child mortality, which is around four times as high as in the EU, has fallen, the decline was only 17 per cent compared to 31 per cent in the EU (WHO, 2001b).

Another crude indicator to look at the association of health status and drug consumption is premature death. Reflected in Figure 13.3, the reduction of life expectancy through death before 65 years is at a noticeably lower level in Slovakia, where drugs of reasonable quality are available and affordable to a considerably higher extent than in the Ukraine.

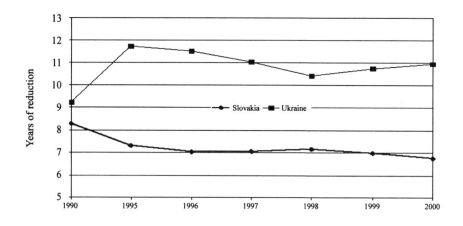

Figure 13.3   Reduction of life expectancy through death before 65 years

Source: WHO Health Database, January 2002; IHS-HealthEcon calculations, 2002.

Aggravating the health consequences of restricted affordability to safe and effective drugs, access to professional care is also limited in transition countries thus multiplying the adverse effects on the health status due to increased co-payments. In Georgia for instance, home treatment without seeking professional care has increasingly become a preferred way to deal with sickness and/or chronic disease (Georgian State Department of Statistics, 2000). This may also contribute to an increased risk of dying. Starting from a lower level compared to other countries in the region, the standardised death rate due to diarrhoeal diseases under the age of 5 was 50 per cent above the 1990 level, the corresponding value in 1995 for the average death rate in the Newly Independent States (NIS) exceeded the 1990 level 11 per cent. The level of all cause maternal deaths are lower in Georgia compared to other NIS-countries but was in 1999 more than twice as high than in 1990. Maternal deaths in NIS countries declined and reached in 1999 86 per cent of its 1990 value (WHO, 2001b).

Corruption and Gratitude Payments are Common

Official data on health and drug spending are likely to underestimate the real financial burden for households in all transition countries. According to a poll in March 2002, carried out by a Slovakian polling agency, 68 per cent of respondents indicated that corruption is most widespread in health care, while as much as 25 per cent of respondents informed of bribes in the health care sector, given in order to secure treatment of a higher quality (Slovenska Tlacova Agentura (Slovak Republic News Agency), 27 May 2002). Paying gratitude money is also a widespread custom in the Georgian health care service. Official estimate indicate that the estimated volume of the health sector consumption would correct the GDP estimates upward by 12.5 per cent, thus explaining about half of the amount of the shadow economy, which was recorded to be at 25 per cent (Georgian State Department of Statistics, 2000).

There appears to be a common sense about the necessity for paying gratitude money. As a consequence, the incentives generated by this common sense are built-in in provider behaviour on each level of care, possibly explaining the persistent wage differential between other professionals and doctors. In Hungary, for instance, public sector real wages have increased 10 per cent between 1995 and 1999 whereas real wage growth in the health sector was lower (Hofmarcher and Orosz, 2001). The willingness to pay higher salaries may therefore be limited. Providers, the government and the purchaser (and ultimately taxpayers) may be reluctant to grant higher salaries since *all* expect physician salaries to be supplemented by an 'appropriate' amount of gratitude money currently and in the future. Apart from the tremendous influence of the 'gratitude money custom' on the overall provider behaviour, it creates a situation that could be termed as 'quality illusion' and that disadvantages patients.

Is There a 'Quality Illusion?

Patients who need health care services demand quality. They are interested in the quality of services that represents a real value. Their concern is not the amount of services. This means that the demand for the amount of services increases in proportion to the increase in the quality level, given all other real factors, for example education, technology, and capacities remain unchanged. An individual whose willingness to pay is affected by an expected or hoped for change in the quality level, all real factors remaining unchanged, 'suffers' from 'quality illusion'. If patients pay gratitude money they presumably suffer from a 'quality illusion' since they expect the provision of higher quality of care though all other factors influencing the improvement and the sustainability of quality may have remained unchanged. Therefore, on average nothing changes and gratitude money has become a pure income supplement without real impacts.

An alternative explanation however can contribute real effects to the gratitude money custom. The elements of quality in a wider sense are: the structure of care (facilities, available technology and education level of the personnel), the process and outcome (in a medical sense). Gratitude money cannot influence the structure and presumably do not influence the medical outcome, however, it can influence the process of care provision by doctors and other personnel, i.e. reduced waiting time, safe medicine. For patients, it is a real element of the quality of care in a wider sense. Furthermore, gratitude money may improve access to care when there is a shortage in certain services or medical goods.

Regulation Deficits are Widespread in Transition Economies

The growing availability of nationally and internationally produced drugs in transition countries is for the most part accompanied by deficits in regulations that are present in the area of quality assurance as well as in distribution and price setting. In addition, prescription practices, in so far as they play a role at all, remain fairly uncontrolled.

In Slovakia, the consumption of pharmaceuticals in volume terms has outpaced the value growth in real terms, reflecting a high propensity to prescribe and to utilise drugs. Due to a major shift in the reimbursement status from fully reimbursed drugs to partially reimbursed drugs, co-payment has increased considerably recently, accompanied by a decline in the consumption of over the counter drugs. Drug supply was discontinued because of payment arrears in some cases; most drugs seem to be readily available in both urban and rural areas, however. In contrast to the internationally observed decline in the number of reimbursable drugs (Rosian et al., 2001) (which are usually only available on prescription) the proportion of expenditure spent on reimbursable drugs in Slovakia, for example, has increased from 80 per cent in 1995 to 84 per cent in 1999 (Hofmarcher, 2000). According to experts this increase was also caused by aggressive lobbying of national and international companies which attempt, as early as the run up to negotiations, to manipulate not only the medical experts but also the political decision-makers about the inclusion of drugs into the Slovakian reimbursement list.

The drug law from 1998 substantially advanced the pharmaceutical sector legislation toward EU standards encompassing regulations for testing of medicines, registration of medicines, approval of medical devices, ensuring and checking quality, efficacy, safety of medicines and medical devices, and the role of the state administration in the area of pharmacy. However, major application deficiencies have remained, the most important of which concerns the coordination in pricing and reimbursement issues between the Ministry of Finance, the Ministry of Health, the categorisation committee and other regulating authorities.

The current regulatory environment in the Ukraine reflects a persistent overlap of responsibilities due to the enforcement of legislation on different jurisdictional levels. Based on constitutional law, jurisdictional hierarchy seemed to have never fully applied to legislation concerning the pharmaceutical sector. As a consequence, different government organisations develop, issue and redesign legislation, all of which appear to be based on the drug law from 1996, however.

Overlaps of responsibilities appear to prevail in the sphere of quality control, licensing, and drug registration, segments of the regulatory system where funds are being obtained from testing and registration fees. The estimated total amount of funds available from both quality control and registration is likely to be in the order of current US\$ 5.52 million in 2000, corresponding to 0.18 per cent of GDP and 0.7 per cent of public expenditures on health (Hofmarcher, 2001a).

Whereas most drugs appear to be readily available, the major barrier in the Georgian pharmaceutical market is affordability and the quality of domestically procured drugs. Addressing access as a top priority of the current national drug policy, the government promotes availability and affordability of drugs via tax reductions. Some drugs in the essential drug list are tax-exempted. Also part of essential drug list, which eventually contains all drugs to be covered by the state health care programmes, narcotic drugs are the only substances whose prices are regulated.

Confronted with a sustained lack of funds, the government appears to pursue conflicting goals: Traditionally a centre of commerce, the government believes that Georgia and in particular Tbilisi delivers all prerequisites for establishing good business opportunities for manufacturing generics to serve the Caucasus region. Thus, to promote private sector development, the Georgian government restrains itself to drug price regulation only within the state health care programmes (Hofmarcher, 2001b).

Conclusions

The present paper examines access, purchasing and market control mechanisms in the pharmaceutical sector in Slovakia, Georgia and in the Ukraine. Although market control mechanisms are evolving, legislation and thus regulation of the pharmaceutical sector including distribution are still inconsistent compared to European standards. Therefore, effective price and volume agreements are inhibited.

Whereas the availability of both domestic and foreign drugs has increased, consumption in volume terms declined perhaps due to low incomes and soaring inflation. The affordability of drugs appears to have diminished in the last years. Limited access is exacerbated by an increase in co-payments and out-of-pocket payments. Moreover, official spending data are likely to underestimate the real financial burden for households, as gratitude payments are common. In addition, in some of the poorer transition countries, access to safe and effective drugs appears to be severely restricted due to poor domestic manufacturing practices.

In transition countries the health expenditure share on pharmaceuticals exceeds the share spent in developed OECD countries and likely to remain relatively high in the future, unless relative prices change quickly. These proportions are about twice as high as in OECD countries. We find this relation to be connected to the global pharmaceutical market. Being traded at international prices, imported drugs drive pharmaceutical expenditure up. As a consequence, the health sector budget appears to be distorted: Services produced domestically yield relatively low prices compared to health care products like pharmaceuticals which have to be imported at international prices. The research based pharmaceutical industry is very concentrated. Further, balancing health policy and industrial policy goals challenges regulations of national drug markets.

Many transition countries have already adopted some form of a national drug policy, however, implementation and application of quality standards in production (GMP) is impeded by a lack of consistent and reliable institution building. This holds particularly true for the low and middle-income-countries.

Although most transition countries have committed themselves to national drug policies following mostly advice from WHO and international donors. However, the scope and the stage of implementation are very divers.

Acknowledgement

This research was funded by the World Bank. We would like to thank Gerald Röhrling for excellent research assistance.

Note

1   It must however be taken into consideration that the size of the shadow economy in the Ukraine is estimated at up to 45 per cent of gross domestic product; thus it can be assumed that both the income and consumption level have been drastically underestimated.

References

Breyer, F. and Zweifel, P. (1997), *Gesundheitsökonomie*, Berlin: Springer Verlag.
European Observatory on Health Care Systems (1999), *HIT-HUNGARY Health Care Systems in Transition – HUNGARY*, Copenhagen: WHO.
Georgian State Department of Statistics (2000), *Medical Service in Georgia. Survey Report on Populations' Health Care Expenditures and Unrecorded Medical Services*, Tbilisi.
Hofmarcher, M.M. (2000), *Access to Pharmaceuticals in Slovakia*, Washington DC: The World Bank.
Hofmarcher, M.M. (2001a), *Access to Pharmaceuticals in Ukraine*, Washington DC: The World Bank.

Hofmarcher, M.M. (2001b), *Access to Pharmaceuticals in Georgia*, Washington DC: The World Bank.

Hofmarcher, M.M. and Orosz, E. (2001), *Resource Allocation and Purchasing in Hungary*, Washington DC: The World Bank.

Jacobzone, S. (2000), 'Pharmaceutical Policies in OECD Countries: Reconciling Social and Industrial Goals', Labor Market and Social Policy – Occasional Papers, No. 40, OECD, Paris.

Kolodko, G.W. (2000), 'Globalization and Catching-Up: From Recession to Growth in Transition Economies', IMF Working Paper WP/00/100, International Monetary Fund, Washington DC.

Lewis, M. (1999), *Who is Paying for Health Care in Eastern Europe and Central Asia*, Washington DC: Human Development Sector Unit Europe and Central Asia, The World Bank.

Noonan, D. (2000), 'Why Drugs Cost so Much', *Newsweek*, 25 September, p. 22f.

OECD (2000), *OECD Health Data 2000 – A Comparative Analysis of 30 Countries*, Paris: OECD.

Rosenberg, T. (2001), 'Look at Brazil, The World's AIDS crisis is Solvable', *The New York Times Magazine*, 28 January, pp. 26–31.

Rosian, I. Habl, C. and Vogler, S. (2001), *Arzneimittel, Steuerung der Märkte in der EU*, Vienna: ÖBIG.

Scherer, F.M. (2000), 'The Pharmaceutical Industry', in A.J. Culyer and J.P. Newhouse (eds), *Handbook of Health Economics*, Amsterdam: Elsevier.

WHO (1998), *How to Develop and Implement a National Drug Policy*, Geneva: World Health Organisation.

WHO (2001a), 'Globalization, TRIPS and Access to Pharmaceuticals', *WHO Policy Perspectives on Medicines*, 3.

WHO (2001b), *WHO Health For All Database*, Copenhagen: World Health Organisation.

Chapter 14

Health Insurance in Iran: Opportunities and Complexities

Mehdi Russel

Introduction

The Islamic Republic of Iran is seeking to reform its health care system, not least through the development of health insurance. Like most developing countries, this has been a response largely due to the economic transition, the financial position of the country, and the need to raise revenue from other than fiscal sources. Demographic transition, developing medical services, and expanding new and expensive medical technologies are some of the other factors, which have accelerated the institution of national health insurance. However, the primary objective of this change in Iran has been to ensure standard access to comprehensive health care services for all its citizens. National health insurance is aimed to improve efficiency, equity and satisfaction in the health care system. On 8 November 1994, the Iranian Parliament passed a law that legislated the introduction of national health insurance.

The Demographic, Economic and Health Situation in Iran

According to the World Health Organisation (2000), Iran is a lower middle-income country with a US$ 1,612 GDP per capita, and a population of more than 60 million persons. The Statistic Centre of Iran (SCI) (1998) reported that 38 per cent of the population live in rural areas and 30 per cent of the population are below the age of 16. The annual population growth rate was 1.9 in 1999 (WHO, 2000). Eighty per cent of the population is literate and over 85 per cent of the population has access to safe drinking water and 80 per cent to sanitation (World Bank, 1999).

The health system in Iran has displayed formidable robustness over many years. Given the country's income and health spending levels (5.7 per cent of GDP), the health outcome is excellent and access to clean water, sanitation, health services, and health insurance are high. About 90 per cent of the population has physical access to medical care and medicines are readily available. Compared to other countries in the region, and to countries around the world with comparable income levels, Iran's performance in terms of health outcomes and population growth is considerable. These results are due to a government focused on primary health care (PHC) (World Bank, 1999).

The Health Care System of Iran

The health care system in Iran has developed over the last century, largely influenced by Western medicine. There are forty regional health authorities responsible for providing health services in Iran. Developing disease prevention and health promotion measures, especially through the rural health houses and their very impressive local health workers (Behvarzes), has been an understandable priority for the Islamic Republic of Iran. Together with a drive to improve literacy and to provide clean water to nearly all households, these measures have resulted in, for example, a fall in the maternal mortality rate in the rural areas from 370 per 100,000 live births in 1974 to 53 per 100,000 live births in 1993. At the same time, there has been a great deal of resource expansion in large provincial hospitals for tertiary care (WHO, 1997).

The public sector dominates in the provision of inpatient services, and the government owns 90 per cent of hospital beds. In outpatient services, the profit-oriented private sector is dominant and it owns 90 per cent of the facilities. Table 14.1 depicts the Iranian health service facilities. Patients who use health services through health insurance can go direct to the specialist and use tertiary levels of health services without first going through a referral system.

Table 14.1   Iran health facilities (1997)

Total population 1997	61,869,884	Laboratory	3,387
Hospital beds	98,669	Rehabilitation centres	936
Hospital	694	Radiology centre	1,562
Hospital beds /1000 population	1. 59	Pharmacy	480
Health clinic	6,218	Medical specialist	12,105
Health clinic/10,000 population	9. 95	GP	37,000
Health centre	15,102	Total number of doctors	49,105

Source: MHTMT, 1999.

Notwithstanding the gains described above, Iran's health care system faces a number of serious challenges, particularly concerning future health outcomes, efficiency, quality and long-term or future sustainability. The World Bank (1999) has cited seven significant issues and complexities in Iran's health system. First, with respect to health outcomes, malnutrition is an extremely serious problem for Iran. Second, the onset of the health transition and the population ageing are shifting the burden of disease to treating non-communicable diseases. This has important implications for both costs and the future configuration of Iran's health financing and delivery system. The cause and number of deaths in 1997, according to the 17 international categories, are shown in Table 14.2. Third, the system is inefficient with a hospital occupancy rate below 60 per cent and continued expansions of both public and private delivery capacity without due regard to underlying needs. Fourth, quality needs to be enhanced and monitored. Fifth, the revenue sources used to finance the multiple public health insurance systems are complex, not transparent, not actuarially sound, and may be inefficient and inequitable. Sixth, the systems used to reimburse medical care providers are insufficient and counter to the more modern system being implemented. Seventh, policy makers lack critical information needed for decision-making.

Health Insurance in Iran

About 100 years ago, the evolution of health insurance in Iran was started by railway workers. The Iranian armed forces' medical services then joined the evolution. The modern health insurance scheme began in 1936 with the implementation of the social security organisation to cover work injuries of persons employed in urban areas. Later, in 1953, it expanded to include cover for sickness, maternity, old age, disability and death. Civil servants' insurance was established in 1970, and made separate from the social security organisation.

The National Health Insurance Act, passed by the Iranian Islamic Consultative Assembly in 1994, legislated the establishment of a medical service insurance organisation in order to prepare for the possibilities of medical service insurance of the civil servants, the needy, the villagers, and other social groups (NHIHC, 2001). According to the Insurance Act, the National Health Insurance High Council (NHIHC) was formed at the Ministry of Health, Treatment and Medical Training (MHTMT). The purpose of the NHIHC is to: develop and popularise the national health insurance; make

Table 14.2   Cause of death in the Islamic Republic of Iran (1997)

Group	Cause of death	Number	Percentage
1st	Infective and parasitic disorders	3,921	1.89
2nd	Cancer and tumors	19,292	9.29
3rd	Allergy and nutritional disorders	2,781	1.34
4th	Blood disorders	1,173	0.56
5th	Psychological disorders	987	0.47
6th	Neurological disorders	2,273	1.009
7th	Cardiovascular disorders	74,557	35.89
8th	Respiratory disorders	7,605	3.66
9th	Gastrointestinal disorders	5,316	2.56
10th	Reno-urological disorders	3,087	1.49
11th	Pregnancy, delivery and birth side effects	406	0.19
12th	Skin disorders	95	0.04
13th	Skeletal disorders	245	0.12
14th	Congenital anomalies	5,252	2.53
15th	Infantile disorders	11,401	5.49
16th	Mal define conditions	40,664	19.53
17th	Accidents, poisoning, suicide	26,086	12.56
18th	Unknown	2,602	1.25
Total		207,744	100.00

Source: MHTMT, 1999.

policies; and, plan and create executive coordination for directing, controlling and evaluating the qualitative level of national health insurance. The Iranian national health insurance system is described as a *voluntary* scheme for all government employees, villagers, self-employed and the vulnerable. The time for covering all groups and individuals of the society was initially determined within five years after the approval date of the Act, with priority to the needy and the villagers. It must be mentioned that the national health insurance legislation attempts to cover parts of population that are not covered by other insurance carriers. Other insurance companies carry their activities according to their own Acts. Every health insurance company covers an individual for treatment, both as an inpatient and outpatient. The cover, however, excludes services like: cosmetic surgeries, transplantation (of, for example, heart, liver and fingers), infertility services, joint replacements, and cochlear implantation. Nonetheless, health insurance companies cover the minimum extent and level of medicines and medical services including emergency, general and specialised medical services. Disease preventive procedures like immunisations and screening tests are provided by the government and are not, therefore, included in the various health insurance packages.

The health insurance *payment system* is based on fee-for-service for all services at all levels.The government plays a major role in setting the fee schedules. According to law, the medical tariffs and diagnostic services have to be approved by the Council of Ministers at the joint suggestion of the Plan and Budget Organisation (PBO) and the Ministry of Health, and with confirmation by the High Council on the basis of actual costs and the approved health insurance premiums. The actual cost of medical services is defined as the cost price of the services plus profits on the capital.

In financing health insurance, an *average risk premium* method is applied to the national health insurance schemes in Iran and people pay the same amount of money as a per capita premium. However, the social security system is still running on the basis of a compulsory payroll tax.

The Iranian government subsidises several social groups by paying a percentage of their premiums (see Table 14.3). In cost sharing, the insured pays *co-insurance* at the time of using medical services; 10 per cent for inpatient services and 30 per cent for outpatient services. For using private services, the insured has to pay the difference between the public and the private tariffs.

Table 14.3   The percentages of premium paid by government (1996–2000)

No.	Group	Government (%)	Insured (%)
1	Martyrs' families	80	20
2	War injured (self-sacrifices)	80–100	0–20
3	Students	50–80	20–50
4	Soldiers' families	100	–
5	Prisoners' families	100	–
6	Vulnerable	100	–
7	Civil servants and army families	70–80	20–30
8	Workers*	1	99
9	Villagers	50	50
10	Self-employed	0–100	0–100

*   Worker and employer pay 99% of contributions.

Source: NHIHC, 1996; The Council of Ministers approvals collection, NHIHC, Health Ministry of Iran.

Achievements to Date of National Health Insurance in Iran

One of the significant goals in establishing national health insurance is to achieve universal coverage. In fact, during the first five years (1995–2000) after the implementation of national health insurance, the villagers, majority of the needy and a section of the self-employed are now covered by heath insurance. The coverage of health insurance has increased from 50–60 per cent in 1994 to 90–95 per cent in 1999 (MSIO, 2000). Based on government subsidies for *villagers* (50 per cent of the premium), the medical service insurance organisation embarked on the distribution of free medical insurance cards to the villagers at a national level in 1997. Consequently, more than 22 million rural people obtained health insurance cards to use inpatient services, specialist and sub-specialist services in outpatient services, with a 25 per cent coinsurance (MSIO, 1998).

Further, more attention than hitherto has been directed to the *poor*, according to national health insurance Act (1994), by the Imam Khomeini Relief Committee (IKRC) that is privileged and duty-bound to prepare health insurance for the needy. Relative to the budget, the IKRC is paid by the government (100 per cent of premiums) to provide medical services for the poor. After implementation of the national insurance Act, IKRC has covered the medical services cost of the majority of needy people. Presently, the IKRC covers more than five million people and this is a significant achievement for Iran. The coverage of the *self-employed* has had less success in national health implementation. The number of self-employed people registered by the social security organisation is less than half a million, and that by the medical service insurance organisation is less than one million. The reasons follow.

Potential Issues and Complexities

There are several important challenges now facing the Iranian health insurance system: sustainability of coverage of the villagers and needy as they are totally dependent on government grants and of coverage of the self-employed based on their voluntary scheme of health insurance; the financing of national health insurance concerning the high dependency on government budgets, but with less attention to mobilise other resources; the health insurance effect on cost and on monitoring the expenditures due to the moral hazard phenomenon; and, the role of private health services in relation to the national health insurance carriers concerning the wide gap between public and private medical tariffs that exists at present (Russel, 2001).

Coverage and Sustainability

In the first two years of NHI implementation in Iran, a considerable number of villagers and self-employed only paid their contributions when they were ill or after they were admitted to hospital. In fact, the majority of these groups that were insured by the medical service insurance organisation (MSIO) when they became sick paid their contributions in order to reduce their own hospital bills to 10 per cent as coinsurance. In the second year of establishment of the medical service insurance organisation, the villagers' coverage was still low, and estimates show that if all-rural populations had participated in the voluntary health insurance scheme, the costs of collecting their contributions would have exceed the total amount of their contributions. The medical service insurance organisation embarked on a national distribution of free medical insurance cards to the villagers at a national level in 1997. Consequently, more than 22 million rural people obtained health insurance cards. That the villagers have no participation in their health insurance fund, and that they are totally dependent on government budgets, are potential challenges. This is because whenever the support of the government funding fluctuates, there is a knock-on effect on the health insurance of the villagers. Some aspects of the arguments related to coverage of the needy are similar to those for coverage of the villagers. The needy do not participate in the payment of their premiums, and government provides 100 per cent of the premiums (see Table 14.3).

The main dilemmas for coverage of the self-employed people are: first, the voluntary nature of the scheme; and, second, the insuring of patients when they are admitted to hospital. It seems that there is no technical reason (in terms of insurance principles) to follow this approach except for political reasons. This method may simply be a means of financing hospitals, which otherwise would likely face financial deficit due to cosufficiency projects. However, there is less probability for sustaining self-employed coverage.

Insufficient Support of the Health Insurance Funds

The nominal amount of the health insurance premium has increased every year by 20 per cent, on average. Table 14.4 shows the health insurance premiums and medical tariffs during 1995–2000. By annually increasing the premiums, some real resources have been mobilised to provide additional funding. Both

Table 14.4 **Iran NHI premiums and illustrative medical tariffs 1995–2000 (Rial currency)**

Year	Premium	GP's visit (public)	Specialist's visit (public)	Internal coefficient	Anesthetic coefficient	Surgical coefficient	First class hospital bed cost per day
1995	4,200	2,000	3,500	400	4,000	7,500	20,000
1996	4,860	–	–	–	–	–	35,000
1997	5,600	3,000	4,500	520	5,200	9,750	47,500
1998	6,350	3,500	5,500	600	6,000	11,000	52,200
1999	9,750	5,000	8,000	800	7,000	12,000	57,200
2000	10,800	6,000	10,000	1,000	8,500	14,500	61,400

Source: NHIHC (2000); the collection of High Council of Ministers related to NHI, NHIHC, Iran.

government and populations' proportions in health care finance have increased in 1995–2000.

Government subsidies provide the majority of financial resources for health insurance carriers. Most subsidies are paid as premiums to health insurance carriers to cover different groups, as shown in Table 14.4. The amount of government subsidies paid to the medical service insurance organisation (MSIO) and to the armed forces medical service organisation (AFMSO) forms 70–80 per cent of the income for these two carriers. The government pays 100 per cent of the insurance premiums received by the IKRC. Except for 30–35 per cent of the population covered in full by the SSO, the rest of the population is insured by an average of 75–85 per cent of government subsidies. Furthermore, the government paid some grants to the insurance carriers in 1997–99 when MSIO, AFMSO, IKRC were faced with financial shortfalls. Financing the NHI has been significantly complex from the very beginning. Insufficient income every year had happened and derailed the insurance carriers, particularly between 1997–99. In these latter years, the insurance carriers – MSIO, AFMSO, IKRC – suffered a 25–35 per cent budget insufficiency, and medical services' reimbursements were delayed for between four to six months. The reasons for the financial shortfalls are linked to several factors. For example, the actual cost of medical services and health insurance premiums have not been accounted for accurately. Hence, the government was unsuccessful in balancing the premiums and the medical tariffs. The medical services' expenditures rose sharply due to increasing use of the medical facilities and other moral hazards. There was, in short, an absolute imbalance between insurance carriers' income and their expenditures. This deeply affected the value of insurance, and reduced the credits between both providers and those insured.

The pivotal role of the government in financing NHI is another key issue to consider. The government influences all aspects of NHI and inevitably makes the NHI hugely dependent on the political and economic situation of the government in office. Government, being the main source of income for all the insurance companies – except the SSO – can resist growth in premiums; yet, it does not have the same power to keep the medical tariffs at (artificially) low rates.

Shifting part of the government's burden of financing and delivering health care onto the private sector has been less successful to date. Insurance carriers cover the cost of private medical services, but only on the basis of public health services tariffs. In other words, the health insurance companies pay out an equal amount of money (to public health services tariffs) for private services; and, hence, those insured people are required to pay the difference, given that private medical tariffs are, on average, 30 per cent higher than the public health services' tariffs.

Cost Inflation

It is well recognised that health insurance can potentially induce a higher growth of health care expenditures (Bogg et al., 1996); equally, it can improve the efficiency of existing services by reducing unnecessary spending and reviewing utilisation and cost containment. Although in the first five years of NHI implementation in Iran, most attention was focused on popularisation, and achievement of nationwide coverage, the continuous rise of medical care expenditures, has obligated both the health insurance carriers and the NHIHC to carry out some cost control methods. After implementation of the co-sufficiency project in the public health sector, the medical services bill has included more details to compensate for service-related costs. The insurance carriers have spent more time concerned with the assessment of bills. Other measures for health insurance cost control have limited the utilisation of health care services. For example, one such policy limits the coverage of the villagers, the needy and the self-employed to public hospital services. To reduce the burden on prescriptions, the NHIHC does not include 19 commonly used medicines (like vitamins) in the health insurance benefits package (NHIHC, 1999).

Limiting the price rise of medical services in order to contain costs has been applied through the DRG tariffs. In this programme, the global tariffs – as average costs for an inpatient treatment courses – are applied for about 60 common surgical services (Russel et al., 1998), and it is going to expand soon to 100 cases. Another method that has been applied in recent years to contain costs is by increasing the percentage of coinsurance for outpatient health services. The outpatient coinsurance increased from 25 per cent of costs in 1999 to 30 per cent at present. In addition, people continue to be charged the difference in price between the public and private medical services when they use the private services (NHIHC, 2001).

There are several other issues that relate to cost containment in Iranian national health insurance and that merit consideration. For example, at present, health insurance carriers have no role in the evaluation of hospitals and medical clinics. Other issues that need to be considered refer to the health market and the role of insurance companies in this market. When the insurance carriers are obligated to cover almost all medical services which exist in the country, they should have a significant role in adopting new services and any changes in the medical services that affect the economy of health care. In practice, however, there is no evidence that they do exert an influence on the health market, its structure or performance.

Conclusion

In developing countries, health insurance is being introduced as an alternative or additional approach of health care financing (alongside public finances, user charges, public/private partnership arrangements and others) to ease the proportionate decline of government funding for health care, due to economic transitions in these countries. Yet, some individuals believe that the current characteristics of most transitional economies suggest that a model of social insurance will, if operating on its own, fail to provide comprehensive cover (Ensor, 1999).

Concerning the results so far in the implementation of the NHI in Iran, can it be said that the NHI programme chosen in 1994 has been an effective alternative or complement to public financing? In other words, should Iran as a low-middle income country have adopted national health insurance as its sole source of funding? The most important lesson from some Asian countries which have achieved success with the implementation of NHI (such as Japan, South Korea and Singapore),, is that they implemented the NHI programme when they had relatively high levels of income, they were largely urbanised, and they had large wage sectors relative to the informal sectors such as villagers and self-employed (Gertler, 1998).

Although Iran was in a relatively high level of economic growth at the beginning of the 1990s, the economic situation changed in the following years. Growth of the real GDP slowed down from 1997 to 2000 by about 30 per cent (IMF, 2000). In fact, wealthy countries that adopted universal health insurance, with relatively small proportions of their national income financing the health care system, had to manage increasing inflation in the cost of medical care in the period following the implementation of NHI. The economy of Iran was at a standstill after the implementation of national health insurance; and, at the same time, the cost of medical care increased. Consequently, the insurance carriers, who are highly dependent on the government, have encountered a critical situation: faced with serious budget insufficiency and long-term delay in reimbursing medical care services.

The social conditions at the time of NHI implementation, was another matter of great concern. Much of the population was living under the poverty line, and a high proportion of people lived in rural areas. The proportion of the wage sector was relatively low. The government took enormous roles in all aspects of the national health insurance, particularly in financing the schemes. These conditions affected the initial design of the NHI.

Concerning the socioeconomic situation during 1995–2000, with hindsight it seems that Iran might have been more successful in its implementation of the NHI programme if had it waited for a more appropriate time i.e. when the social composition was improved and the economic situation was more stable. Further, a higher level of effectiveness and efficacy of the programme might have been reached had the socio-economic conditions been conducive.

Of course, it does not mean that the significant achievements of the programme can be overlooked. Obviously, Iran is still yet in the early stages of the NHI programme, and needs to analyse and evaluate the progress of the programme to answer the questions above. Nevertheless, as with other national projects, the NHI is currently faced with several challenges, ranging from managing the existing issues to improving the NHI system overall. Recommendations suggested to improve the system, include:

- developing national health insurance (NHI) arrangements further, on the basis of equity and access of population to health services, as resources allow;
- decentralising NHI and reducing the state burden on health financing and utilisation;
- developing private medical services and mobilising community participation to guarantee sustainability of the NHI;
- empowering cost control policies, by granting health insurance carriers' the authority to audit and evaluate medical services and giving them enhanced roles in the health market; and,
- by promoting NHI information systems and research studies to develop the management performance of national health insurance.

Acknowledgements

The author gratefully thanks Professor K. Lee, the Director of the Centre for Health Planning and Management of Keele University, UK, for his guidance and support. The author would like to acknowledge the Iranian Ministry of Health, particularly the NHI High Council members and secretariat, for their cooperation and support.

References

Bogg, L., Hengjin, D., Keli, W., Wenwei, C. and Diwan, V. (1996), 'The Cost of Coverage: Rural Health Insurance in China', *Health Policy and Planning*, 11 (3), pp. 238–52.

Ensor, T. (1999), 'Developing Health Insurance in Transitional Asia', *Social Science and Medicine*, 48, pp. 871–9.

Gertler, P.J. (1998), 'On the Road to Social Health Insurance: The Asian Experience', *World Development*, 26 (4), pp. 717–32.

IMF (2000), 'Islamic Republic of Iran: Statistical Appendix', Report. No. 99/37.

Iranian Secretary of NHIHC (2001), 'Annual Report', Ministry of Health, Treatment and Medical Training of Iran.

MSIO (1997), The Public Medical Service Insurance Act and Articles of Association of Medical Service Insurance Organization,Tehran.

MSIO (1998), *MSIO Annual Report*, MSIO, Tehran.

MSIO (2000), *MSIO Annual Report*, MSIO, Tehran.

NHIHC (2001), 'The Collection of the NHIHC Approvals', Ministry of Health, Treatment and Medical Training of Iran.

NHIHC (2001), 'The Collection of the Council of Iranian Ministers' Approvals', Ministry of Health, Treatment and Medical Training of Iran.

Russel, M.(2001), 'National Health Insurance: Theory and Reality in Developing Countries – A Case Study of the Islamic Republic of Iran', mimeo, Keele University.

Russel, M. et al. (1998), 'Study of Accounting Global Medical Tariffs for 100 Common Surgical Operations', Secretariat of National Health Insurance Council, Iran.

SCI (1998), Population Report, http://www.sci.com/htp/parto.

SSPTW (1999), http://www.ssa.gov/statistics/ssptw99.

UNDP(1998), *Human Development Report*, Oxford: Oxford University Press.

World Bank (1999), 'Iran – Second Primary Health Care and Nutrition Project', Report No. PID8574, Washington DC.

WHO (1997), 'Visit to Iran', *RCGP International Newsletter*, http://www.rcgp.org.uk/rcgp/international/newsletters/jun97/who.asp.

WHO (2000), *The World Health Report 2000: Health System Improving Performance*, Geneva WHO.

SECTION IV
ORGANISING INNOVATION

Improving the Operation of Operating Theatres: Data Triangulation, Change Management and Action Research in Operating Theatres

R.J. Boaden and J. Bamford

Introduction

This chapter describes the results of some empirical work involving the reorganisation of operating theatre management in a large teaching hospital. The theatre suite consists of ten operating theatres, along with two further operating theatres in a newly built bespoke Day Surgery Unit. The theatre suite accommodates all types of surgery and maintains a 24-hour emergency theatre. The theoretical context for this work is both the management of change literature and also the literature on quality improvement and performance measurement. The conclusions demonstrate that both quantitative and qualitative information are important in identifying causes of delay and that measuring performance is multi-faceted and influenced by a wide range of factors.

Objective

The objective of the empirical work was to identify the major causes of delay in operating theatre schedules, and to explore how these causes could be verified. In particular, the work focused on delays to the start of these schedules, and aimed to develop methods to address some of these, as well as developing a method for measuring performance.

Background

The empirical work reported in this chapter forms part of a larger project focusing on the re-engineering of both business and information systems in the operating theatres at Manchester Royal Infirmary. This work is funded by the Teaching Company Directorate (http://www.tcsonline.org.uk) as a TCS Programme and has already yielded significant benefits for the organisation. It is also informally linked with a national project on improving theatre operation, funded by the Modernisation Agency (www.modernnhs.nhs.uk) and the results of both studies will be compared in future work. The research is also part of an ongoing and developing partnership between the Health Organisations Research Centre, Manchester School of Management, UMIST and Central Manchester and Manchester Children's University Hospitals NHS Trust.

Methodology

In order to obtain the clearest picture regarding the nature of the causes for delay it was decided to collect both qualitative and quantitative information (Gill and Johnson, 1997). The overall methodology used could be termed action research: 'generating knowledge about a social system while, at the same time, attempting to change it' (Meyer, 2001, p. 173). Three methods were used:

- process mapping (Martin and Henderson, 2001) – this was used to identify bottlenecks and inefficiencies in the processes carried out within the theatres (from the point at which the theatre list commences and the patient is summoned for treatment). The data from which to develop the process maps was gathered from interviews with a range of staff involved at all stages of the process; both clinical and administrative, as well as any available documentation and procedures. Because the main researcher was based full-time in the department concerned he was also able to use informal methods of data gathering, for example, brief conversations to clarify particular points, as well as formal interviews;
- root cause analysis (Slack et al., 2001) – this was used to identify the multiple causes of any problems discovered. Data for this was also gathered through interviews and four focus groups composed of a variety of clinical staff;
- information flow mapping – this was used to enable more efficient scheduling of operations and to identify problems. The data for this was

gathered using the same methods as that used to gather data for the process maps, and at the same time.

Results

Perception of the reasons for delay in the operating theatres had been included in interviews carried out as part of an earlier study at the hospital (Nuttall, 1999). The reasons for delay from this study were combined with new qualitative data collected during the course of a series of informal interviews structured around a process-mapping exercise. Interviewees in each study were asked to list all the causes of delay in the running of an operating theatre schedule and to give their opinion as to which had the biggest impact. Figure 15.1 shows those reasons for delay most often identified as having the largest impact.

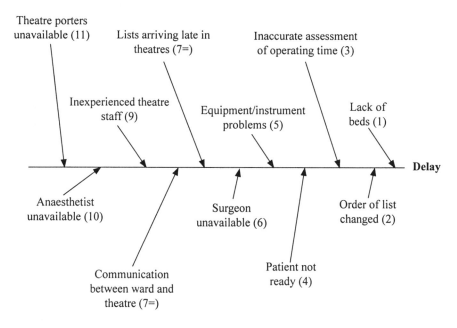

Figure 15.1   Reasons for delay in starting theatre sessions – what people said

Note: numbers in brackets indicate the relative importance, in terms of the number of times these reasons were mentioned by interviewees, with the most frequently mentioned being no. 1.

The process maps that were created were used as part of an information flow analysis to identify the key controls of the system and where the key performance information could be collected. With this knowledge a computerised management information system (MIS) was developed to provide accurate, historical key performance indicators (KPIs) for activity in each of the 12 operating theatres in the directorate. This MIS, for the first time, was able to accurately report reasons for the delays within the operating theatres, and the amount of operating time that has been lost as a result. The data put into the system was obtained from the paper records kept at each operation and theatre session. Although this data had been collected manually for some time, it was not normally input into a computer system (the main hospital IT systems did not require such a level of detail) and so analysis of the data was both time-consuming and likely to be only carried out on request, rather than routinely. The most common causes of delays identified for the historic data that was put onto the MIS have been summarised in Figure 15.2.

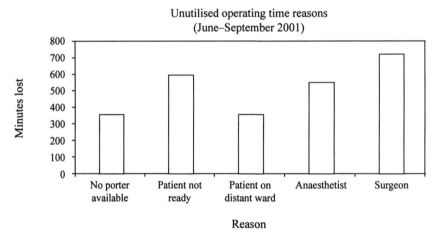

Figure 15.2   Reasons for delay in starting theatre sessions – what the MIS said

The qualitative data collected in the two sets of interviews painted a rather confusing picture. Other than a lack of surgical beds, a common problem through the entire Trust, being the most important cause of delay, little other agreement could be found. The patient not being ready on time and the order of the operating list being changed both would appear to also be important. However, no agreement as to the ranking of these and the other causes of delay could be drawn from these two sets of opinions.

The reasons for the discrepancies in these two sets of data are not known. However the interviews took place over two years apart and a list of the staff interviewed in the earlier study was unavailable when planning the second interviews. It is possible that if such a list had been used to ensure that same people had been interviewed on both occasions the results would have been more comparable. However, as the results of this opinion data are broadly in line with that reported in other studies they have been summarised together for ease of comparison with the quantitative information discussed below (Buchanan and Wilson, 1996).

A comparison between the opinion data gathered from the interviews and the quantitative data gathered from the MIS is given in Figure 15.3.

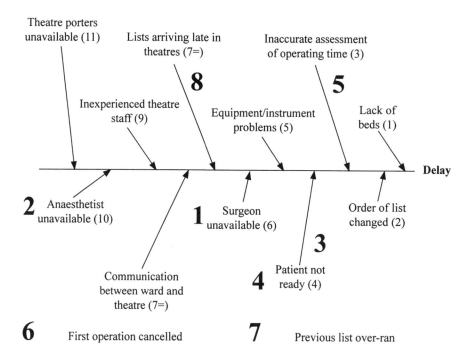

Figure 15.3   Comparison between interview and MIS data

The major causes for delay identified by the MIS differ greatly from those identified in both sets of interviews. The top two reasons are both people related, the surgeon and anaesthetist being delayed; with the lack of surgical beds a lesser issue. This is possibly due to the limitations of the MIS in that it records only the activity that takes place within the operating theatre department; many patients have their operation cancelled before the operating list is seen in theatre. This will not be recorded by the MIS, but is something that people may remember as a reason for delay. This, along with the Trust wide problems with bed availability, help to explain why it is ranked as the most important reason in the qualitative information. However, overall the issues are around 'people' related factors.

Discussion

The differences in the results from the qualitative and quantitative data lead to the debate of which is the more accurate. However, what needs to be considered is the limitations of the two methods of data collection.

Although during the interviews total confidentiality was guaranteed, a marked reluctance to place blame on individuals and groups of staff (particularly senior clinical staff) was observed. This may explain why resource (lack of beds, equipment problems ...) and communication (changes to the order of lists, lists arriving late in theatre ...) issues were cited as frequently as they were.

In contrast the MIS, due to the way the information was collected (by receptionists, not frontline clinical staff), and when it was collected (as each delay occurred), seems to have avoided this issue of an unwillingness to blame groups or individuals. Possibly this is due to the fact that as no-one was being singled out for interview, staff felt more secure that there would be no retaliation for any comments they have made, or that as the data is being collected continuously a truer picture may emerge.

As useful and comprehensive as the KPIs and delay reasons provided by the MIS are, they do not provide a complete picture. If delays caused by the anaesthetist arriving late are considered as an example, all the MIS indicates is that this is one of the most common reasons for delays in theatre. It does not offer any explanation as to the reasons behind the delay. There are a multitude of reasons why an anaesthetist could be delayed: a ward round running late, responding to a request for a visit by a worried patient, or other apparently conflicting clinical responsibilities. As most of these factors are beyond the control of the theatre management, further investigation into them was decided to be unnecessary at this stage, since change could not be effected. However, this limitation needs to be considered when deciding which issues to focus any change effort on.

Deciding What to Change

There are many difficulties associated with studying the activities of an operating theatre. Not least of which are: the complexity of the overall system, and the 'them and us' culture that seems to exists between the operating theatres and other areas of the hospital (McAleer et al., 1995; Drife and Johnston, 1995).

In order to overcome these difficulties two further questions were considered by the researchers: 1) what actually needs changing; and 2) what is it possible to change?

To a large extent much of the first question has already been discussed. However, what needs to be considered is that just because an issue has been identified as causing a delay, it does not automatically follow that this issue must be investigated and a change programme initiated.

For example, to decree that the order of the operating list could not be changed once the theatres had received it would remove much of the flexibility that is needed to deal with issues such as the variability of the patient's condition. When the need to accommodate patients who require emergency surgery is added to this picture, it could even be argued that to remove the flexibility inherent in the existing system will result in more delays and cancelled operations.

The scope of any proposed changed also needed to be decided. As the reorganisation effort is currently solely focused within the boundary of the operating theatres, wider issues such as bed management cannot be addressed. However, it was decided after consultation with key stakeholders that issues focusing around communication would be looked into, and where, possible action taken.

The second question – 'what is it possible to change?' – could actually be rephrased as – What can easily be changed? Indeed as the reorganisation was viewed as a series of incremental changes it was important to focus initially on issues that would not have a large impact on the front end operation, that is, the performance of the operation itself.

To assist with this decision a summarised cause and effect diagram, shown in Figure 15.4, was produced. This groups the delay reasons into four broad categories. This tool was used to help decide which issue to focus upon.

The decision was made to focus upon people and communication factors as these contained the main reasons that caused most delay. A further reason for choosing the people factors to focus upon was that this group included the issue of theatre porters being available. This is one of the few issues that is

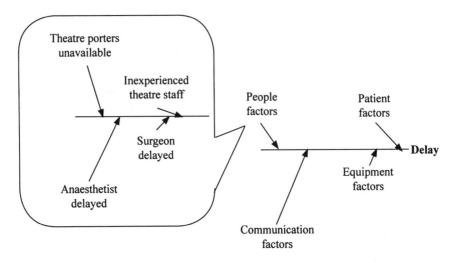

Figure 15.4   Summary of reasons for delay

wholly under control of the theatres directorate, and as such the investigation and any necessary adjustments could be carried out outside the arena of inter-directorate politics. The other factors were also considered and some action taken: equipment factors were addressed by re-engineering of the theatre stores and purchasing processes and the reorganisation of roles and responsibilities. The investigation of, and action on, patient factors is the focus of the next stage of the research.

Examples of Change Programmes Initiated

Theatre Porters

The first issue chosen for further investigation was the availability of theatre porters. The investigation included shadowing porters, discussing their role both with them and other members of theatre staff and management, and recording their availability at key times. The findings indicated that, for the present level of demand, there is a sufficient establishment of porters. Occasionally, at key times, a delay was caused due to all the porters being busy. It was decided that this was acceptable, as there was a surplus of availability during the slower times.

    This investigation was viewed as successful even though it did not result in a change programme. The results of the findings were communicated to the staff, who were told the reasons for the investigation and given the opportunity to contribute with any further improvement ideas.

Weekly Theatre Utilisation Meetings

Whilst it had been agreed to focus effort upon the people factors, it was felt that several of the communication factors could be addressed at the same time. A weekly theatre utilisation meeting was instigated. This meeting, which brought together Surgical Specialty Managers, Bed Managers, the Anaesthetic Rotamaster and the theatre management, has a broad remit: discuss proposed theatre activity up to two weeks in advance, discuss any issues arising from the previous weeks theatre activity, where possible utilise any cancelled theatre sessions, agree late start or late finishes to operating lists, discuss bed availability, identify unusual equipment requirements, discuss the actual content of each proposed operating list, and so on.

These utilisation meetings have now become an accepted part of the weekly management activity. There has been little resistance to their implementation, although there was initially very poor attendance by several groups of non-theatre staff. This issue has now been addressed by the gradual diffusion of the benefits achieved through these meetings. They are helping to ensure the smooth running of the lists and have had the effect of indirectly starting to solve issues that are not directly under the control of the operating theatres, such as the content of theatre lists.

This success seems to be in direct contradiction with the generally held belief that conflicts within the NHS are very difficult to resolve (Drife and Johnston, 1995). This new method of communication is viewed as one of the major contributing factors to the, on average, 8 per cent reduction in cancelled operating lists over the period October to December 2001 when compared with the period October to December 2000. Although it can be argued that what is needed in the NHS is less meetings, this example demonstrate the effectiveness of targeted meetings, with a clear objective, relevant information available and a remit to take action as required.

MIS

The MIS is being developed to have a key role in addressing some of the key causes of delay, in particular the people factors. Information regarding delays in theatre will, for the first time, be able to be fed back to managers and individuals. The plan is for KPIs, which will include delay information, to be reported to the theatre staff, and each individual surgeon and anaesthetist regarding the their theatre sessions. KPIs will also be reported to the managers of the surgical specialities and hopefully this information will be utilised as part of the consultant appraisal process. More general, summary information will be reported to the Theatre Users Group, Theatre Managers Group, and the Trust board. All parties involved have agreed to this.

It is hoped that peer pressure will bring about a marked improvement in the two key causes of delay, surgeon or anaesthetist being delayed. However, if corrective action is not voluntarily taken on an individual basis, then a more formalised approach may be used, This may be included as part of the annual appraisal process, or as part of a more regular performance review system.

Conclusions

Don't Trust what People Say?

The key to understanding and measuring the causes for delay, in this instance, has been the development and maintenance of a Management Information System. Without accurate, timely and focused information it was impossible to gain a true picture of the causes and reasons for delay in the running of an operating schedule. Anecdotal, qualitative, data often paints a distorted picture as individuals remember those reasons that most affect them, not those reasons which actually most affected the smooth running of the operating schedule. However, asking for the views of individuals and investigating them is still important in effective change (Burnes, 2000) and should arguably never be discarded in favour of only quantitative data. It is not a question of not trusting what people say, but being able to put it in context and triangulate it with other data sources: 'the researcher's role ... is not "to adjudicate between participants' competing versions" (Dingwall, 1981) but to understand "the situated work that they do" (Silverman, 1985)' (Fulop et al., 2001, p. 11).

Too much Data but not Enough Information?

It is important to recognise the limits inherent in any department based information system. It can only collect information regarding the activities of that particular department, and cannot be used to get an accurate representation of the 'big picture'. This weakness is somewhat outweighed by having the facts and figures 'at your fingertips' when presenting an argument for a change programme. The vast range of methods by which data is collected and stored within the NHS and the relative lack of IT infrastructure across the NHS (Department of Health, 2002) means that developing systems that analyse data and produce useful information is a key step in effective change.

Is Communication the Real Issue?

The change programmes that have been instigated although supposedly aimed at reducing the people factors have in fact been mainly communication exercises. In one case arranging a forum for open and honest discussion of theatre related issues, and in the other communicating the KPIs generated by the MIS. Indeed, it is foreseen that most of the other outstanding delay reasons can be reduced somewhat through proper communication of the effects of the delays, or simply through more effective communication. That is not to say that a comprehensive, effective, communication system would be the solution to all the outstanding issues, but at the very least all the affected parties would be aware of the problems and able to consider how best to tackle them. This is well supported by other evidence: 'People need information; if they are not given it, they will create it for themselves' (Upton and Brooks, 1995, p. 35).

Where is the Whole Systems Approach?

This research, like much of the other work going on across the NHS under the banner of 'modernisation', is focused on one part of a much larger system. To attempt to effect whole systems change (Harrison, 2001) is beyond the scope of this project, or others like it, and it could be argued that it would not be achievable. However, this research demonstrate the limitations of this type of approach – some of the key reasons for delay (delay in arrival of senior clinicians) are often due to factors outside the theatres, and until these are also addressed, the overall performance of the theatres cannot be improved beyond a certain point.

Are the Results Generalisable?

One test of research validity is the generalisability of results, although it is acknowledged that this is different in action research (Meyer, 2002). The results in this chapter are inevitably limited by the small sample size and lack of detailed quantitative analysis, but this is only a key issue if a purely positivistic view of research methodology is taken. The research activity reported in this chapter is not dissimilar to much of the modernisation activity currently taking place in the NHS. However, there does not seem currently to be very much research evidence to support this, although some national initiatives are now beginning to fund work in this area (Service Delivery Organisation, 2002). The key conclusions from this chapter centre on the importance of triangulation of research data (Patton, 1987) not only to ensure data validity and to compensate for weaknesses in the various types of methodology used, but also where the evidence is to be used as the basis for a change programme. In order for change to be successful, most authors (Iles and Sutherland, 2001), and many practitioners (for example, CHI) agree that staff involvement is crucial and data triangulation is one way to achieve this.

Acknowledgements

The authors would like to acknowledge the help and support of all the theatre staff at MRI, and in particular the Theatres Manager, Heather Bonnebaigt, as well as Jill Alexander who initiated the project.

References

Buchanan, D. and Wilson, B. (1996), 'Re-engineering Operating Theatres: The Perspective Assessed', *Journal of Management in Medicine*, 10 (4), pp. 57–74.

Burnes, B. (2000), *Managing Change*, Harlow: Financial Times/Prentice Hall.

Department of Health (2002), *Delivering the NHS Plan*, London: Department of Health.

Dingwall, R. (1981),'The Ethnomethodoligcal Movement', in G. Payne, J. Dingwall, J. Payne and M. Carter (eds), *Sociology and Social Research*, London: Croom Helm.

Drife, J. and Johnston, I. (1995), 'Management for Doctors: Handling the Conflicting Cultures in the NHS', *British Medical Journal*, 310, pp. 1054–6.

Fulop, N., Allen, P., Clarke, A. and Black, N. (2001), 'Issues in Studying the Organisation and Delivery of Health Services', in N. Fulop, P. Allen, A. Clarke and N. Black (2001) (eds), *Studying the Organisation and Delivery of Health Services: Research Methods*, London: Routledge.

Gill, J. and Johnson, P. (1997), *Research Methods for Managers*, London: Paul Chapman Publishing.

Harrison, A. (2001), *Making the Right Connections: The Design and Management of Health Care Delivery*, London: Kings Fund.

Iles, V. and Sutherland, K. (2001), *Organisational Change*, London: National Co-ordinating Centre for NHS Service Delivery and Organisation R&D.

Martin, V. and Henderson, E. (2001), *Managing in Health and Social Care*, London: Routledge/ Open University Business School.

McAleer, W., Turner, J. Lismore, D. and Naqvi, I. (1995), 'Simulation of a Hospital's Theatre Suite', *Journal of Management in Medicine*, 9 (5), pp. 14–26.

Meyer, J. (2001), 'Action Research', in N. Fulop, P. Allen, A. Clarke and N. Black (2001) (eds), *Studying the Organisation and Delivery of Health Services: Research Methods*, London: Routledge.

Nuttall, P. (1999), 'Hospital Operating Theatre Delay; Causes, Effects and Potential Solutions', MSc thesis, University of Manchester Institute of Science and Technology, Manchester.

Patton, M.Q. (1987), *How to use Qualitative Methods in Evaluation*, Newbury Park, CA: Sage.

Service Delivery Organisation (SDO) (2002), http://www.sdo.lshtm.ac.uk, accessed on 26 April 2002.

Silverman, D. (1985), *Qualitative Method and Sociology*, Aldershot: Gower.

Slack, N., Chambers, S. and Johnston, R. (2001), *Operations Management*, 3rd edn, Harlow: Financial Times/Prentice Hall.

Upton, T. and Brooks, B. (1995), *Managing Change in the NHS*, Buckingham: Open University Press.

Chapter 16

Job Satisfaction and the Modernisation Project: A Longitudinal Study of Two NHS Acute Trusts

Colin Fisher, Lynette Harris, Susan Kirk, John Leopold and
Yvonne Leverment

Introduction

The underlying theme of this chapter is the contradictions between the 'best fit' approach to the modernisation project that the government is proposing for the National Health Service (NHS) and the findings of recent Chartered Institute of Personnel and Development (CIPD) research which calls for a more tailored approach to introducing human resources (HR) practices to bring about improved work performance. In particular we explore the relationship between the job satisfaction perceptions of staff within the NHS and performance.

The intention to modernise the NHS was set out in the *NHS Plan* in July 2000 stating that the NHS 'is a 1940s system operating in the twenty-first century' (Department of Health, 2000a). The basis of the modernisation project is an inferred cycle of cause and effect with the assertion that there is a correlation between levels of staffs' job satisfaction and their performance at work. Thus it is seen as critical that senior management seek to improve job satisfaction in the belief that this will in turn lead to improved work performance resulting in the achievement of the modernisation objectives. This, it is asserted by the government, can be realised by focusing on seven key areas.

The findings reported in this chapter are based on a research study into staff's perceptions of job satisfaction in two NHS Hospital Trusts. They suggest that the actual state of employees' perceptions of job satisfaction with respect to these seven aspects may contradict the managerial imperatives of the modernisation project.

Moreover, it is argued that the adoption of a 'one size fits all' strategy is overly simplistic in that it overlooks differences in local contexts and cultures that may benefit from a more flexible approach within different parts of the Service.

The Modernisation Imperatives

The broad claim essayed in the introduction, that the government sees improvements in job satisfaction, as part of the imperative of modernisation needs to be justified. In September 1998 the NHS's first human resources framework, 'Working Together: Securing a Quality Workforce for the NHS' emphasised the importance of involving staff in the planning and delivery of local services. One key strategic aim introduced in this document stressed the need to:

> Ensure that people who work in the NHS are able to make the best possible contribution, individually and collectively, to improving health and patient care (Department of Health, 1998, p. 5).

The document recognised a link between quality service delivery and quality management of staff. In particular it claimed there was research evidence from within the NHS that poor staff management, amongst other things, exacerbated low morale, work-based stress and exhaustion, and that organisations following 'progressive HR policies' were more efficient and productive (Department of Health, 1998, §2.3).

Further initiatives to achieve the 'next generation of health care professionals' to modernise the Service, were implemented. The Improving Working Lives (IWL) campaign and a review of the workforce planning were launched in 1999. The former local modernisation reviews were to be the mechanism for improving services with the aim that, by April 2001, all Trusts would have achieved at least the first stage of IWL accreditation (NHS Executive, 2000). The IWL standard includes Trusts having a range of policies in place that enable staff to manage a healthy balance between work and their commitments outside work, development and training opportunities, and valuing and supporting staff according to the contribution they make to patient care.

The workforce planning review team was tasked with identifying the 'opportunities and barriers which currently exist for effective and efficient workforce planning' across all roles and responsibilities at all levels within the NHS and the NHS Executive looking at staff as 'teams of people rather than as different professional tribes' (Department of Health, 2000b, p. 9).

Inter alia, this report desired that NHS Trusts, 'in developing strategies for continuing professional development, should gear their thinking and resourcing to supporting greater career flexibility and development of additional skills for staff '(ibid., p. 35). These are themes to which we shall return.

The voice of NHS staff is heard in the 'Report of the NHS Taskforce on Staff Involvement' (Department of Health, 1999b, pp. 3, 4), in which the authors, all practising NHS employees, argue:

> that employers in the NHS who involve their staff in decisions, planning and policy making – improve patient care though better service delivery, manage change more effectively, and have a healthier, better motivated workforce and reduces a staff turnover.

The link between staff attitudes, motivation and performance is again asserted.

The resource pack for modernisation reviews (Department of Health, 2001) included a template press release that local managers in Trusts and authorities could use to inform their staff, via in-house newsletters, of the importance of these reviews. One senior NHS manager was quoted in this press release as saying 'staff need to view this (review process) in a positive light and start thinking about how they deliver services now and how they can be re-designed'.

There is a hint in this quotation of what Oakes et al. (1998, p. 271), following Bourdieu, called 'symbolic violence'. This is a process of excluding some ideas and including others in an agent's mind by the use of subtle and hidden force, of which the agent is unaware. Government ministers, on the other hand, perhaps aware of the possibility of staff obtaining this coercive impression, have carefully avoided claiming a direct connection between job satisfaction and improvement in the quality of services to patients. The then health minister John Denman, for example (Department of Health, 1999a) talked of job satisfaction as a right rather than as a lever to bring about modernisation and improvement, thus avoiding the implication that employees need to be enticed to accept reform. Initiatives such as the introduction of 'NHS Performance Ratings' rolled out in acute hospital Trusts in 2000/2001, may also be viewed as seeking to force the pace of change with the 'carrot' of 'more rewards for good performance' and the 'stick' of 'more support to sort out poor performance' (Department of Health, 2000a).

The government was clearly determined that Trusts should deliver job satisfaction as a lever to bring about modernisation. An item in the action plan in 'Working Together', requiring Trusts to survey staff satisfaction and establish a baseline against which future progress could be assessed, was the trigger for the empirical work which this chapter reports. The senior managers of Trusts are obliged to respond to ministerial wishes. As Pollitt and Bouckaert (2000, p. 18) pointed out once the rhetoric of managerial improvement, known in the UK as modernisation, 'has gained hold, it can become, like other reform movements, a 'community of discourse' with its own logic, vocabulary and internal momentum'.

Confirmation of the general approach taken by the government came in *Reforming our Public Services* (Office of Public Service Reform, 2002) launched by the Prime Minister in March 2002. In this document it was asserted that 'successful public services have flexible employment and working practices to be able to respond quickly to the rapidly changing world' (p. 18). More specifically it was claimed (p. 21) that this meant that staff must:

- be *recognised* for their contribution;
- be *rewarded fairly*, but for their *individual contribution* and performance;
- have more *flexible systems of pay and working*;
- feel *valued* at work by being treated fairly;
- have managers who are capable of *tackling poor performance*;
- be *supported by high quality training and development*;
- represented by *trade unions* who know that the future is about *partnership*.

Each of the seven italicised areas are covered in our survey which gives us an opportunity to examine the extent to which staff in two large city NHS Trusts believe that these features are applied in practice. The experience of these trusts will give some indication of the extent of the problem that the government still has to address in order to achieve the conditions in which its aspirations may be met.

A Link between Job Satisfaction and Performance?

The premise, which underpins the government's modernisation project within the NHS, is that a link exists between job satisfaction, improving performance and the realisation of the aims of the *NHS Plan*. While intuitively the existence of positive feelings associated with the rewarding aspects of a job (Legge and Mumford, 1978, p. 3) might be believed to lead to improved work performance, this is not conclusively borne out by research findings. Most studies into the statistical connection between job satisfaction and job performance indicate a positive, but low, correlation. Iaffaldano and Muchinsky (1985), who reviewed a range of these studies, found an average correlation coefficient of only 0.17. Researchers generally concluded that changes in performance were not much affected by job satisfaction.

Many of these studies were done in the 1960s and 1970s and more recent work has indicated that the lack of a linear relationship does not mean there is no relationship between the two variables. Katzell et al. (1992, pp. 210–12) argued that both job performance and job satisfaction were determined by a large number of variables and that the lack of any linear relationship did not mean that there were not important relationships between them that were moderated by other factors. They tested this proposal using a path analysis technique and argued that intervening factors (such as goal setting and job involvement) create indirect causal links between job satisfaction and performance. Somers et al. (2001) used a different technique (neural nets) but also found non-linear relationships between work attitudes and job performance. Their study was conducted using American staff nurses as respondents. They concluded that the relationship between satisfaction and performance might be higher than previously claimed but only under optimal conditions, when all the other factors impinging on performance were right.

On the other hand, the seven prerequisites which Tony Blair asserts are required to ensure that public services are successful, are key to the establishment and maintenance of a positive psychological contract at work. In fact, the development of a positive psychological contract is where managers should start. The psychological or implicit contract can be defined as:

> The tacit agreement between an employer and the employee about what the employee will 'put in' to the job and the rewards and benefits for which this will be exchanged (Watson, 1995, p. 139).

The psychological contract is central in defining the nature of the employment relationship that develops between employers and employees. It impacts upon both parties' expectations of the work experience and influences how they both perceive and prioritise their work and balance this with their interests outside the work setting.

Patterson et al.'s (1997) study observed a positive relationship between employee attitudes, organisational culture, human resources management (HRM) practices and company performance and concluded that employee commitment and a satisfied workforce are fundamental to improving performance. This connection, which mirrors those in the Prime Minister's pamphlet and is a bolder statement of the more tentative findings from earlier research reviewed above, was re-emphasised by the CIPD who claimed that 'good people practices generate greater satisfaction, satisfaction yields greater motivation, which in turn is reflected in better performance' (CIPD, 2001, p. 11).

Yet the CIPD went on to argue that despite relevant bundles of human resource practices:

> they will not deliver the goods if the psychological contract is weak. Putting it positively, the stronger the employees' faith in the company's willingness to live up to their promises, the greater the satisfaction and the positive spillover into performance are likely to be (ibid.).

However, what is important is the approach adopted to achieve effective personnel and development strategies. CIPD research studies (CIPD, 2002) describe three main approaches: the 'best practice' approach, which posits a 'universal model' of HRM suitable for all; the 'best fit' or contingency approach which takes the opposite stance, that is the most appropriate approach depends on contingent factors, for example, context and culture; and; the 'configurational' approach which argues the need to achieve a horizontal or internal fit. This strategy is realised by 'bundling' personnel and development practices together as described by MacDuffie (1995, p. 5):

> implicit in the notion of a 'bundle' is the idea that practices within it are interrelated and internally consistent, and that 'more is better' with respect to the impact on performance, because of the overlapping and mutually reinforcing effect of multiple practices.

So ad hoc or 'faddish' practices are viewed as detrimental to the achievement of a coherent HR strategy.

The seven prerequisites for modernisation identified by the government are redolent of the 'best fit' model in that they appear to prescribe a universal remedy for the NHS. This is in opposition to a more tailored approach as argued for in the latest research which calls for organisations to bundle together HR practices which are both mutually supporting and that are contingent with that organisation's particular circumstances.

Notwithstanding the fact that the rationale for the government's 'best fit' approach is clearly questionable in the light of recent research findings, this chapter seeks to measure employee attitudes within two NHS hospitals to ascertain to what extent there is evidence that the imperatives which the government claim are essential to achieving the desired modernisation of the Service are being met in practice.

Research Methods

The empirical basis of the chapter is derived from two questionnaire surveys of job satisfaction in two NHS Trust hospitals conducted two years apart. The questionnaire was designed around two dimensions; the five 'C's and the three 'P's. The five 'C's are a modification of the five contracts defined by Gowler (Legge and Mumford, 1978) as the dimensions of the quality of working life. The three 'P's (priority, policy and practice) concern staff's perceptions of the importance of job satisfaction and their employer' intentions and subsequent actions with regard to job satisfaction.

Gowler suggested that the contracts could be related to each other as shown in Figure 16.1. The values contract is an overarching one. It concerns the degree of congruence between the staff's values and those espoused by the organisation. The other four contracts look at particular aspects of the experience of working in the organisation:

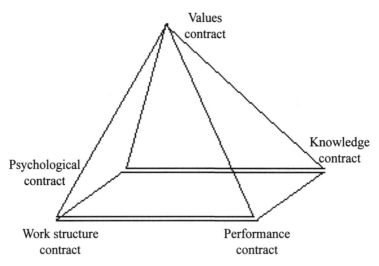

Figure 16.1   The five dimensions on which the survey questionnaire is based

Source: Gowler in Legge and Mumford (1978).

- the knowledge contract relates to the way in which the organisation values and utilises the knowledge and skills of staff and how it facilitates their learning;
- the performance contract concerns the way in which staffs' work is managed and how they are rewarded;
- the psychological contract is concerned with the expectations that staff have about how they should be managed and treated (as discussed above);
- the work contract addresses the way in which work processes are organised and structured including such issues as empowerment and job flexibility.

The 'three Ps' questions explore potential gaps between:

- employers' and employees' priorities;
- employees' understanding of employers' priorities; and
- employees' perceptions of employers' actions.

Priority concerns the importance respondents give to the factors that make up each of the contracts. The policy questions are to determine whether employees know which factors it is the Trust's policy or intention to deliver and which factors Trusts are not committed to. The practice questions ask whether employees think the Trusts deliver on the factors.

The questionnaire was used in two district general hospital trusts, General and Infirmary, in the same, large UK city late in 1999 and again in late 2001. Both Trusts obtained an above-average two star rating in the 2000/2001 NHS Performance Ratings. The names used in this chapter are not the actual ones. The questionnaires were sent to *all* the employees of the two Trusts in employment on the survey dates so that those still employed at the time of the second survey would have had the opportunity to complete two questionnaires. Questionnaires were returned by 1,364 staff (28 per cent of the staff) in the Infirmary in 1999, and by 1289 (24 per cent) in 2001. In the General, 1,011 staff (18 per cent) responded in 1999 and 1535 (25 per cent) in 2001.

These response rates, while slightly disappointing, are within the bounds of similar large surveys. Moreover, on checking the achieved sample against the known population, it was discovered that the sample was broadly representative of the population in terms of gender, age, and, ethnicity, but that staff groups with formal educational qualifications were over-represented at the expense of those with fewer, or no, formal educational qualifications. Nonetheless there is no reason to believe that the results that follow are biased in any way that would render them invalid. The 2001 sample is in broadly the same proportions as that achieved in 1999. (See appendix 1 for details of both surveys).

The wider survey revealed a number of strengths and weaknesses in staff perceptions of the way that the two Trusts were being managed, but here we only use data directly relevant to the government's seven criteria. These are *recognition, fair rewards for individual contribution, flexible systems of pay and working, being values at work, dealing with under performance, high quality training and development and a partnership with unions* which The Prime Minister's Office of Public Services Reform claimed are essential conditions to bring about the successful modernisation of the NHS (Office of Public Service Reform, 2002) and which echo earlier NHS documents discussed above.

Expectations and Perceptions of Job Satisfaction: Analysis of Survey Results

In this section the results from both questionnaire surveys are used to assess staff's perceptions of their job satisfaction specifically in relation to the seven factors identified by the government. Linkages to our five contracts are shown in parenthesis. The implications of these findings will be explored in the terms of their potential impact upon the imperatives underpinning the NHS modernisation programme.

Recognition

The first factor concerns the extent to which staff perceive that they are recognised for their contribution. There are numerous ways in which individuals might measure the degree of recognition given to them, for example, through tangible or extrinsic mechanisms that is, pay; promotional opportunities etc. or through psychological or intrinsic means, that is, being treated with care and consideration, receiving appreciation from managers etc. The surveys sought staffs' perceptions regarding both of these dimensions. Thus, staff were asked to evaluate the extent to which they felt that their pay recognises their contribution (*performance contract*) and also, to assess the degree to which their efforts are praised and to what extent they are treated with respect and dignity (*psychological contract*).

In the survey in 1999 staffs' perceptions of the extent to which pay recognised individual contribution were not positive, with 65 per cent of staff in the Infirmary and 47 per cent of staff in the General rating this aspect negatively. In both cases the figures worsened slightly in the second survey with five-percentage point increase in dissatisfaction in the case of the former and a seven-percentage point increase in the case of the latter.

With regard to the amount of praise they receive for their efforts, staff in both Trusts hold a similarly negative view. In the Infirmary, in both surveys, 67 per cent of staff feel that their efforts are *not* praised sufficiently frequently. There is a slight improvement in perceptions amongst staff in the General with regard to this aspect, with a decrease from 72 per cent to 68 per cent of staff feeling that their efforts are *not* praised regularly enough.

In terms of being treated with respect and dignity, results in both surveys give cause for concern, as over half of staff in both Trusts are either negative or neutral in their views of this factor.

Rewarded Fairly

Questions in the *performance contract* section asked staff to consider the extent to which they feel that their pay system is fair and equitable and to what degree it supports team working.

Responses indicate that many staff in both Trusts do not feel that their pay systems are fair and equitable. In the Infirmary, 45 per cent of staff felt negatively about this in both surveys. In the General, the situation had worsened slightly from 47–54 per cent. With regard to staff feeling that pay recognises individual contribution, the picture is quite negative and has become more so since the previous survey. Within the Infirmary, the number of staff feeling negative about this had increased from 55 per cent to 60 per cent and in the General, from 65–68 per cent.

This dissatisfaction with pay and conditions in general was mirrored in a survey reported in IDS Study Plus (Winter, 2001) into staff attitudes within the London Ambulance Service NHS Trust.

Given the increasing emphasis on collaboration and team-working within the NHS (Department of Health, 1999b) it is concerning to report an overall increase in the number of staff in both Trusts reporting that the pay system actually undermines team-working. In 1999, 39 per cent of respondents commented negatively on this in the Infirmary. This figure rose to 42 per cent in 2001. A similar picture emerged in the General with an increase in dissatisfaction from 36 per cent of staff making negative responses in 1999 to 47 per cent in 2001.

This apparent contradiction, where staff paradoxically feel that the pay system at the same time does not reward individual contribution fairly and equitably and undermines teamworking, can be fairly simply explained by reference to equity theory (Adams, 1965). This theory states that people are satisfied or dissatisfied by the extent to which they feel that they are being treated fairly *in comparison to other people*. While staff may feel that in absolute terms their individual efforts are being undervalued in terms of pay, that is, the degree of *external competitiveness* of the pay system, their perceptions of differentials, that is, *internal equity* may be the real cause for concern.

This feeling of inequitable treatment may be further exacerbated by the apparent failure of managers to deal with under-performance within the Trusts. This aspect is explored in further detail below.

Flexible Pay Systems and Ways of Working

Given that current reward systems are largely determined through national mechanisms, asking staff about flexibility of their current arrangements seemed inappropriate. However, in the area of working patterns Trusts have more local discretion so staff were asked to comment on the extent to which the Trust encourages flexible working patterns (*work contract*). An additional question relating to the degree of staff choice over working hours was added to the most recent survey after discussions with management at both Trusts but there is no comparative data from the first survey with which to contrast results.

Although there has been an improvement in staff's perceptions about the availability of flexible working patterns, less than half of those surveyed (42 per cent in the General and 48 per cent in the Infirmary) were positive about this aspect, but in both cases this was an improvement on 1999. Staff working weekdays as opposed to shifts and weekends are more likely to be positive about this issue and part-time staff are more positive than full-time staff. In general a finding from the 2001 survey was that staff who have a choice over their working patterns have more positive scores over a range of measures compared with those who do not.

Feeling Valued and Fair Treatment

As a measure of the degree to which staff feel valued, they were asked to comment on the extent to which the Trust treats staff as if they were the most important assets. In terms of fair treatment, this was translated in two ways; firstly in relation to fairness and equity of pay systems (outlined above) and secondly, in relation to equal opportunities and fair treatment on the grounds of sexism, racism or disability (*values contract*). Previous questions regarding the degree to which staff feel that they are treated with respect and dignity and the extent to which they believe their efforts are praised are also relevant to how valued individuals may feel, however these questions relate to the relationship staff have with their managers as opposed to at a broader Trust level.

There was little change in terms of staffs' perceptions about the degree to which the Trust treats them as the most important asset. In both surveys staff at the two Trusts were decidedly negative about this issue. In the General, 90 per cent of staff were either neutral or negative about this aspect and in the Infirmary, 83 per cent expressed the same views. This mirrors conclusions reached by Guest et al. (2000, p. 6) who state, 'in the majority of organisations people are not viewed by top managers as their most important assets'.

In terms of discrimination and equal opportunities, there is a more positive picture with over 80 per cent of staff in both Trusts feeling that they are treated fairly on the grounds of racism, sexism and disability. However those who classify themselves as an ethnic minority have greater experience of being treated unfairly, especially at Infirmary. In terms of gender, there is little gap in the experiences of men and women, if anything men feel a little more unfairly treated than women.

Tackling Poor Performance

In both surveys, staff were asked to comment specifically on whether or not managers deal with underperformers (*performance contract*).

In both Trusts, perceptions amongst staff have become more negative about the extent to which under-performance is being managed. In the General, from 1999 to 2001 staff perceptions that managers do not tackle this aspect have grown from 56–60 per cent. This picture is mirrored in the Infirmary with negative comments in this respect increasing from 50 per cent to 58 per cent in the most recent survey. As mentioned previously, this perceived failure to deal with under-performers may be seen as a further source of inequity and a cause of dissatisfaction to staff, which may lead to poor team-working and dysfunctional conflict.

Training and Development

Both within the *knowledge* and the *performance contracts* staff were asked questions relating to the support they receive in terms of '*high quality training and development*'. Specifically, staff were asked to comment upon the extent to which they are supported in terms of their professional and wider development needs, are offered opportunities to learn new skills, have developed and maintained a personal development plan, are effectively appraised and receive coaching from their line managers.

Overall, staff with a professional identity were found to be more positive about this aspect than those who were not members of a profession. The results from the General hospital showed a slight improvement from the previous survey, whereas those from the Infirmary indicated a slight deterioration, although neither presents a wholly positive picture. For example, within the General, 60 per cent of staff surveyed made neutral or negative comments in relation to the support that they receive for professional development, just under half feel that Trust does not offer opportunities to learn new skills and over 80 per cent feel that resources are not made available for development opportunities. In addition, 44 per cent of staff feel that they do not have opportunities to stretch their skills and 58 per cent of staff feel that they are given no encouragement to stretch their knowledge and skills.

In terms of the judged effectiveness of the appraisal systems in operation and the degree to which line managers offer coaching, staff were still not positive about these issues. There was a decrease in satisfaction from 40–45 per cent relating to the perceived contribution of performance appraisals to the development process. On the other hand, although there was a three-percentage point improvement in perceptions regarding coaching, 64 per cent of staff still scored this element negatively.

Looking at results from the Infirmary, there is a similarly pessimistic picture. Staffs' perceptions of the following dimensions have worsened slightly since the previous survey; support for continued professional development (from 41 per cent negative to 47 per cent), encouragement to stretch knowledge and skills (from 44 per cent negative to 51 per cent), opportunities to learn new skills (from 28 per cent negative to 35 per cent) and establishing and maintaining a personal development plan (from 58 per cent negative to 61 per cent) Only 6 per cent of staff believe that there is a healthy budget for staff development activities.

In relation to performance appraisals and coaching from line managers, the picture is also a negative one. As with the previous survey, 40 per cent of staff feel that their appraisal has not helped their personal development and 64 per cent stated that their managers spend little or no time coaching them.

The lack of success in terms of performance appraisals is not uncommon in other parts of the NHS. Redman and Wilkinson (2001, p. 89) report on the experience within a Trust in the northeast of England. They observe that the process of linking appraisals to training and development is similarly weak with 12 per cent of staff surveyed asserting that this was not discussed at all. While all respondents stated that their personal development plans did form part of the appraisal discussion, they claimed it to be, 'a relatively unfocused and vague discussion'.

The survey undertaken within the London Ambulance Service NHS Trust (IDS Study Plus, 2001) also highlighted staff concerns over the lack of regular feedback on performance and training and development needs.

In short, the picture in relation to the quality of training and development provided in both hospitals does not project a positive image in terms of achieving the government's stated aims in this regard, not, by implication, realising the NHS modernisation objectives.

However, notwithstanding the degree to which the results of these surveys indicate a robust infrastructure to facilitate the desired changes, it is perhaps of more interest to note the implications for performance as indicated by the recent series of CIPD surveys. Guest et al. (2000) assert the most effective people management practices are 'those concerned with skills acquisition and development'.

Partnerships with Trade Unions

Staff were asked to evaluate the extent to which they perceive that the Trust works well with trade unions/professional associations (*values contract*).

In both Trusts views regarding relationships with trade unions/professional associations remain static. In the General Trust, 28 per cent and in the Infirmary, 30 per cent of respondents believe that improving these relationships is something that the Trusts are actively pursuing. Thus the majority of staff in both Trusts are not positive about the degree to which the Trusts are developing these partnerships.

Conclusion

The success of the government's NHS modernisation programme has been premised on the presence of a motivated, satisfied staff to deliver this. Evidence from research literature suggests that there is a weak link between job satisfaction and performance. But recent CIPD research into the connection between performance and human resource management reasserts that link (CIPD, 2002). However, the findings from this study shows that in areas highlighted in a number of NHS reports, and particularly by the prime minister himself, there is a gap between aspiration and practice in these two NHS Trusts. This evidence suggests that in nearly all of the seven areas much work still needs to be done. But the CIPD research further suggests that a 'configurational' or 'bundles of practice' approach might be more effective than the 'best fit' approach implied by government policy and exhortation. This means that Trusts should be left to develop their own appropriate bundle of employment policies and practices rather than have a list imposed upon them.

References

Adams, J.S. (1965), 'Inequality in Social Exchange', in L. Berkowitz (ed.), *Advances in Experimental Social Psychology*, Vol. 2, New York: Academic Press.

Chartered Institute of Personnel and Development (2001), *The Change Agenda*, London: CIPD.

Chartered Institute of Personnel and Development (2002), *The Case for Good People Management: A Summary of the Research*, London:CIPD.

Department of Health (1998), 'Working Together – Securing a Quality Workforce for the NHS', London: Department of Health, http://www.open.gov.uk.doh/newnhs/hrstrat.htm.

Department of Health (1999a), 'Two Human Resource Beacons awarded to Trusts in Eastern Region', press release, http://www.doh.gov.uk/euro/jun29press.htm.

Department of Health (1999b), 'Report of the NHS Taskforce on Staff Involvement', London: DofH.

Department of Health (2000a), *The NHS Plan. A Plan for Investment. A Plan for Reform*, Cmnd. 4818–1, Norwich: The Stationery Office.

Department of Health (2000b), *A Health Service of all the Talents: Developing the NHS Workforce*, London: DoH.

Department of Health (2001), 'Local Modernisation Reviews: Support Pack and Toolkit', http: //www.doh.gov.uk/nhsperformance/modreview.

Guest, D., Michie, J., Sheehan, M., Conway, N. and Metochi, M. (2000), *Effective People Management, Initial Findings of the Future of Work Study*, London: Institute of Personnel and Development.

Iaffaldano, M. and Muchinsky, P. (1985), 'Job Satisfaction and Job Performance: A Meta-amalysis', *Psychological Bulletin*, 97, pp. 251–73.

Incomes Data Services Study Plus (2001), *Staff Attitude Surveys*, London: IDS.

Katzell, R.A., Thompson, D.E. and Guzzo, R.A. (1992), 'How Job Satisfaction and Job Performance are and are not Linked', in C.J. Cranny, P.C. Smith and E.F. Stone (eds), *Job Satisfaction: How People Feel about their Jobs and how it Affects their Performance*, Oxford: Lexington Books.

Legge, K. and Mumford, E. (1978), *Designing Organisations for Satisfaction and Efficiency*, Farnborough: Gower.

MacDuffie, J.P. (1995), 'Human Resource Bundles and Manufacturing Performance', *Industrial Relation Review*, 48 (2), pp. 199–221.

NHS Executive (2000), *Human Resource Performance Framework*, London: NHS Executive.

Oakes, L.S., Townley, B. and Cooper, D.J. (1998), 'Business Planning as Pedagogy: Language and Control in a Changing Institutional Field', *Administrative Science Quarterly*, 43 (2), pp. 257–92.

Office of Public Service Reform (2002), *Reforming our Public Services*, London.

Patterson, M.G., West, M.A., Lawthom, R. and Nickell, S. (1997), *Impact of People Management Practices on Performance*, London: CIPD.

Pollitt, C. and Bouckaert, G. (2000), *Public Management Reform. A Comparative Analysis*, Oxford: Oxford University Press.

Redman, T. and Wilkinson, A. (2001), *Contemporary Human Resource Management*, Harlow: Pearson Education.

Somers, M.J., Dormann, C., Janssen, P.P.M., Dollard, M.F., Landeweerd, J.A. and Nijhuis, F.J.N. (2000), 'Thinking Differently: Assessing Nonlinearities in the Relationship between Work Attitudes and Job performance Using a Bayesian Neural Net', *Journal of Occupational and Organizational Psychology*, 74 (1).

Watson, A.J. (1995), *Sociology, Work and Industry*, London: Routledge.

Appendix

2001 questionnaire returns matched against staff groups
Infirmary

Staff group	Population 2001	Achieved sample 2001	Achieved sample 1999
Ancillary staff	14	05	05
Administrative and clerical	16	21	17
Maintenance and works	01	01	01
Medical and dental (career grade)	05	05	04
Medical and dental (training grade)	04	03	02
Medical and dental (honorary)	<1	<1	Not included
Nursing and midwifery (registered)	25	33	36
Nursing and midwifery (unregistered)	16	06	06
Professions allied to medicine	07	13	12
Senior manager	03	05	06
Technical, scientific, professional	09	08	10
	100	100	99
Total number of staff	5,405	1,289 (24%)	1364 (28%)
Gender			
Male	20	21	21
Female	80	79	79
Manager/supervisor*			
Yes	15	52	24
No	85	48	76
Member of ethnic minority group?			
Yes	07	07	06
No	93	93	94
Age			
16–20	02	01	01
21–35	35	35	38
36–49	41	45	42
50+	22	20	19

*   In 1999 question asked: Are you a manager/supervisor?
*   In 2001 question asked: Do you supervise or manage staff?

2001 questionnaire returns matched against staff groups
General

Staff group	% population 2001	% achieved sample 2001	% achieved sample 1999
Ancillary staff	10	05	06
Administrative and clerical	20	22	25
Maintenance and works	02	02	02
Medical and dental (career grade)	04	06	06
Medical and dental (training grade)	07	02	02
Medical and dental (honorary)	02	02	Not included
Nursing and midwifery (registered)	31	36	30
Nursing and midwifery (unregistered)	09	04	04
Professions allied to medicine	05	10	09
Senior manager	01	02	02
Technical, scientific, professional	11	09	13
	102	100	99
Total number of staff	6,123	1,535 (25%)	1,011 (18%)
Gender			
Male	23	24	26
Female	77	76	74
Manager/Supervisor*			
Yes		53	24
No		47	76
Member of ethnic minority group?			
Yes	07	07	05
No	93	93	94
Age			
16–20	01	<1	01
21–35	38	38	37
36–49	41	41	45
50+	20	21	18

*   In 1999 question asked: Are you a manager/supervisor?
*   In 2001 question asked: Do you supervise or manage staff?

Chapter 17

The Relation between Patient Volume, Staffing, Workload and Adherence to Selected National Standards and Risk-adjusted Outcomes in UK Neonatal Intensive Care Units: A Prospective Study

Janet S. Tucker, Gareth J. Parry, Chris McCabe, Paula Nicolson
and William Tarnow-Mordi

Introduction

The effect on outcomes of levels of neonatal intensive care throughput (patient volume), staffing levels and workload was uncertain. Although clinical and nursing skills were believed to be best developed and supported in higher volume units, performance might also deteriorate due to staff shortages or at high workload. The UK Neonatal Staffing Study (UKNSS) investigated the relation between the directly alterable organisational characteristics of volume, staffing levels and workload and risk-adjusted hospital mortality and morbidity in this prospective UK-representative study. Secondary analyses also assessed risk-adjusted outcomes in relation to selected contemporary recommended standards of the British Association of Perinatal Medicine (BAPM) (BAPM, 1996).

Centralisation of specialist neonatal intensive care services in the UK has been supported in the belief that it would improve effectiveness and efficiency. (ibid.) The proportion of maternity hospital births in the UK resulting in very sick or premature infants who require *intensive* care is around 0.05 to 0.1 per cent, although definition of intensive care varies and data is not routinely collected (Macfarlane and Mugford, 2000: BAPM, 1996) In this type of low volume, high cost specialty the aim is to provide specialist care of demonstrable highest quality, as efficiently as possible, and maintain access. The Short Report (1980) recommended a tiered neonatal care system at a time of rapid technological advances in obstetrics and neonatal intensive care (NIC). (Short, 1980) Policy documents in the last decade continue to support the tiered neonatal intensive care network and the concept that higher patient volume and accrued clinical and nursing expertise would optimise outcomes. (Clinical Standards Advisory Group (CSAG) 1993: Clinical Standards advisory Group (CSAG) 1995) It is clear that what constitutes intensive care changes with evolving technology, but in general maternity units have associated neonatal care provision that could be classified thus (Clinical Standards advisory Group (CSAG) 1993):

1   non-intensive care – special care baby units (SCBUs);
2   limited intensive care – some NIC but transfer complex problems;
3   all intensive care for inborn babies but accept no transfers in (non-trading NICUs);
4   all NIC for both inborn and accept transfers in (both in utero and postnatal).

In 1996/97 NICUs throughout the UK demonstrated wide variation in annual levels of neonatal intensive care activity, staffing levels and skillmix (Tucker et al., 1999). Contemporary BAPM recommendations stated that NICUs: should be appraised against national criteria, develop clinical guidelines, have specified staffing and equipment levels, and be designated as neonatal intensive care units only if they attained a minimum number of 500 intensive care days per annum (BAPM, 1996). This latter recommendation implied further centralisation of neonatal intensive care services. The Standards document however also noted that more empirical evidence was needed to support these recommendations (ibid.).

The evidence to date in the UK of the relation between NICU performance and volume of neonatal intensive care activity was contradictory and raised the question of change in comparative performance through time. For example, reports comparing tertiary (and higher volume) and non-tertiary centres in both Scotland (International Neonatal Network, 1993) and Trent (Field et al., 1990) for the years 1987 to 1990 suggested improved risk-adjusted mortality in tertiary centres. However, more recently-reported regional UK studies (de Courcy Wheeler et al., 1995: Field and Draper, 1999) detected no significant differences in risk-adjusted outcome by unit size.

Research Objectives

To assess whether risk-adjusted mortality and morbidity outcomes of UK neonatal intensive care are related to:

- differences in primary organisational characteristics of volume, medical and nurse staffing levels, and workload;
- adherence to national standards of service provision.

Methods: Design, Setting, and Patients

Phase 1

A UK-wide census of neonatal care units in 1997 allowed identification of neonatal intensive care units (NICUS) and stratification by primary organisational characteristics.

Phase 2

A prospective, risk-adjusted study of a cohort of 14,611 infants consecutively admitted (March 1998 to April 1999) to a random sample of 54 UK neonatal intensive care units. Occupancy and workload measures were also prospectively recorded twice daily at participating NICUs.

Descriptive data for the 54 NICUs, included unit profile data collected at site visit in 1998 (WTM, JT). Each phase 2 NICU also returned a detailed anonymous staff profile in 1998. The staff profiles listed each post within their nursing and medical establishment; the highest specialist qualifications of post-holders, grades, specialist roles and responsibilities. Whether posts were currently unfilled and where staff were on long-term sick leave were also recorded.

Comparisons for eligible, attributable and risk-adjusted infant outcomes were by hospital type, and for infants exposed to varying workload measures. Our study aimed to examine workload using a cross-sectional and longitudinal approach. The cross-sectional approach examined whether overall average unit workload during the study period was related to the primary outcomes. The longitudinal approach aimed to examine whether variations in workload and infants' exposure to variations within each unit during the study period were related to the primary outcomes. Workload was measured as both occupancy and nurse-infant ratios per shift.

The following outcomes were assessed in relation to the primary organisational characteristics:

- death before hospital discharge or planned deaths at home (excluding lethal malformations);
- major brain damage on cerebral ultrasound (excluding damage of probable onset before birth);
- bacteraemia or septicaemia of probable nosocomial origin more than 48 hours after birth (excluding vertical transmission).

Secondary clinical hypotheses were related to adherence to national standards: that the three risk-adjusted outcomes are independently related to:

1   whether one consultant is designated for the direction and management of the Unit, monitoring clinical policies, practice and standards, with the majority of his or her clinical sessions committed to neonatal care;*
2   whether a doctor with at least 6 months training in neonatal intensive care is continuously resident in the same building as the NICU;*
3   whether a doctor with at least two years' full time equivalent training in neonatal intensive care is continuously resident in the same building as the NICU;*
4   implementation of regular audit;*
5   implementation of systematic training programme for junior medical staff;*

or that risk-adjusted rates of probable nosocomial bacteraemia are independently related to:

6   appointment of an infection control nurse or link nurse for the unit.

(* in accordance with recommendations from the BAPM document on Standards for Hospitals Providing Neonatal Intensive Care (BAPM, 1996).)

Results

Phase 1 Census

A 1997 census of unit activity and staffing achieved responses from all identified 246 UK neonatal units. There was substantial variation between units with 186 (76 per cent) who reported delivering sustained neonatal intensive care. (Tucker et al., 1999) These 186 units were identified as neonatal intensive care units (NICUs) and stratified into 12 types by the three primary organisational characteristics in a 3 x 2 x 2 factorial matrix using the following variables and cut-off points: (Table 17.1):

1   patient volume (by annual number of VLBWT infants (high ≥ 58, medium 35–57, low ≤ 34));
2   neonatal consultant availability (by number consultants with > 50 per cent clinical sessions in neonatal care (higher ≥ 2, and lower < 2));
3   nurse provision (using calculated nurse cot ratios of recommended vs actual nurse establishment (higher ≥ 0.84, lower < 0.84)).

Thus primary organisational characteristics were categorised using UK norm-referenced cut-off points, derived from the census distributions rather than arbitrary judgement. High volume NICUs and high nurse and neonatal consultant provision were defined as the upper third and upper halves of the distributions of admissions of very low birth weight infants and of nurse and consultant provision respectively. Fifty-four NICUs were randomly selected from the stratified matrix (Table 17.1).

Phase 2 Clinical Results

Primary organisational characteristics Of 14,611 infants consecutively admitted to 54 NICUs, information was available for 14,343 infants (98.2 per cent). Of those, 13,515 were eligible admissions, with abstracted data for 13,401 (99 per cent). There were 393 hospital deaths (2.9 per cent), of which 322 (2.5 per cent) were attributable to the participating hospitals of care (71 non-attributable deaths included lethal congenital conditions or complex cardiac and organ transplant surgery). *Crude* mortality rates were significantly higher in high volume NICUs than in low volume NICUs (OR 0.58 (0.38–0.87). Following risk-adjustment, the observed mortality, and mortality and cerebral abnormality outcomes by patient volume, and by clinical and nurse staffing levels were not significantly

Table 17.1 186 UK NICUs stratified by volume, consultant availability, and nurse staffing

Census variable	Volume (annual no. VLBWT infants (<1500g)	Availability of neonatal consultants (consultant with > 50% sessions in neonatal care)	Nurse provision (nurse cot ratio)*	Number of NICUs stratified to cell type per cell	Number of NICUs randomly selected
Cut-off values	*High ≥ 58* *Medium 35-57* *Low ≤ 34*	*High ≥ 2* *Low < 2*	*High ≥ 0.84* *Low < 0.84*		
Group					
1	high	✓	✓	16	3
2	high	✓	✗	29	3
3	high	✗	✓	6	3
4	high	✗	✗	12	3
5	medium	✓	✓	12	4
6	medium	✓	✗	12	4
7	medium	✗	✓	11	4
8	medium	✗	✗	19	4
9	low	✓	✓	14	5
10	low	✓	✗	7	5
11	low	✗	✓	14	8
12	low	✗	✗	34	8
Total				186	54

✓ high, ✗ low.

* See Tucker et al., 1999 for the method of calculating the nurse–cot ratio (0.84 was the UK median value). A value less than 1 indicates the nursing establishment was less than that recommended for the unit's cot establishment.

different to that expected given the illness severity of their populations (for example, OR for adjusted mortality and major cerebral abnormality in high volume vs low volume, 0.99 (0.69–1.43)). Full risk-adjustment models and detailed data of the primary results are reported elsewhere. (Tucker et al., 2002) Here we illustrate adjusted mortality results by the primary organisational characteristics (see Figures 17.1–17.3). Findings for risk adjusted mortality and major cerebral abnormality of postnatal origin showed similar non-association with the primary organisational characteristics as mortality alone. However, risk-adjusted nosocomial bacteraemia was lower than expected in NICUs with lower consultant availability (see Figures 17.4–17.6).

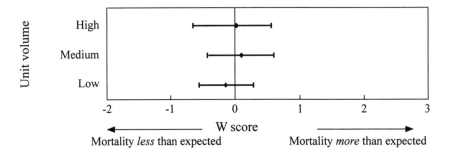

Figure 17.1   Risk-adjusted mortality by NICU patient volume

Note: Observed mortality is *no different* to that expected (taking account of illness severity) in high, medium and low volume units.

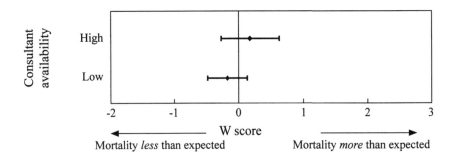

Figure 17.2   Risk-adjusted mortality by consultant availability

Note: Observed mortality is *no different* to that expected (taking account of illness severity) in high vs low consultant availability.

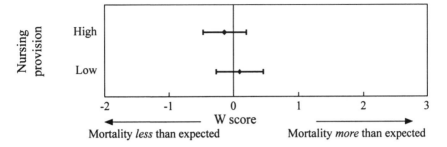

Figure 17.3   Risk-adjusted mortality by nursing provision

Note: Observed mortality is *no different* to that expected (taking account of illness severity) in high vs low consultant availability.

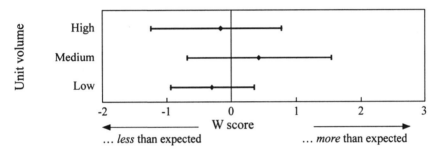

Figure 17.4   Risk-adjusted nosocomial bacteraemia by NICU volume

Note: Observed hospital acquired infection is *no different* to that expected (taking account of illness severity) in high, medium and low volume NICUs.

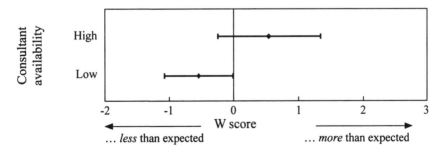

Figure 17.5   Risk-adjusted nosocomial bacteraemia by consultant availability

Note: Observed hospital acquired infection is *lower than* expected (taking account of illness severity) in NICUs with low availability of specialist consultants.

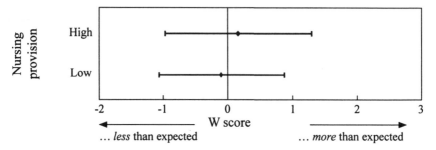

Figure 17.6   Risk-adjusted nosocomial bacteraemia by nursing provision

Note: Observed hospital acquired infection is *no different* to that expected (taking account of illness severity) in NICUS by low vs high nursing provision.

The average workload values over the study period varied by unit characteristic. High volume units (median 0.70) tended to be operating closer to maximum occupancy than medium (median 0.61) and low (median 0.57) volume units. There were no apparent differences in occupancy between high and low consultant availability and high and low nursing provision.

For nurse to infant ratio, a value of one or more indicated that the number of nurses to infants had reached the recommended BAPM levels. Overall the nurse to infant ratio was less than that recommended the BAPM. (BAPM, 1996) The standard was not reached on 57 per cent of time periods. There was some evidence of improved nurse to infant ratio with high unit volume compared to medium and low unit volume. However the percentage of time periods the BAPM standards were *not met* for high, medium and low volume units were 58 per cent, 56 per cent and 58 per cent respectively.

There were no significant associations between cross-sectional unit-based workload measures and risk-adjusted outcomes. However, in infant-based analysis, risk-adjusted mortality did increase with increasing occupancy of cots in all NICU types. For every 10 per cent increase in percentage maximum occupancy at time of admission for each infant, the odds of mortality increased by 1.09 (1.01-1.18).

Secondary Organisational Characteristics

1 Whether one consultant is designated for the direction and management of the NICU, monitoring clinical policies, practice and standards, with the majority of his or her clinical sessions committed to neonatal care The majority of NICUs did have a consultant designated for the direction and management of the unit in accordance with the standards recommended by BAPM (BAPM, 1996). More of the high volume NICUs (83 per cent) had a dedicated consultant compared with medium (56 per cent) or low volume (57 per cent) NICUs (Table 17.2). There was no significant relation between NICUs having a designated consultant and risk-adjusted mortality or risk-adjusted mortality and brain damage. However, there was a significant relation between having a designated consultant and increased nosocomial bacteraemia (Table 17.8 (odds ratio 1.56, 1.03 to 2.36)).

Table 17.2 Designated consultant by cell type and patient volume

Cell type	No Designated consultant	Yes Designated consultant	Volume	No. NICUs
1	0	3		3
2	0	3	high	3
3	1	2	(83%)	3
4	1	2		3
5	2	2	medium	4
6	1	3	(56%)	4
7	2	2		4
8	2	2		4
9	3	2	low	5
10	0	5	(57%)	5
11	3	5		8
12	5	3		8
Total	20 (37%)	34 (63%)		54 (100%)

2 Whether a doctor with at least six months training in neonatal intensive care is continuously resident in the same building as the NICU The majority of units did have a doctor with at least six months specialist training continuously in the NICU building (Table 17.3). However there were no differences in any of the risk-adjusted outcomes between those units with and without a doctor with 6 months experience continuously in residence (Table 17.8).

3 Whether a doctor with at least two years' full time equivalent training in neonatal intensive care is continuously resident in the same building as the NICU Only 20 per cent of units had a doctor with at least two years

Table 17.3   Doctor with six months specialist training continuously in the NICU building by cell type and patient volume

Cell type	Always	> 50% time	< 50% time	Never	No. NICUs
1	3	0	0	0	3
2	2	0	1	0	3
3	2	0	1	0	3
4	2	1	0	0	3
5	3	1	0	0	4
6	3	0	1	0	4
7	4	0	0	0	4
8	3	1	0	0	4
9	2	2	1	0	4
10	4	1	0	0	5
11	7	0	1	0	8
12	4	2	1	0	8
Total	39	8	6	0	53
	(72%)	(15%)	(12%)		(98%)*

*   One non-response.

specialist training continuously in the NICU building (Table 17.4). There were no differences in any of the risk-adjusted outcomes between those units with and without a doctor with two years' training continuously in residence (Table 17.8).

4 Implementation of regular audit The great majority of NICUs (83 per cent) had a member of staff responsible for clinical audit. Those without such an identified member of staff were more likely to be low volume NICUs (Table 17.5). There was no association between having identified staff for clinical audit and risk adjusted measures of mortality or morbidity (Table 17.8). Similar results were obtained in analysis of risk adjusted outcomes in comparisons of units with and without an audit neonatal nurse (Table 17.8).

5 Implementation of systematic training programme for junior medical staff and hospital teaching status Evaluation of training programmes and training status of NICUs was complex. It became clear that many units would use their unit protocols and guidelines as texts, but these were held at or near the nursing station. Trainees would rarely be provided with personal copies or specifically prepared clinical training texts. Similarly, only the broad content

Table 17.4 Doctor with two years specialist training continuously in the NICU building by cell type and patient volume

Cell type	Always	> 50% time	< 50% time	Never	No. NICUs
1	1	1	0	0	3
2	1	0	0	0	3
3	1	0	1	1	3
4	0	2	0	0	3
5	1	0	2	2	4
6	2	0	0	0	4
7	0	0	1	1	4
8	0	0	1	1	4
9	1	0	2	2	4
10	1	3	0	0	5
11	1	1	5	5	8
12	2	1	3	3	8
Total	11	8	19	15	53
	(20%)	(15%)	(35%)	(28%)	(98%)

* One non-response.

Table 17.5 Identified member of staff responsible for clinical audit by cell type and patient volume

Cell type	Yes Identified clinical audit	No Identified clinical audit	Volume % with clinical audit	No. NICUs
1	3	0	High	3
2	3	0	92%	3
3	3	0		3
4	2	1		3
5	4	0	Medium	4
6	3	1	88%	4
7	4	0		4
8	3	1		4
9	3	2	Low	5
10	3	2	77%	5
11	6	2		8
12	8	0		8
Total	45	9		54
	(83%)	(17%)		(100%)

of topics included in training were available for most NICUs and these were reported as being often supplemented. Few records or copies of supplementary material covered were available. Quality of post-graduate specialist training programmes needs closer systematic examination than was possible in this study.

Units had overlapping responsibilities for training SpR Paedatricians and General Practitioners as well as those SpR's intending to become neonatal intensive care specialists. NICUs were divided into University Teaching Hospitals, those who claimed training status with placements of trainees, and those with no training. Most NICUs with no training were medium or small volume NICUs (Table 17.6).

Table 17.6   Training status of NICUs by cell type

Cell type	University teaching hospital	Training	No Training	No. NICUs
1	2	1	0	3
2	2	1	0	3
3	1	2	0	3
4	1	2	0	3
5	0	1	3	4
6	0	1	3	4
7	0	1	3	4
8	0	1	3	4
9	0	3	2	5
10	0	4	1	5
11	0	6	2	8
12	0	2	6	8
Total	6	25	23	54
	(11%)	(47%)	(42%)	(100%)

There were no significant relationships between these training status categories and risk-adjusted outcomes (Table 17.8).

There were 402 (3 per cent) infants observed who, following negative results of blood cultures at birth to 48 hours, had positive blood cultures after 48 hours. These were taken as probable cases of nosocomial bacteraemia. These cases were evenly distributed throughout the NICU types (33 per cent in high volume NICUs, 36 per cent in medium volume NICUs and 32 per cent in low volume NICUs).

6 Appointment of an infection control nurse or link nurse for the unit The majority of all types of NICU had an appointed infection control nurse or link nurse (Table 17.7).There was a significant relation between having an infection control nurse and reduced incidence of risk-adjusted nosocomial bacteraemia, odds ratio 0.53 (0.35 to 0.79) (Table 17.8).

Table 17.7 Appointed infection control nurse or link nurse by cell type and patient volume

Cell type	Yes Infection control nurse	No Infection control nurse	By volume	No. NICUs
1	2	1		3
2	2	1		3
3	3	0	(83%)	3
4	3	0		3
5	3	1		4
6	3	1	(75%)	4
7	3	1		4
8	3	1		4
9	3	2		5
10	5	0	(77%)	5
11	5	3		8
12	7	1		8
Total	42	12		54
	(78%)	(22%)		(100%)

Thus tests for association between prespecified secondary organisational characteristics, (for adherence to BAPM national recommendations) showed few independent, significant relation to risk-adjusted outcome measures, with a notable exception that risk-adjusted nosocomial bacteraemia was lower in units with an infection control nurse (OR 0.53 (0.35-0.79)) (Table 17.8).

Discussion

The UK Neonatal Staffing Study (UKNSS) results indicated that high volume NICUs in the UK cared for sicker infants, were busier and had higher crude mortality and morbidity than medium and low volume units. Adjusting for initial clinical risk and illness severity, the performance of high volume NICUs was comparable to that of medium and low volume NICUs. How these UKNSS results might impact on clinicians' beliefs and service change is explored further in a Bayesian analysis (Parry and Tucker, this volume).

The quality of the risk adjustment models are central to the study quality and models were empirically developed from the whole dataset. Technical specifications in modelling are fully discussed elsewhere (Tucker et al., 2002).

Previous reports of the relation between NICU patient volume and performance are not consistent in the direction and size of effect in the literature. Improved hospital survival was reported for one UK region in 1990 for infants ≤ 28 weeks gestation cared for in NICUs with more than 500 ventilator days per annum. (Field et al., 1990) A similar study for the same region in 1994–96 (Field and Draper, 1999) reported that relation was no longer evident. The authors suggested that might be due a number of factors: to major developments in perinatal care such as use of surfactant and maternal steroids or to increased investment in equipment and specialist staff in neonatal care in district general hospitals. The later study also more fully adjusted for clinical risk. (Field and Draper, 1999) Good adjustment for case mix, clinical risk and illness severity has been suggested to remove the apparent relationship between increased volume and improved outcome.(NHS Centre for Reviews and Dissemination, 1996) This has been borne out in some clinical settings but not in others (Tilford et al., 2000).

In the UKNSS, mortality increased with measures of increasing workload in all types of NICU. It should be noted that NICUs in our study experienced a rate of maximum occupancy which was greater than the number in its official cot establishment. These workload findings have implications for staffing policy in all types of NICU in the UK, and are consistent with previous reports of increased adverse outcomes in relation to high workload in intensive and emergency care (Tarnow-Mordi et al., 2000; Goldfrad and Rowan, 2000; Griffith et al., 1999; Miro et al., 2000).

Allowance for multiple testing of the secondary hypotheses had been made in the study protocol in sample size estimation. The descriptive results for the variables in the secondary hypotheses related to adherence to national recommendations (BAPM, 1996) and indicate the extent of variation in clinical expert availability, training settings, audit practice and infection control nurse provision. There were two statistically significant independent associations between individual secondary characteristics of NICUs and risk-adjusted outcomes, namely:

Table 17.8   Secondary clinical hypotheses: the relation between selected process and organisational characteristics and risk-adjusted outcomes (odds ratios and 95% confidence intervals)

	Death		Death or brain damage		Nosocomial bacteraemia	
Unit has a designated consultant	0.88	(0.65, 1.19)	0.86	(0.63, 1.16)	1.56	(1.03, 2.36)
Doctor with at least 6 months training						
Always						
> 50%	1.30	(0.92, 1.83)	1.43	(1.07, 1.92)		
< 50%	0.92	(0.66, 1.30)	0.78	(0.48, 1.27)		
Doctor with at least 2 years training						
Always						
> 50%	0.76	(0.44, 1.32)	1.02	(0.63, 1.65)		
< 50%	0.76	(0.46, 1.25)	0.81	(0.50, 1.33)		
Never	0.78	(0.44, 1.37)	0.97	(0.60, 1.57)		
Unit has an audit nurse	1.16	(0.86, 1.56)	1.14	(0.81, 1.61)	1.10	(0.70, 1.75)
Unit has an audit clinician	1.15	(0.86, 1.53)	0.93	(0.64, 1.35)	0.76	(0.41, 1.40)
Unit has self-reported training status	0.95	(0.66, 1.36)	0.88	(0.62, 1.25)	1.14	(0.73, 1.78)
University teaching						
Training (not university)	0.90	(0.60, 1.35)	1.32	(0.89, 1.97)	0.93	(0.54, 1.61)
No teaching, no medical training	0.82	(0.58, 1.17)	1.17	(0.79, 1.73)	0.81	(0.49, 1.35)
Unit has an infection control nurse					0.53	(0.35, 0.79)

- that those units with infection control nurses or link infection control nurses had significantly reduced risk-adjusted nosocomial bacteraemia;
- And that those NICUs with a designated consultant for the clinical management of units had significantly higher risk-adjusted nosocomial bacteraemia.

These findings appear consistent with the earlier primary finding that lower consultant availability was associated with lower risk-adjusted nosocomial bacteraemia. Our defined cases of probable nosocomial bacteraemia excluded all cases of vertical transmission. These results are also consistent with observations in the literature that suggest some invasive procedures (Brodie et al., 2000), overcrowding and understaffing in periods of increased workload (Harbarth et al., 1999), poorer compliance with handwashing by clinicians compared with nursing staff (Pittet et al., 1999) and poorer compliance within intensive care settings (ibid.) may be associated with increased levels of hospital acquired infections. We cannot exclude the alternative possible explanations of existing variation between hospital types in either rates of contaminated blood cultures or case ascertainment.

Conclusions

The UK Neonatal Staffing Study (UKNSS) results indicated that high volume NICUs in the UK cared for sicker infants, were busier and had higher crude mortality and morbidity than medium and low volume units. Adjusting for initial clinical risk and illness severity, the performance of high volume NICUs was comparable to that of medium and low volume NICUs. There was no independent relation, in this UK-representative study, of risk-adjusted outcomes of mortality and mortality or cerebral damage to unit characteristics of patient volume and simple establishment staffing levels. Similarly, individual elements of recommended best practice from expert-defined standards did not appear to have a measurable independent impact on performance. However, when infants were admitted at times of increasing within-unit maximum occupancy risk-adjusted mortality increased. Furthermore risk-adjusted nosocomial bacteraemia was more likely in units with higher consultant availability and in NICUs with no infection control nurse.

These results may inform policy and practice as the key areas highlighted for potential improvement in neonatal clinical outcomes involve management of unit workload and nurse staffing, and infection control.

Acknowledgements

The UK Neonatal Staffing Study (UKNSS) was funded by the NHS R&D Executive, Mother and Child Health Programme (grant number MCH:6–7), and the work was endorsed by the British Association of Perinatal Medicine, the Neonatal Nurses Association (UK) and Scottish Neonatal Nurses Group. We thank all UK neonatal units and staff for their help. We thank link research nurses, nurse managers and clinicians who collected the prospective data on our behalf. We are also grateful to research midwives, secretarial and data management team in the Tayside Institute of Child Health, University of Dundee: and staff at ScHARR in Sheffield for their support We thank the UKNSS steering group and in particular Drs Alan Gibson, Sandy Calvert, John Davies, Joanne Meran, David Milligan, Harry Baumer, and Neil Marlow for their work on the consensus panel for diagnostic severity categories.

References

BAPM (1996), *Standards for Hospitals providing Neonatal Intensive Care*, London: British Association of Perinatal Medicine.

Brodie, S., Sands, K., Gray, J., Parker, R., Goldmann, D., Davis, R. and Richardson, D. (2000), 'Occurrence of nosocomial Bloodstream Infections in Six Neonatal Intensive Care Units', *Pediatric Infectious Disease Journal*, 19, pp. 56–62.

Clinical Standards Advisory Group (CSAG) (1993), *Neonatal Intensive Care, Access to and Availability of Specialist Services*, report to CSAG (Clinical Standards Advisory Group) by a working group chaired by Professor Sir David Hull, London: HMSO.

Clinical Standards Advisory Group (CSAG) (1995), *Neonatal Intensive Care, Access to and Availability of Specialist Services*, 2nd Report to CSAG (Clinical Standards Advisory Group) by a working group chaired by Professor Sir David Hull, London: HMSO.

De Courcy-Wheeler, R.H.B., Wolfe, C.D.A., Fitzgerald, A., Spencer, M., Goodman, J.D.S. and Gamsu, H.R. (1995), 'Use of the *Clinical Risk Index for Babies* Score in Prediction of Neonatal Mortality and Morbidity', *Archives of Disease in Childhood*, 73, F32–6.

Field, D., Hodges, S., Mason, E. and Burton, P. (1990), 'Survival and Place of Treatment after Premature Delivery', *Archives of Disease in Childhood*, 66, pp. 408–11.

Field, D. and Draper, E.S. (1999), 'Survival and Place of Delivery following Pre-term Birth (1994–96)', *Archives of Disease in Childhood*, 80, F111–14.

Griffith, C.H., Wilson, J.F., Desai, N.S. and Eugene, C.R. (1999), 'Housestaff Workload and Procedure Frequency in Neonatal Intensive Care Unit', *Critical Care Medicine*, 27, pp. 815–20.

Goldfrad, C. and Rowan, K. (2000), 'Consequences of Discharges from Intensive Care at Night', *Lancet*, 355, pp. 38–42.

Harbarth, S., Sudre, P., Dharan, S., Cadenas, M. and Pittet, D. (1999), 'Outbreak of Enterobacter Cloacae related to Understaffing, Overcrowding and Poor Hygiene Practices', *Infectious Control and Hospital Epidmiology*, 20, pp. 598–603.

International Neonatal Network (1993), 'The Clinical Risk Index for Babies Score: A Tool for assessing Initial Neonatal Risk and comparing Performance of Neonatal Units', *Lancet*, 342, pp. 193–8.

McFarlane, A. and Mugford, M. (2000), *Birth Counts: Statistics of Pregnancy and Childbirth*, 2nd edn, London: Stationery Office.

Miro, O., Sanchez, M. and Milla, J. (2000), 'Hospital Mortality and Staff Workload', *Lancet*, 356, pp. 1356–7.

NHS Centre for Reviews and Dissemination, University of York and Nuffield Institute for Health, University of Leeds. (1996), 'Hospital volume, health care outcomes, costs and patient access.' *Effective Health Care Bulletin*, 2, (8).

Pittet, D., Mourouga, P. and Perneger, T.V. (1999), 'Compliance with Handwashing in a Teaching Hospital', *Annals Internal Medicine*, 130, pp. 126–30.

Short Report (1980), *Perinatal and Neonatal Mortality: Second Report from the Social Services Committee*, London: HMSO.

Tarnow-Mordi, W.O., Hau, C., Warden, A. and Shearer, A. (2000), 'Hospital Mortality in Relation to Staff Workload: A 4-year Study in an Adult Intensive-care Unit', *Lancet*, 356, pp. 185–9.

Tilford, J.M., Simpson, P.M., Green, J.W., Lensing, S. and Fiser, D.H. (2000), 'Volume-outcome Relationships in Pediatric Intensive Care Units', *Pediatrics*, 106, pp. 289–94.

Tucker, J., Tarnow-Mordi, W., Gould, C., Parry, G. and Marlow, N. (1999), 'UK Neonatal Intensive Care Services in 1996', *Archives of Disease in Childhood*, 80, F233–4.

Tucker, J., Parry, G., McCabe, C., Nicolson, P. and Tarnow-Mordi, W. on behalf of the UK Neonatal Staffing Study Group (2002), 'A Prospective Evaluation of the Relation between Patient Volume, Staffing and Workload and Risk-adjusted Outcomes of Neonatal Intensive Care in 54 UK Neonatal Intensive Care Units', *Lancet*, 359, pp. 99–107.

Index